Shrewsbury School.

—————

Roll of Service

1914=1918.

—————

1921.
—
Wilding & Son, Ltd.,
Shrewsbury.

STATISTICS.

O.SS. Serving	..	1850
Killed	..	321
Prisoners	..	44
Wounded once	..	274
twice	..	42
three times	..	15
four times	..	5
Interned at Ruhleben 1914 to 1918	..	4
Mentioned in Despatches, once	..	194
twice	..	57
three times	..	22
four times	..	11
five times	..	7
six times	..	2
seven times	..	1

Distinctions—

V.C.	2	D.S.O. Bars to	..	3
K.C.B.	1	D.S.C.	..	3
K.C.M.G.	4	O.B.E.	..	33
K.B.E.	3	M.C.	..	184
C.B.	8	,, Bars to..		21
C.S.I	1	D.F.C.	..	3
C.M.G.	12	Air Force Cross	..	1
C.I.E.	4	M.B.E.	..	6
C.B.E.	9	T.D...	..	25
D.S.O.	64	D.C.M.	..	3

Croix de Guerre	..	18
,, ,, avec palmes	..	2
Cross of Chevalier of Legion of Honour	..	2
Legion of Honour	..	4
Chevalier of the Legion of Honour and Crown of Italy	..	1
Officer of the Order of the Crown of Italy ..	..	2
Italian Silver Medal for Military Valour	..	2
Chevalier of the Order of Leopold with Croix de Guerre	..	3
Grand Officer of the Order of Leopold	..	1
Order of Leopold	..	1
Croix de Guerre (Belgium)	..	6
Chevalier de l'Ordre de Mérite Agricole	..	1
Russian Order of St. Anne with Swords	..	2
Cross of the Order of St. Anne	..	1
Order of St. Vladimir ..	..	1
Order of the Nile	..	7
Ordre de l'Etoile Noir	..	2
Cavalier of the Order of the Redeemer (Greek)	..	1
Order of St. John of Jerusalem	..	1
Commander, Ordre de la Couronne	..	1
Cavalier of SS. Maurice and Lazarus	..	1
Order of Medjidieh	..	1
Officer of Military Order of Savoy	..	1
Serbian Order of White Eagle	..	2
Chevalier of the Military Order of Aviz	..	2
Order of St. Sava	..	1

PREFATORY NOTE.

———

The Roll of Service consists of : (1) an alphabetical list of all Old Salopians who are known to have served in the armed forces of the Crown during the War of 1914–1918. (2) Obituary notices of nearly all those who fell.

No effort has been spared in the heavy task of making it complete and accurate. For the greatest part of the work of compiling the list and seeing the book through the press, Salopians are indebted to T. E. Pickering, who has received valuable assistance from C. R. N. Routh, A. F. Chance, J. E. Auden, and the printer, W. O. Wilding.

The Roll was compiled for the Old Salopian Club. The cost of printing and circulating it is being borne by the Shrewsbury School War Memorial Committee.

February, 1921.

Rank shown is the highest held at any one time in the War.

D.   Mentioned in despatches (the numeral denotes if more than once).

W.   Wounded or Gassed (the numeral denotes if more than once).

P.   Prisoner of War.

The names of those who have fallen are printed in loaded type.

* Shows those who have died since November, 1918.

The last two columns show the House and the date of leaving.

	Name / Rank	Award	Code	Year
	Ackroyd, Edward, Lieut. R.D.C.		A.F.C.	1894
	Ackroyd, Harold, M.D. Capt. R.A.M.C.	**V.C. M.C.**	A.F.C.	1896
W.	Acton, Owen Henry, Capt. Connaught Rangers.		C.J.S.C.	1908
	Adams, George Norman, Capt. S. Staffs. Regt.		C.J.S.C.	1905
	Adams, Lawrence Kingston, Lieut. K. Liverpool Regt.		A.F.C.	1903
	Adams, Wilfrid George, Lieut. K. Liverpool Regt.		A.F.C.	1904
	Adamson, Herbert Middlebrooke, Trooper, Herts Yeo.		E.B.M.	1907
W.	**Addie, John Heathcote Forrester,** Col., R. Welch Fus.	**C.B.E. D.**	E.B.M.	1892
	Addy, James Carlton, Capt. E. Yorks Regt.	**M.C.**	C.J.S.C. and T.E.P	1910
	Addy, Roland, Capt. E. Yorks Regt.		C.J.S.C. and T.E.P.	1910
	Addleshaw, Harold Leslie, Private, Artists' Rifles.		W.D.H.	1914
	Adye, Frederick Robert, Lieut. Remount Service.		C.J.S.C.	1886
	Ainslie, Henry, 2nd Lieut. Labour Corps.		F.M.I.	1914
	Aitchison, Andrew Leslie, 2nd Lieut. K.O.S.B.		T.E.P.	1915
	Aldous, Wilfrid Temple, Lieut. Nagpur Rifles, I.A.		C.J.S.C.	1904
	Alexander, Charles Leslie, I.C.S. Corporal, Indian Cavalry.		S.H.	1894
	Alexander, Cyril Wilson, Lieut. W. African Frontier Force.		S.H.	1898
	Alington, Noel Stanley, Lieut. K.G.O. Central India Horse.	**M.C. (Bar)**	S.H.	1916
	Alison, Charles William Lepper, Pte., London Regt.		W.D.H.	1905
	Alison, Douglas Smythe, Lieut. London Regt. and R.A.F.		W.D.H.	1907
W.	Allan, Alexander William, Lieut. Rifle Bde.		J.B.O.	1916
	Allen, David Drenen Trevor, 2nd Lieut. M.G.C.		W.S.I. and A.F.C.	1910
	Alltree, Charles Derek, Lieut. R. Welch Fus.		D.B.	1912
	Alltree, Ernest Woodbourne, Lieut. R.N.R.		D.B.	1904

For explanations and abbreviations, see page 4.

	Alltree, William George, Engineer Lt.-Commander, R.N.		D.B. 1903
P.	Ambrose Smith, John, Lt.-Col. Lancs. Fus.	**D.²**	A.F.C. 1894
P.W.	Amis, Henry Glennie, Capt. Yorks. Regt. and R.A.F.		W.D.H. 1913
	Anderson, Charles Rae, Lieut. R.F.A.		S.H. 1894
	Anderson, Hew Graham, Lieut. Brit. Columbia Regt.		S.H. 1905
	Anderson, Norman Ruthven, Major, I.A.		D.B. 1892
	Andrews, Ronald H., 2nd Lieut. R.A.F.		T.E.P. 1916
W.²	Annand, Archibald Walter, Capt., Gordon Highlanders.	**M.C.**	D.B. 1901
	Anthony, Charles Vaughan, Corporal, R.A.F.		F.E.B. 1900
	Apperley, Henry Wynne, Lt.-Col. I.A.		S.H. 1868
	Appleton, Charles Egerton, Sergeant, R.A.S.C.		A.F.C. 1896
	Appleton, The Rev. James Ashley, Chaplain to the Forces.		A.F.C. 1906
	Armstrong, Gordon, 2nd Lieut., R.G.A.		W.D.H. 1916
W.	Armstrong, Richard Acland, Lieut. R.A.S.C.		A.F.C. 1915
	Arnold, Oliver Vaughton, 2nd Lieut. Worcs. Regt.		W.D.H. 1905
	Aron, Charles James, Pte., R. Fus.	**D.C.M.**	G.T.H. and W.D.H.1904
	Aron, Frederick Adolph, Capt., S. Lancs. Regt.		G.T.H. and W.D.H. 1906
	Arthur, William Alfred, Capt. L.N. Lancs. Regt. and M.G.C.		F.S. and F.M.I. 1910
W.	Ashdown, Roger Harding, Capt. K.S.L.I.		F.M.I. 1911
	Ashford, Cyril (formerly Potts), Lieut. S. Staffs. Regt.	**M.C.**	D.B. 1899
	Ashton, William, Capt. Herts. Yeo.		G.T.H. 1892
	Ashworth, Harold, Capt. E. Lancs. Regt.		F.S. 1902
	Aston, Frederic Marriner, Capt. D.C.L.I.		S.H. 1886
	Attfield, Arthur James, Lieut. (Adjutant), R.A.O.C.		D.B. 1893
	Auden, The Rev. John Ernest, Chaplain to the Forces.	**T.D.**	D.B. 1880
	Auden, Reginald Stockenstrom, 2nd Lieut. R.A.F.		F.M.I. 1917
	Austin, Geoffrey Langshaw,		A.F.C. 1903
W.	Babb, Charles Herbert, 2nd Lieut. E. Yorks. Regt.		D.B. 1910
	Backhouse, Gerald Lovell, Lieut. R.A.F.		T.E.P. 1914

For explanations and abbreviations, see page 4.

	Backhouse, Henry Weston, Lieut. R.F.A.			T.E.P.	1913
W.	Badger, Kenneth Howard Collins, Capt. Suffolk Yeo.			C.J.S.C. and T.E.P.	1912
	Bagshaw, William Hounsfield, Major, E. Surrey Regt.			E.B.M.	1886
	Bagshawe, Leonard Vale, Capt. K.O.S.B.			E.B.M.	1896
	Bailey, Richard Fitzroy, 2nd Lieut. Shrewsbury School O.T.C.			Master	
	Bailey, Walter Arthur Francis, 2nd Lieut. Ox. and Bucks L.I.			F.T.P.	1915
	Bainbrigge, Philip Gillespie, 2nd Lieut. Lancs. Fus.			Master	
	Bainton, Arthur William, R.N.V.R. Anti-Aircraft Corps.			S.H.	1879
W.	Baird, Arbuthnot George Muir, Capt. R.F.A., A.D.C.			C.J.S.C. and T.E.P.	1910
	Baird, William Douglas, Lieut. R.A.F.			W.D.H.	1916
	Baker, John Cotter, Trooper, N. Bengal Mounted Rifles.			A.F.C.	1899
W.	Bald, John Arthur, Lt.-Col., I.A.	**C.M.G.**	**D.**	F.E.B.	1894
	Ball, Sir Charles Arthur Kinahan, Bart., M.D., Major, R.A.M.C.			S.H.	1895
	Banks, Arthur Chaplin, 2nd Lieut. R. Welch Fus.			T.E.P.	1914
	Banks, Charles Chaplin, Capt. R. Welch Fus. and R.A.F.	**D.F.C.**	**M.C. D.**	E.B.M. and F.T.P.	1913
	Banning, Henry Druce, Lieut. R.G.A.			C.J.S.C.	1895
	Barber, Eric Arthur, Lieut. K.S.L.I. Staff.	**D.**		W.D.H.	1906
	Barbosa, Alberto Antonio, R.E.			F.M.I.	1911
	Barbour, John Humphrey, M.B., Major, R.A.M.C.	**Commander of the Military Order of Aviz. D²**		G.T.H.	1890
	Barchard, Leslie Burnett, Lieut. York Regt.			A.F.C.	1911
	Barker, Allaen Noel Birkett, Sergeant, R.G.A.			S.H.	1909
	Barker, Edward Robert, Capt. R.A.F.	**D.S.C.**		A.F.C.	1916
	Barker, Greville Birkett, Lieut. R. Warwicks. Regt. and R.A.F.			S.H.	1910
	Barker, John Raymond, Pte., Central London Vol. Regt.			S.H.	1888
	Barker, Samuel Lionel Philpotts, Capt., The Buffs. R. of O.			G.T.H.	1892
W.	Barlow, Frank Collins, Lieut. Somerset L.I.	**M.C.**		F.E.B.	1895
	Barlow, Harold Loftus, Lieut. R.E. and R.A.F.			F.E.B.	1905
	Barlow, John Lancashire, 2nd Lieut. R.A.F.	**D.**		J.B.O.	1914
	Barlow, Percy Douglas, Major, S. Staffs. Regt.	**T.D.**		F.E.B.	1895

	Barlow, Walter Northey Cecil, Capt. and Adjutant, I.A.	**M.C.**	F.T.P.	1913
	Barnard, Henry de Vere Vane, Lord (the late), Hon. Col. D.L.I.		Governor	
	Barnes, Ernest, Major, I.A. (ret.) and R.F.A.	**D.**	S.H.	1886
	Barnett, Sydney Herbert, 2nd Lieut. H.L.I.		F.E.B. and C.J.B.	1909
	Baron, John, Major, E. Lancs. Reg. and M.G.C.	**Croce di Guerra**	W.D.H.	1907
	Bartleet, Thomas Edwin, 2nd Lieut. I.A. R O.		S.H.	1916
	Bartlett, Robert Arthur, Sub.-Lieut., R.N.		W.D.H.	1916
	Bartley, Eric Oswald, 2nd Lieut. Labour Corps.		S.H.	1911
	Barton, Cecil Molyneux, LL.D., Capt., R. Dublin Fus.		G.T.H. and W.D.H	1902
	Barwell, Ernest, 2nd Lieut., Labour Corps.		T.A.B. and S.H.	1887
	Bate, Thomas, Capt. R. Welch Fus.	**D.**	E.B.M.	1908
	Bath, John Euel Witherden, Capt., R. Berks. Regt.		S.H.	1912
	Bayley, Arthur George, Col., Ox. & Bucks. L.I., G.S.O.	**D.S.O. C.B.E. D⁴**	C.J.S.C.	1894
P.	Bayliss, William Murray Forbes, Lieut. 4th and 5th Lancers & R.A.F.		T.E.P.	1915
	Baynes, Philip Heacock, Sergeant, Rifle Bde.		S.H.	1897
	Bearcroft, Ernest Charles Lister, Lieut., R.M.	**D.**	F.M.I.	1916
	Beardmore, Charles Leslie Halifax, The Rev., Chaplain to the Forces.	**Serbian Order of White Eagle**	C.J.B. and G.T.H.	1895
P.W²	Beazley, Eric Bertram, Capt., K. Liverpool Regt.		F.E.B.	1895
	Becker, John Edward, Lieut., London Divl. Engineers.		·C.J.S.C.	1906
	Belk, Eric Herbert, Pte., Scottish Rifles (The Cameronians.)		E.B.M.	1911
	Bell, Alan Thorpe, L/Corpl., R.A.S.C. (M.T.)		F.E.B. and C.J.B.	1909
	Bell, Benedict Godfrey Allen, 2nd Lieut. R.A.F.		A.F.C.	1908
	Bell, Thomas Geoffrey, Capt. and Adjutant, Tank Corps.		C.J.B.	1916
W.	Benham, William George, Sub.-Lieut., R.N.V.R.		T.E.P.	1913
	Bennett, Arnold John, The Rev. Chaplain to the Forces.	**M.C.**	S.H.	1900
	Bennett, George Robert, 2nd Lieut., Connaught Rangers.		T.E.P.	1914
P.	Bennett, Herbert John, Major, Ox. and Bucks. L.I.	**M.C.**	F.E.B.	1895
	Bennett, John William, 2nd Lieut., R. Munster Fus.		S.H.	1908
	Bennett, Norman Butler, Capt. I.A.		C.J.S.C.	1908

	Bennett, Risdon, Lieut. Herts Regt. Staff.		S.H. 1901
	Bennitt, Harry Pynson Capt., Seaforth Highlanders.		C.J.S.C. 1887 †
	Benson, Percy Hugh, M.B., C.M., Surgeon-General, I.M.S.		S.H. 1869
P.W.	Beresford, Charles Venables, Major, Worcs. Regt. and R.A.F.	**D.**	S.H. 1895
P.	Beresford, Marcus de la Poer, 2nd Lieut. R.F.A.		S.H. 1899
	Berkeley, Rowland Broughton, Lieut-Commander, R.N.V.R.		S.H. 1892
	Best, John Arrowsmith, Major, R.A.S.C.	**M.C. D.**	F.E.B. 1903
	Best, John Samuel, Capt. Assam Valley Horse, I.A.		F.E.B. 1902
	Beswick, Harry, Capt. R. Welch Fus.		F.S. 1908
	Beswick, Wilfrid Thomas, M.R.C.S., Surgeon-Lieut. R.N.V.R.		F.E.B. and C.J.B. 1909
W.	Beswick, William, Lieut.-Col., R. W. Kent Regt.	**Croix de Guerre, D.**	F.S. 1904
	Bethell, Thomas Henry, Capt. R. Warwicks. Regt.	.	S.H. 1902
	Bevan, Henry Edward Jones, The Ven. Archdeacon, Chaplain to the Forces.		D.B. 1873
W.	Bevan, Temple Percy Molesworth, Lieut. Grenadier Guards.	**M.C.**	S.H. 1916
	Bevan, William, Capt. Transport Workers Bn.		D.B. 1898
W.	Beverley, Frank LL.B., Capt. R.G.A.	**M.C. Croce di Guerra**	E.B.M. 1900
	Bevir, Raymond, 2nd Lieut. R. Fus.		S.H. 1907
	Bickersteth, John Richard, Capt. Yorks. Hussars.		S.H. 1915
W.	Bidwell, Leonard Muriel Capt. Canadian Exped. Force.	**D.**	C.J.B. and E.B.M. 1900
W.	Biggar, James Maxwell Rawline, Capt. K.O.S.B. and T.M.B.		C.J.S.C. 1895
W³.P.	Bigland, Eric Walter, Capt. Cheshire Regt.		F.E.B. and C.J.B. 1907
	Bigwood, Ernest Guy, 2nd Lieut. R.M.	.	E.B.M. 1902
	Bird, Charles John Gwynne, Major, I.A.		. S.H. 1895
W.P.	Birds, Vernon Gilbert Moss, L/Corpl. Middlesex Regt.		T.E.P. 1914
	Birtwistle, William, Major, R.F.A.	**D.S.O. D²**	R.J.D. and A.F.C. 1901
	Blackledge, Geoffrey Glynn, Major, K. Liverpool Regt.	**M.C. (Bar). D.**	S.H. 1913
	Bladon, Harold Russell, Lieut. Cheshire Regt. and M.G.C.		F.M.I. 1914
W.	Blake, James Raymond . Capt. Worcs. Regt.	**D²**	S.H. 1904
	Blair, Alexander Macpherson, Capt. S. Lancs. Regt.		G.T.H. 1980

For explanations and abbreviations, see page 4.

10

	Bland, Valentine Stevens,	**M.C.**	E.B.M.	1905
	Capt. R.F.A.			
W.	Blaxland, Alan Bruce,		D.B.	1911
	Capt. and Adjutant, I.A.			
	Blaxland, Lionel Bruce,		D.B.	1916
	Capt. R.A.F.			
	Blease, Walker Lyon,		S.H.	1902
	Service with Red Cross Hospitals.			
	Blore, John Lawrence,		Master.	
	Major, K.S.L.I. Staff Capt.			
	Blundell, Arthur Walmsley,		E.B.M. and	
	Pte., K. Liverpool Regt.		F.T.P.	1912
	Blunt, Denzil Layton,		S.H.	1909
	Lieut. R.A.S.C.			
W.	Blunt, Hubert Porter,	**M.B.E. D.**	D.B.	1898
	Major, R. Warwicks.Regt.and			
	R.A.O.C.			
	Bock, John Vincent,		E.B.M.	1902
	Pte., K.R.R.C. attchd. Cheshire Regt.			
	Boddington, Myles,	**M.C.**	S.H.	1910
	Capt. K.S.L.I.			
	Boddington, Oswald William,		E.B.M.	1907
	Lieut. N. Staffs. Regt.			
	Boddington, Vincent Coke, The Rev.		G.T.H. and	
	Chaplain to the Forces.		W.D.H.	1901
	Bolton, Harry Hargreaves,		E.B.M.	1904
	Capt. E. Lancs. Regt.			
	Bolton, Maurice Baldwin,	**M.C.**	E.B.M.	1911
	Capt. E. Lancs. Regt.			
	Bond, George Douglas,	**M.C. (Bar)**	F.M.I.	1912
	Capt. K. Liverpool Regt.			
	Bone, Geoffrey Foster,		C.J.S.C.	1909
	Capt. Devon R.E. and R.A.F.			
	Bone, John,		C.J.S.C.	1900
	Capt. and Adjutant, Devon R.E.			
	Boote, Charles Edmund,		E.B.M.	1891
	Lt.-Col. N. Staffs. Regt.			
W.	**Booth, Frank Hardinge Follett,**		W.D.H.	1908
	Capt. Worcs. Regt.			
	Booth, Walter Richard Baxter,		F.T.P.	1916
	2nd Lieut. D. of Lancaster's Own Yeo.			
	Booth, Gerald,		F.E.B.	1896
	Lieut. Cheshire Regt.			
W.	Bornemann, Max E.,	**D²**	S.H.	1911
	Lieut. W. Riding Regt.			
	Bornemann, Oscar Louis,		S.H.	1908
	Corporal, Singapore Rifles.			
W.	Bosvile, John Godfrey Bolle,	**D.**	D.B.	1911
	Major, K.S.L.I. Army Cyclist Corps.			
	Botham, Arthur Frederick,	**D.**	Former Master	
	Lieut. and Adjutant, R.F.A.			
	Bottomley, George Rhodes,		S.H.	1911
	Capt. R.F.A. and T.M.B.			
	Bottomley, Edwin Rhodes,		E.B.M. and	
	Lieut. R.A.F.		F.T.P.	1913
	*Boucher, Bazil Edward Creswell,	Croce di Guerra. **D.**	T.E.P.	1916
	Lieut. R. Welch Fus.			

For explanations and abbreviations, see page 4.

Boucher, William Armstrong, Major (Hon.) Senior Assistant Surgeon, I.M.S.			D.B.	1879
Boumphrey, Arthur Noel, Capt. K. Liverpool Regt.	**D²**		F.E.B.	1906
Boumphrey, Colin, Capt. R.A.F.			A.F.C.	1915
Boumphrey, Donald, Major, M.G.C.	**M.C. D.**		A.F.C.	1912
P. Boumphrey, Joseph Whalley, Lieut. Cheshire Hussars and R.A.F.			F.E.B.	1901
Boumphrey, Roy, Capt. Cheshire Hussars Yeo. and R.A.F.			F.E.B. and C.J.B.	1908
Boutflower, Geoffrey, Capt. and Bt. Major, R.A.S.C.	**O.B.E. D.**		E.B.M.	1902
Bowden, John Hadfield, 2nd Lieut. R.G.A.			F.M.I.	1917
Bowden, Tom Rose, Capt. R.G.A.			F.M.I.	1915
Bower, Richard, Capt. K. Liverpool Regt., Adjt. Lancs. Vol. Regt.			A.F.C.	1893
Bowdler, John Charles Henry, Pte., Shropshire Vol. Regt.			D.B.	1888
Bowdler, John Ernest Benjamin, 2nd Lieut. R.F.A.			D.B.	1918
W. Bowen-Cooke Victor Rashleigh, Lieut. R.E.			W.D.H.	1914
Bowles, Humphry Charles Bradshaw, Capt. R.F.A.			E.B.M.	1899
Bowring, Charles Thurston, Lieut. Canadian Infantry, M.G.C.	**D.**		C.J.S.C.	1899
Bowring, Cyril, Capt. K. Liverpool Regt., Adjutant.	**D.**		C.J.S.C.	1905
Bowring, Frank Harvey, Major, K. Liverpool Regt.			C.J.S.C.	1898
W. Bowring, Edgar Rennie, 2nd Lieut. R.F.A.			T.E.P.	1917
Bowring, Frederick Clive, Capt. and Adjutant, K. Liverpool Regt.	**D²**		T.E.P.	1914
Bowring, Harold, M.B., Major, R.A.M.C.			C.J.S.C.	1901
Boxwell, Ambrose, Major, I.A.	**C.I.E. D²**		G.T.H.	1894
Boxwell, William, Capt., R.A.M.C.			G.T.H.	1893
W. Boyd, Laurence Chadwick, Lieut. R.A.F. and R. Munster Fus.			S.H.	1905
Boyd, Winnett Wornabe, Lieut. Canadian Artillery and R.A.F.			S.H.	1906
Bracewell, Charles Hargreaves, Capt. E. Lancs. Regt.			C.J.S.C. and T.E.P.	1911
Brace, George Bedford, 2nd Lieut. R.G.A.			D.B.	1902
Bradburn, Thomas Stratford, M.R.C.S., Temp. Surgeon, R.N.	Russian Order of St. Anne with Swords.		S.H.	1899

For explanations and abbreviations, see page 4.

	Bradley, Cuthbert Wilding,		S.H.	1909
	Capt. K.O.R. Lancaster Regt.			
W.	Bramall, Kenneth George McLeod,		W.D.H.	1911
	Capt. Royal Scots Fus. & I.A. R.O.			
	Bramall, Francis Marmion,		W.D.H.	1915
	Lieut. R.M.L.I.			
	*__Bramwell, Edward Hargreaves,__		W.D.H. and	
	Lieut. R.A.F.		G.T.H.	1896
	Brancker, Thomas, The Rev.,		C.J.S.C.	1896
	Chaplain to the Forces,		W.D.H.	
W.	Brassey, Laurence Percival, M.B.	**D²**	C.J.S.C.	1893
	Lt.-Col., I.M.S.			
	Brassey, Robert Egerton,		A.F.C.	1904
	Capt. Cheshire Hussars Yeo.			
W.	Brashaw, Arthur Clement,		F.T.P.	1916
	2nd Lieut. K.S.L.I.			
	Breese, Charles Edward,		S.H.	1881
	Hon. Major, Training Reserve.			
	Bremner, Rupert Henry,		C.J.S.C.	1902
	Capt, R.H. and R.F.A.			
	Bremner, Stewart Bruce Macduff,		F.E.B.	1907
	Lieut. N. Irish Horse.			
	Brennand, Cecil Walter,		G.T.H.	1900
	Capt. Dragoon Guards.			
	Brewis, Arthur,	**D.**	C.J.S.C.	1890
	Major, S. Lancs. Regt.			
	Bridge, Philip Sydney Rabnett,		D.B.	1895
	Lieut. R.A.S.C. (M.T.)			
	Bridges, Arthur Edmund,		S.H.	1918
	2nd Lieut. R.M.			
	Bridges, Philip Harriot,		S.H.	1914
	2nd Lieut. Glos. Regt. and R.A.F.			
	Bridges, William Robert,		S.H.	1913
	2nd Lieut. Beds. Regt.			
	Brierley, Henry,	**M.C.**	W.D.H.	1916
	Capt. Rifle Bde.			
W.	Brierley, James,	**D.**	F.M.I.	1914
	Lieut. Manchester, Regt.			
P.	Brierley, Richard,		W.D.H.	1911
	Capt. I.A.R.O.			
W²	Briggs, Thomas William,	**D.**	J.B.O.	1914
	Major, R.F.A.			
	Brindle, John Lawrence,		W.D.H.	1913
	Capt. L. N. Lancs. Regt.			
	Briscoe, Arthur John Trevor,		S.H.	1890
	Lieut. R.N.V.R.			
	Briscoe, Frederick Ernest Trevor,		S.H.	1893
	Capt. R.A.S.C. (M.T.)			
	Britton, Noel Edward,		D.B.	1903
	Lieut. R.E.			
W.	Britton, William Lewis,		S.H.	1915
	Lieut. Yeo. and M.G.C.			
	Broadbent, Harold,		S.H.	1908
	Pte., Rifle Brigade.			
	Brocklehurst, William Argyll,		C.J.S.C.	1897
	Capt. Cheshire Regt.			
	Brodie, Eric Brownlee,		F.M.I.	1914
	Lieut. R.A.F.			

For explanations and abbreviations, see page 4.

	Brook, Arthur Kenneth, Lieut. W. Riding Regt.		S.H.	1907
	Brook, Arthur King, Lieut. R.A.S.C. (M.T.)		S.H.	1886
	Brooke, Frederick William, Pte., York and Lancaster Regt.		T.E.P.	1913
W.	Brown, Austin Charles, Lieut. R.F.A.		C.J.S.C.	1902
	Brown, Arthur Graham, Lieut. London Regt.		F.E.B.	1896
	Brown, Charles Reginald, Major, R.F.A.	**D.**	S.H.	1904
	Brown, Cecil Arthur, Lieut. Sherwood Foresters.		W.D.H.	1913
	Brown, David, Capt. S. Lancs. Regt.		E.B.M.	1904
	Brown, George Bolney, 2nd Lieut. R.E.		S.H.	1908
P.	Brown, Herbert Cecil, Lieut. K.O.R. Lancaster Regt.		S.H.	1910
	Brown, Horace George, Surgeon, R.N.		F.E.B.	1896
	Brown, Maurice Buchanan, Capt. E. Lancs. Regt.		S.H.	1915
W²	Brown, Thomas Ward, Lieut. K.O.R. Lancaster Regt.		S.H.	1907
	Brown, William Anthony, Capt. Wilts. Regt.	**Order of the Nile, D.**	C.J.S.C.	1895
	Brown. William Leonard, 2nd Lieut. Sherwood Foresters.		W.D.H.	1909
	Browne, Arthur Symonds, Major, Shropshire Vol. Regt.	**D.**	D.B.	1891
	Browne, Barwick Sharp, Major, R.G.A.		C.J.S.C.	1898
W.	Browne, Thomas Lyster, 2nd Lieut. Burmah Rifles.		W.D.H.	1910
W.	Brownell, Walter Robinson, Major, K. Liverpool Regt.	**M.C.** **D.**	C.J.B. and F.E.B.	1901
	Brundrit, Percy Wright, Hon. Capt. Vol. Bn. R. Welsh Regt.		E.B.M.	1894
	Brunskill, Gerald, Lieut. R. Sussex Regt., Staff Capt.	**M.C.** **D.**	A.F.C.	1914
	Buchanan, Basil Roberts, 2nd Lieut. Labour Corps.		W.S.I.	1914
	Bulman, Andrew, Lieut. K.O.S.B.		S.H.	1907
	Bulmer, Geoffrey Percival, Lieut. K.S.L.I. and R.A.F.	**M.C.**	S.H.	1913
	Bunney, Frederick William Edward, Lieut. T.F.R.		D.B.	1893
	***Burbury, Francis William,** Lt.-Col. R.W. Kent Regt.		S.H.	1884
W.	Burdass, Frederick George, Lieut. Herefordshire Regt.		D.B.	1913
	Burdekin, Alan Stockdale, Lieut. Suffolk Regt.		F.E.B.	1901

14

	Burdekin, Arthur Hugh, Lieut. K.O.R. Lancaster Regt. Staff Capt.		F.E.B. 1905
	Burge, Cecil Gerard, Paymaster Lieut. R.N.V.R.		S.H. 1915
W.P.	Burgess, Jack Stanley, Sergt. K. African Rifles.		F.S. 1908
	Burney, Gilbert Edward, **D.** Lieut. Gordon Highlanders. A.D.C.		C.J.S.C. 1910
	Burnie, John Gilchrist, Pte., R. Fus.		S.H. 1911
W²	Burnyeat, William Maurice Brownlie, **M.C. D²** Capt. Monmouths. Regt.		F.S. 1902
	Burrough, John, The Rev. Chaplain to the Forces.		G.T.H. 1892
	Burton, David Stuart Gaselee, **Croix de Guerre** 2nd Lieut. Motor Ambulance Dvr. **French.** and Flying Officer, R.A.F.		C.J.S.C. 1906
	Burton, Kenrick Hamond, Lieut. K. Liverpool Regt.		T.E.P. 1914
	Burton, Percy Merceron, A.B. Anti-Aircraft Corps, R.N.V.R.		A.F.C. 1888
	Burton, Ronald Cowper, Capt. R.A.S.C.		C.J.S.C. 1910
	Burton, William Edward Alan, Pte. Inns of Court O.T.C.		F.M.I. 1915
	Bury, John, Lieut. R.F.A.		E.B.M. and F.T.P. 1911
	Butterworth, Harold, **M.C.** Lieut. R.F.A.		F.T.P. 1915
	Byrd, Hugh Linley, A.M.I.C.E., Lieut. R.M. (Engineers).		A.F.C. 1901
	Bythell, John Francis, Sergt.-Instructor, London Scottish Regt.		T.E.P. 1918
	Calcott, Charles David, Lieut. K. Liverpool Regt.		D.B. 1910
	Caldicott, John Moore, Prob. Flight Officer, R.N.A.S.		F.M.I. 1918
	Cameron, The Hon. Edward John, K.C.M.G., Governor and Commander-in-Chief of the Gambia.		S.H. 1873
W.	Campbell-Jones, Mervyn, Lieut., R.A.S.C.		S.H. 1913
W.	Campbell, Cecil James Henry, **D²** Major, R.A.S.C.		S.H. 1910
	Campbell, Edward, Lieut. N. Staffs. Regt.		C.J.B. 1914
W.	Campbell, Charles William (of Boreland), **M.C.** Major, R.F.A.		W.D.H. 1905
	Cant, Frederick Vaudrey, Capt. R.A.M.C.		C.J.S.C. 1909
W.	Cant, Geoffrey Yeld, Lieut. E. Lancs. Regt.		F.T.P. 1916
	Cardwell, Norman, Lieut. K.O.Y.L.I.		S.H. 1910
	Carrow, Harry Frederick, Ceylon Planters' Rifle Corps.		W.D.H. 1905
P.	Carter, Guy Lloyd, **D.** Lieut. R.A.F.		S.H. 1917

For explanations and abbreviations, see page 4.

W²	Carter, Henry Gordon, Major, R. Welch Fus.	M.C.	S.H.	1912
	Carter, Harold Leslie Mark, Lieut. R.G.A. and I.A.		A.F.C.	1907
	Carter, W. Hamilton, Lieut. Welsh Guards.		S.H.	1914
W.	Cartman, John Philip Chabert, Lieut. Dorset Regt.		S.H.	1894
	Carus-Wilson, Trevor, Lt.-Col. D.C.L.I.	**D.S.O. T.D. D³**	G.T.H.	1887
	Carver, Edmund Tucker, Major, R.A.S.C.	**D.**	E.B.M.	1903
	Case, George Ronald Ashburner, 2nd Lieut. S. Lancs. Regt.		E.B.M. and F.T.P.	1914
	Catterall, Sidney, 2nd Lieut. London Regt.		W.D.H.	1899
W.	Cattlow, Hugh Ford, Gunner, R.G.A.		D.B.	1892
	Cave Browne, William, Major, R.E.	**D.S.O. M.C. Order of the Nile 4th Class. D⁴**	S.H.	1903
	Cave-Browne Cave, Norman, Capt. R. Welch Fus.		C.J.B.	1909
	Cemlyn-Jones, Elias Wynne, Capt. R. Welch Fus.	**M.B.E.**	E.B.M.	1907
	Chadwick, Archibald Eustace, Lieut. D.L.I. and R.A.F.		S.H.	1901
	Chadwick, Brian Lloyd, Lieut. R.G.A.		E.B.M.	1910
	Chadwick, Charles Eric, The Rev., Chaplain to the Forces.		G.T.H.	1894
	Chadwick, Cyril, Corporal, Signal Service.		E.B.M.	1906
W²	Chadwick, Frank, Major, K.R.R.C.	**D.S.O. (Bar). M.C.**	E.B.M.	1910
	Chaffers, Hubert, Trooper, K. Edward's Horse.		F.E.B. and C.J.B.	1907
	Chaloner, John Cole, Lieut. R.A.S.C.		C.J.S.C.	1908
	Chambers, Corney Royston, Capt. R.F.A.		F.M.I.	1913
	Champion-Jones, Douglas, Lt.-Col. R.E.	**D.S.O. Cross of Chevalier of Legion of Honour D²**	S.H.	1894
	Chance, Harry, Col. Res. of Officers.		S.H.	1873
	Chandler, Ernest L. Lieut. R.F.A.		C.J.B.	1916
W²	Channer, George Kendall, Lt.-Col. Gurkha Rifles.	**D.S.O. D.**	S.H.	1891
	Charlesworth, Edward Adams, Pte. R.A.M.C.		C.J.S.C.	1887
	Chaytor, Charles Grainger, 2nd Lieut. R. Innis. Fus.		F.T.P.	1918
	Chell, Harold, Lieut. R. Fus.		A.F.C.	1908
W.	Childe, Edwyn Ralph, Lieut. Worcs. Regt.		F.T.P.	1915

For explanations and abbreviations, see page 4.

	Christophers, Edgar St. John, Major, Northumberland Fus. (attd.)	**D.S.O. D.**	T.A.B. 1876
	Church, John Victor, Lieut. K.S.L.I.		S.H. 1915
	Christie, Arthur, Capt. T.F.R.		S.H. 1910
W.	Churton, Harry Leslie, Capt. Cheshire Regt.	**D.**	W.D.H. and A.F.C. 1897
	Churton, John Gaitskill, Lt.-Col. R.A.M.C.		E.B.M. 1892
	Churton, William Arthur Vere, Lt.-Col. Cheshire Regt.	**D.S.O. T.D. D³**	A.F.C. 1895
	Churton, Thomas, M.D., M.R.C.S., Major, R.A.M.C. (T.F.R.)		S.H. 1854
W.	Clapham, John Walker, Capt. West Riding Regt. and M.G.C.	**M.C.**	F.T.P. 1913
	Clark, Charles Frederick, Jun., Lieut. Cheshire Yeo.	**Croix de Guerre (French).**	T.E.P. 1911
	Clark, Edwin Kitson, Lt.-Col. W. Yorks Regt.	**T.D.**	S.H. 1885
	Clark, Thomas Jackson, 2nd Lieut. R.A.S.C.		C.J.B. 1914
	Clarke, Edward Francis Routh, Lieut. Gen. List.		G.T.H. 1901
	Clarke, Geoffrey 2nd Lieut. I.A.R.O.		G.T.H. 1899
	Clarke, Henry Harold, Capt. R. Welch Fus. and R.A.F.		D.B. 1900
	Cleaver, Claude Rex, Capt. and Adjutant, I.A.		C.J.S.C. 1903
	Cleaver, Eric Arnold, Lieut. E. Yorks Regt., Balloon Commander, R.A.F.		W.D.H. 1896
	Cleaver, Geoffrey Harris, Capt. R.F.A.		C.J.S.C. 1909
W.	Cleaver, Percy Alan, Lieut. Glos. Regt.		C.J.S.C. 1896
	Clifford, Arthur William (formerly Phelps), Capt. Glos. Regt. Staff Capt.		G.T.H. 1897
W.	Climo, Skipton Hill, Maj.-Gen., I.A.	**C.B. D.S.O. Order of the Nile. D⁵**	C.J.S.C. 1886
W²	**Climo, Verschoyle Crawford,** Major, Manchester Regt.	**D²**	D.B. and S.H. 1885
	Clover, Alan, The Rev., Chaplain and Pte. Vol. Bn. Glos. Regt.		G.T.H. 1892
	Clover, Henry Edward, Lt.-Col. R.E. Staff.	**O.B.E. D²**	F.E.B. 1901
	Clover, Martin, Capt. R.A.M.C.		G.T.H. 1890
	Cobb, Alan, Lieut. R. Warwicks. Regt.		C.J.S.C. 1900
	Cobbett, Herbert Richard, Lt-Col. Lancs. Fus.		S.H. 1888
W.P.	Cobden, Hugh, Major, K.O.S.B.		E.B.M. 1899
	Cochran, Alexander, Capt. Indian Defence Force.	**C.B.E. O.B.E.**	C.J.S.C. 1897
W.	Cochrane, Duncan Evers, Lt. Dragoon Guards.		S.H. 1901

	Cochrane, Ralph, 2nd Lieut. R.E.		C.J.B.	1917
P.	Cock, Geoffrey Hornblower, Capt. R.A.F.	**M.C.**	D.B.	1912
	Cockburn, George, Lieut. R.F.A.	**Croix de Guerre (French).**	W.D.H.	1908
	Cockburn, William Bingham, Capt. K. Liverpool Regt.		W.D.H.	1907
	Cocksedge, Thomas Abraham Bryan, Major, A.V.C.,	**D.**	F.E.B.	1902
	Coey, Edward, Jun., Capt. M.G.C.		F.E.B. and C.J.B.	1909
W.	Coey, George Hamilton, Lieut. R. Irish Rifles.		C.J.B.	1902
	Coey, James Arthur, Capt. N. Irish Horse.	**D.**	C.J.B.	1910
	Coke, Desmond Francis Talbot, Capt. and Adjt. L. N. Lancs. Regt.	**D.**	C.J.S.C.	1899
	Coldwell, Guy Hope, Lieut. R.A.S.C.		D.B. and F.E.B.	1902
	Coleridge, George Selwyn Campbell, Lieut. Ox. and Bucks L.I. and R.D.C.		C.J.S.C.	1886
W.	Coles, John Lord, Lieut. York and Lancaster Regt.		S.H.	1910
	Collier, Ashton Nelson, Capt. R.A.M.C.		C.J.B.	1894
	Collier, James Luke, Lieut. Northants Regt.		C.J.B.	1913
W.	Collins, Edward Duppa, Capt. K.S.L.I.		C.J.B.	1912
	Colquhoun, Arthur Hugh, Capt. R.A.O.D.	**O.B.E. D³**	S.H.	1894
	Colt, Thomas Archer, Commdnt. Branksmere Aux. Hospital, Southsea.	**C.B.E.**	S.H.	1871
	Comins, Richard Innes, Lieut. 12th Cavalry, I.A.		W.D.H.	1915
	Conran, Owen Mostyn, Major, R.A.F.		W.D.H.	1896
	Cooke, Arthur Ingram, Capt. Staff Surgeon, R.A.M.C.		E.B.M.	1899
	Cooke, Ernest Maitland, The Rev., Chaplain to the Forces.		E.B.M.	1902
	Cooke, Herbert Edward, The Rev. Chaplain to the Forces.		E.B.M.	1899
	Cooke, John Howard, Lieut. R.A.S.C. attchd. R.G.A.		E.B.M.	1910
W.	Cooke, Wilfrid Edward, Lieut. R.F.A.	**M.C.**	D.B.	1915
	Coombs, Charles John Plumbe, Sergt., Carnarvonshire Vol. Regt.		G.T.H.	1876
W.	Cooper, Alan Withington, Major, Manchester Regt.		E.B.M.	1905
	Cooper, Charles D'Oyley, 2nd Lieut. Res. Regt. of Cavalry.		C.J.S.C.	1890
W.	Cooper, Frank Sandiford, Col. and Bt. Lt.-Col. Suffolk Regt.	**D.S.O. D⁴**	D.B.	1891

	Cooper, Robert Henry, Lieut. Suffolk Regt.				D.B.	1891
	Corbett-Lowe, William Sydney, Capt. and Adjutant, K. Liverpool Regt.				C.J.S.C.	1896
W⁴	Corder, Terence Spence, Lieut. R.F.A.				C.J.B.	1915
	Corfield, John Wilmot, Pte. British Columbia Regt.				W.D.H.	1910
W.	Corfield, Ralph Tregoning Channer, Lieut. R.H. and R.F.A.				W.D.H.	1912
W.	Corser, Eric Edward, Lieut. K.S.L.I.				S.H.	1914
W.	Corser, Frederick George, Lieut. R.F.A.				D.B.	1904
	Corser, John Sidney, LL.B., Lieut. Hamps. Regt.				F.E.B.	1897
W.	Cort, James Russell, Lieut. Seaforth Highlanders.				W.D.H. and F.S.	1902
	Cort, John Leonard Patchit, Lieut. R.A.F.				W.D.H.	1900
	Cosgrave, Alexander Kirkpatrick, M.B.	**M.C.**			G.T.H. and W.D.H.	1902
W.	Cotterell, George Cecil Blencowe, Flight Sub.-Lieut., R.A.F.				W.D.H.	1915
	Cotterell, John Nicholas Franklin, 2nd Lieut. R.F.A.				W.S.I. and T.E.P.	1918
	Cottrell, George Swinfen, 2nd Lieut. R.A.S.C.				S.H.	1904
	Coulman, Edward Raymond, 2nd Lieut. R.A.S.C. (M.T.)				T.E.P.	1917
	Court, Christopher Charles Cole, M.B.	**D.**			D.B.	1904
	Major, R.A.M.C.					
	Court, Harold Darlington Henry, Capt. R.E.	**D.**			E.B.M.	1909
W.	Coverdale, Miles, Lieut. D.L.I.				W.D.H.	1912
	Cowie, Henry Edward Colvin, Lt.-Col. R.E.	**D.S.O.**	**C.B.E.**	**D.**	S.H.	1891
W.	Cowie, John, Lieut. W. Riding Regt.				S.H.	1901
	Cowlishaw, Frederick Clifford, Lieut. York and Lancaster Regt.				T.E.P.	1914
	Cowlishaw, Leslie, Pte. Inns of Court O.T.C. and R.A.S.C.				T.E.P.	1916
	Cox, John Ward, Lieut. Sherwood Foresters.				W.D.H.	1908
	Cox, Thomas Allard, 2nd Lieut. R.A.S.C.				E.B.M.	1891
	Coxon, Richard Humphrey, Pte. London Regt.				E.B.M.	1908
W³	Cragg, William Gilliat, Lt.-Col. L. N. Lancs. Regt.	**D.S.O.**	**D²**		C.J.S.C.	1901
	Craig, John, V.D. Temp. Major, Recruiting duties.	**T.D.**	**D.**		D.B.	1871
W.	Craig, John Francis, Col., R.F.A.	**C.M.G.**	**D²**		D.B.	1873

	Craig, William Henry Pryse,	**M.C. D³**	G.T.H.	1895
	Capt. R.E., Brigade Major on R.E. Staff.			
	Cramer-Roberts, Francis William Henry **D.**		S.H.	1893
	Capt. R.A.O.D.			
	Cramsie, Robert Alexander,		S.H.	1905
	Capt. R.A.S.C.			
W³	Cranage, Roger William,		E.B.M. and	
	Capt. Northumberland Fus.		F.T.P.	1913
	Cranstoun, Gordon,		C.J.S.C.	1905
	Capt. R.A.F. (M.S.)			
	Craven, William Cecil,		E.B.M.	1910
	Capt. R.M.A.			
	Crawford, Denzil,		T.E.P.	1918
	2nd Lieut. R.A.F.			
	Crawford-Clarke, Richard William Bunney, **M.C. D²**		S.H.	1912
	Capt. and Adjt. R.G.A. Staff Lieut.			
	Crawford-Clarke, Walter Harley,	**M.C.**	S.H.	1913
	Capt. R. Monmouths. R.E.			
	Crawford-Clarke, William Richard,	**D.**	D.B.	1879
	Pte. Shrops. Vol. Regt.			
	Crawley, Frank Hubert Macarthy Chetwode,		A.F.C. and	
	Capt., R.A.M.C.		S.H.	1887
	Cree, Arthur Thomas Crawford,		S.H.	1900
	Lieut. D.L.I.			
W.	Cree, John Francis George,		S.H.	1900
	Capt. Welsh Regt. (attchd.)			
	Cresswell, Cyril Eystein,	**D.**	S.H.	1907
	Lieut. Herefords. Regt.			
	Cresswell, George Edmund,		S.H.	1905
	Sergt. A.V.S.			
	Crew, Denis Merville,		T.E.P.	1912
	Lieut. Cheshire Regt.			
W³	Crocker, Herbert Edmund,	**D.S.O. C.M.G. D⁵**	S.H.	1894
	Bt. Lt.-Col. Essex Regiment.			
	Croft, Henry Page, M.P.,	**C.M.G. T.D. D²**	S.H.	1899
	Hon. Brig. Gen. T.F.R.			
	Crook, John Frederick,		W.D.H.	1907
	Lieut. Lancs. Fus.			
W.	Crosfield, Eric Oliver,		A.F.C.	1911
	Major, S. Lancs. Regt. : Egyptian Army.			
	Crosfield, Guy Henry Goad,		A.F.C.	1915
	Lieut. Rifle Brigade.			
	Crosfield, Leonard Mellor,		T.E.P.	1916
	2nd Lieut. Ox. and Bucks L.I.			
W.	Cross, Charles Norman,	**M.C. (Bar)**	C.J.B. and	
	Major, R.F.A.		A.F.C.	1904
	Cross, Ernest Llewellyn,		D.B.	1806
	Corporal, Manchester Regt.			
W²	Cross, George Henry,	**D.**	C.J.S.C.	1901
	Lieut. K. Liverpool Regt.			
	Cross, Robert Singlehurst,		A.F.C.	1906
	Lieut. K. Liverpool Regt.			
	Cross, William Gowen,		D.B.	1864
	Pte. Shrops. Vol. Regt.			

For explanations and abbreviations, see page 4.

	Cross, William Gowen, Jun., Pte. Shrops. Vol. Regt.		D.B.	1899
	Crosthwaite, Charles Gilbert, Major, I.A.	O.B.E.	S.H.	1894
	Crosthwaite, Vivian Forsyth, Pte., London Regt.		F.M.I.	1917
	Crowther, Edgar, Lieut. R.N.V.R.		S.H.	1897
	Cullimore, William, Lieut. Cheshire Regt. and R.A.F.		C.J.S.C.	1906
	Culverwell, George Hugh, M.D., Major, R.A.M.C.		S.H.	1905
	Culverwell, Oliver Gerald, Lieut., R.A.S.C.		C.J.S.C.	1910
	Cunliffe, Sir Foster Hugh Egerton, Bart. Major, Rifle Brigade.		Governor.	
	Curtis, Frank Archibald, Lieut. R.A.S.C.		F.S.	1905
	Da Costa, Augustus Edward, Capt. Hants. Regt.		E.B.M.	1907
	Dale, Alwyn Percy, Major, W. Yorks. Regt.	O.B.E.	S.H.	1898
	Daniel, William Glyn, Capt. R. Welch Fus.		W.S.I.	1915
W.	Dansey, Guy Reginald, Pte., Canadian Infantry.		G.T.H.	1893
	Darbishire, Charles Stephen, Capt. R.E.		E.B.M.	1906
	Darbishire, Harold Dukinfield, LL.B. Major, R.F.A.		E.B.M.	1900
	Darley, Harold Pim, Lieut. and Adjutant, R.A.S.C.		F.M.I.	1912
	Darlington, Henry Clayton, Lt.-Col. Manchester Regt.	C.M.G. T.D. Officer of the Order of the Crown of Italy. D³	S.H.	1895
W²	Darlington, William Aubrey Cecil, Capt. (Adjt.) Northumberland Fus.		F.E.B. and C.J.B.	1909
W.	Dashwood, Gerald Raikes, Lieut. R.F.A. Anti-Aircraft Battery.		W.D.H.	1912
W.	Dashwood, Richard Raikes, 2nd Lieut. Northumberland Fus.		W.D.H.	1909
·	David, Charles John Evan, Major, R.E. Tunnelling Co.		C.J.S.C.	1899
W.	Davies, Alfred John Mackenzie, Capt. Welsh Regt.		A.F.C.	1911
W³	Davies, Arthur Lloyd, Capt., R.F.A.	M.C. (Bar).	J.B.O.	1914
W.	Davies, Daniel Gordon, Lieut. Welsh Horse Yeo. attchd. Welsh Regt.		F.S.	1906
	Davies, David, The Rev. Canon, Chaplain to the Forces.		S.H.	1876
	Davies, Gwilym Merion, Lieut. R. Welch Fus.		D.B.	1898
	Davies, John Ambler, 2nd Lieut. Welsh Guards.		W.D.H.	1917
W.	Davies, John Harold Twiston, 2nd Lieut., R.A.F.		J.B.O.	1917

	Davies, John Norman,		S.H.	1912
	Lieut. R. Welch Fus.			
	Davies, John Taylor,		D.B.	1894
	Capt. Montgomeryshire Yeo. Staff Officer.			
	Davies, Thomas Henry,		D.B.	1896
	Lieut. K.S.L.I.			
	Davies, Walter Ambler,		W.D.H.	1912
	2nd Lieut. E. N. Lancs. Regt.			
W²	Davies, William Twiston,	**M.C.**	A.F.C.	1910
	Capt. Highland L.I.			
W.	Davis, Ivor Aneurin, The Rev.	**M.C.**	G.T.H. and	
	2nd Lieut. Yorks. Hussars.		W.D.H.	1903
	Chaplain to the Forces.			
	Dawson, Ernest Edward,		S.H.	1905
	Major, Cheshire Regt.			
	Day, Jack Hamilton,		S.H.	1906
	2nd Lieut., Yorks. Regt.			
	Deakin, Geoffrey Ward,		D.B.	1905
	Capt., R.E.			
	De Crespigny, George Arthur O. Champion,		F.M.I.	1911
	Lieut. Suffolk Regt. and Tank Corps.			
W.	De Hamel, Egbert Alexander,	**M.C. D.**	E.B.M.	1906
	Capt. S. Staffs. Regt.			
	Delap, Alexander,		C.J.B.	1910
	2nd Lieut. Leinster Regt.			
	De la Hey, Cyril James Oldridge,		T.E.P.	1914
	Capt., Jacob's Horse, I.A.			
W²	Dempsey, Miles Christopher,	**M.C. D.**	A.F.C.	1914
	Capt. (Adjutant) R. Berks. Regt.			
W²	Dempsey, Patrick Henry Delafosse,		A.F.C.	1913
	Capt. R. Irish Fus. Staff Captain.			
	Demuth, Robert Arthur,		F.E.B.	1893
	Sub-Lieut. Hawke Bn. R.N.R.			
	Dendy, Edward Herbert ,M.B.		C.J.S.C. and	
	Capt. R.A.M.C.		T.E.P.	1910
	Densham, Walter Henry,	**M.C.**	W.S.I.	1915
	Lieut. R.F.A.			
P.	Denton, Richard Angrave,		G.T.H.	1894
	L./Corpl., Canadian Mounted Rifles			
	Deuchar, Gordon E.,		E.B.M. and	
	Corporal, Northumberland Fus.		F.T.P.	1912
	DeWoolfson, Albert Henry Frederick,	**O.B.E. D⁴**	D.B.	1896
	Engineer Lt.-Commander, R.I.M.			
	Inland Water Transport.			
	Dickin, Edwin Spencer,	**D.**	S.H.	1891
	Major, Queen's Bays (Res.)			
W³	Dickins, Arthur Richard Anson,		S.H.	1911
	Capt. S. Staffs. Regt. Staff Capt.			
	Dickson, Arthur Hubert,		S.H.	1902
	2nd Lieut. Recruiting Duties.			
	Dickson, Gerald Hector,		E.B.M.	1897
	Capt. (Adjutant) L.N. Lancs. Regt.			
P.	Dickson, Thomas Henry		S.H.	1894
	Sub-Lieut. R.N.			
	Dickinson, Geoffrey Garbutt,		W.D.H.	1916
	2nd Lieut. R.F.A.			

W²	Dixon, John Bowey, Capt. R.E.	**D.**	F.E.B.	1900
	Dixon, John Vibart, 2nd Lieut. R.F.A.		S.H.	1915
	Dixon-Nuttall, Thomas, Lieut. R.E.		S.H.	1912
	Dobson, Robert Arthur, Officers' Cadet Unit, R.F.A.		C.J.B.	1918
	Dobbs, George Eric Burroughs, Lt.-Col. R.E.	**Cross of Chevalier of the Legion of Honour. D³**	G.T.H. and W.D.H.	1901
W.P.	Dobbs, John Fritz Kivas, Capt. R. Dublin Fus.	**M.C.**	W.D.H.	1906
	Dobbs, William Evelyn Joseph, I.C.S. Major, I.A. (Res. of Officers).		G.T.H.	1899
W.	Dobell, Alfred Temple, 2nd Lieut. K. Liverpool Regt.		E.B.M.	1899
W.	Dobell, Robert Lyle, Capt. (Adjutant) K. Liverpool Regt. A.D.C.		E.B.M.	1908
	Dodd, Ernest Leigh, Major, R.F.A.	**M.C.**	W.D.H.	1908
	Douglass, James Henry, Major, R.A.M.C.	**O.B.E.**	A.F.C.	1893
	Douglas, Malcolm, Major, M.G.C.	**D.**	D.B.	1909
	Dove, Ernest Percy, Lieut. I.A. and R.A.F.		C.J.S.C.	1895
W.	Dowson, William Head, Pte. Yorks. Regt.		S.H.	1893
P.	Doyle, David Colquhoun, 2nd Lieut. R.A.F.		A.F.C.	1915
W.	Draper, John Godfrey Beresford, 2nd Lieut. Yorks. L.I.		S.H.	1914
W.	Draper, Robert Maurice, Pte. Australian Force.		A.F.C.	1915
W.	Dresser, Harold Bruce, Lt.-Col. R.F.A.	**D.S.O. D²**	E.B.M.	1892
	Dreydel, Alfred Joseph, Capt. R.A.F.		C.J.B. and G.T.H.	1899
	Drinkwater, Frederick Andrew Worsley, Major, R.A.M.C.		D.B.	1893
	Druce, Vere Powys, Lt.-Col. Beds. Regt.		C.J.S.C.	1894
	Duffin, John Terence, Major, D.A.A.G. Staff Capt.	**M.C. (Bar).**	C.J.S.C.	1902
	Dulley, Edward Henry, Lieut. R.A.S.C.		S.H.	1904
W.	Duncan, Francis John, Major-General, R. Scots Fus. Mil. Attaché.	**D.S.O., C.B., C.M.G., D⁵, Croix de Guerre (Belgian), Officer Legion d'Honneur.**	G.T.H.	1887
	Duncan, George Henry Frederick, Lieut. County of London Vol. Regt.		S.H.	1886
	Duncan, Norman, 2nd Lieut. R.A.F.		D.B.	1917
W.	Dunn, William Norman, Capt. Leicestershire Regt.		T.A.B. and S.H.	1892

Durant, William Beresford, Pte. Artists' Rifles.		T.E.P.	1916
Dutton, Charles, Lieut. London Regt.		F.E.B. and C.J.B.	1907
Dwyer, Charles Henry, Capt. (Adjt.) Worcs. Regt.	**D.**	F.M.I.	1914
Dyer, Gilbert, 2nd Lieut. K.S.L.I.		J.B.O.	1918
W. Dymond, Frank Jeffcott, Capt. York Regt. Staff Lieut.		W.D.H. and C.J.S.C.	1898
Dyson, William Lionel, Lieut. and Adjt., Border Regt. Depôt.		S.H.	1905
Ealand, Arthur Noel, O.S. Motor Ambulance Driver, 2nd Lieut. R. Regt. of Cav., 2nd Lieut. R.A.F.		E.B.M.	1902
Eardley, Raymond Faucit Wilmot, Capt. R.E.		S.H.	1909
Eccles-Holmes, James Francis, Capt. I.A.		W.D.H.	1915
Eddowes, Alfred, M.D., Capt. and Medical Officer, County of London Vol. Regt.		D.B.	1867
Eddowes, Hugh Mortimer, Lieut. R.E. Tunnelling Co.	**D.S.O. D.**	D.B.	1895
Edge, Herbert Parry Harris, Major, T.F.R.	**T.D.**	G.T.H.	1888
Edge, Thomas William Jenkinson, L/Corp. M.G.C.		J.B.O.	1917
Edwards, Arthur Meuric Powell, Motor Ambulance Driver (with the French).		D.B.	1916
Edwards, Charles Bertram, Lieut. K.S.L.I.	**D.**	S.H.	1915
Edwards, Edward Robert Hamilton, Lieut. R. Innis. Fus. Staff Lieut.		J.B.O.	1914
Edwards, Francis Hyde, Lt.-Col. (Bt. Major) Bed. and Herts Regt.	**D.S.O. M.C. D.**	G.T.H.	1890
W. Edwards, Geoffrey Dixon, Capt. R. Welch Fus.		W.D.H.	1909
Edwards, Graham Thomas George, Hon. Brig.-General, Hussars.	**C.B. D³**	S.H.	1883
Edwards, Kenneth Vaughan, 2nd Lieut. R.G.A.		E.B.M. and F.T.P.	1912
Elley, Stanley, Temp. Capt. S. African Vet. Corps.		C.J.S.C.	1894
Elliott, George Keith, Lieut., R. Welch Fus.		D.B.	1916
Ellis, Basil Herbert, Lieut. K.S.L.I.		S.H.	1914
Ellison, Harold Blades, M.B., Capt. R.A.M.C.		G.T.H.	1900
Elwin, Frank Harold, 2nd Lieut. Wilts. Regt.		S.H.	1914
England, John Humphrey, Capt. R.G.A.		S.H.	1905
W³ England, Norman Ayrton, Lieut.-Col. (Bt. Major) W. Yorks. Regt.	**D.S.O. D³, Croix de Guerre avec Palm (French).**	W.D.H.	1904

For explanations and abbreviations, see page 4.

	England, Sydney Ayrton, Lieut. R.A.S.C.		W.D.H.	1900
	English, Joseph Oxley, Major, R.A.		S.H.	1873
	Eustace, Seton George Legge, Trooper, Calcutta Light Horse.		E.B.M.	1890
	Evans, Arthur Frederic, Lieut. R. Welch Fus. and R.A.F.		F.E.B.	1904
	Evans, Arthur Lees, Major. S. Lancs. Regt.	**T.D.**	F.E.B. and S.H.	1890
	Evans, Charles Wilmot, Capt. S. Staffs. Regt.	**M.C. D.**	W.D.H.	1909
	Evans, Evan Richard, Lieut. R.F.A.		C.J.S.C.	1900
	Evans, Francis Allen Dorset, Capt. R. Welch Fus.	**M.C.**	D.B.	1898
W.	Evans, Gerard Sherriff, Pte. Ox. and Bucks. L.I.		C.J.S.C.	1902
	Evans, Jeffrey Williams Dorset, Pte. Canadian Infantry.		D.B.	1900
	Evans, Rees Tudor, Capt. (Adjutant) Welsh Regt.		S.H.	1906
	Evans, Richard Stanley, Lieut. Welsh Regt.		S.H.	1911
	Evans, Stephen Morris, Lieut. Army Audit Staff.		D.B.	1901
	Evans, Thomas Fanning, Lieut. R. Welch Fus.		E.B.M.	1888
	Evans, William Howard Dorset, Pte. Inns of Court O.T.C.		D.B.	1894
	Evans, William Lees, 2nd Lieut. R.F.A.		F.E.B.	1902
	Evers-Swindell, Eric Theodore, Lieut. R.G.A.		F.S.	1902
W.	Faber, Edward Waring, Lieut. Durham L.I.		C.J.S.C. and T.E.P.	1913
	Fairer, Christopher, Lieut. K.S.L.I.		A.F.C.	1915
	Fairweather, Francis Harold, Capt. R.A.S.C. (Adjutant).	**O.B.E. D.**	C.J.S.C.	1890
W³	Falkner, Arthur Henry, Major, R.A.M.C.	**D.S.O. D²**	D.B. and S.H.	1894
	Fairclough, William, Lieut. K. Liverpool Regt.		S.H.	1911
	Fairrie, Geoffrey, 2nd Lieut., Tank Corps.		S.H.	1906
	Farbridge, Stanley Brisco, The Rev. Chaplain to the Forces.	**D.**	S.H.	1896
W.	Farr, Edmund Thomas Cobbold, Lieut. R.F.A.		W.D.H.	1901
	Fawsitt, Thomas Rubie, 2nd Lieut. York and Lancaster Regt.		A.F.C.	1903
	Fell, Ronald Gillies, Capt. W. Yorks Regt. Staff Capt.	**D.**	E.B.M.	1909
W.	Fenn, Andrew George Thomas, Lieut. K.S.L.I.		D.B.	1909
	Ferguson, Spencer Charles, Major, Northumberland Fus. D.A.A.G.	**O.B.E. D.**	S.H.	1887

W⁴.	Fernyhough, John, Lieut. W. Yorks Regt.	**M.C.**	F.E.B.	1902
	ffoulkes, Charles John, F.S.A., Lieut. R.N.V.R.		G.T.H.	1885
	ffoulkes, Edmund Andrew, Capt. (Adjutant) Oxfordshire Vol. Regt.		G.T.H.	1883
	Field, Harry Hubert, Capt. Manchester Regt. L.T.M.B.	**D.**	T.E.P.	1914
	Fielding, George Rudolf, Major, Sherwood Foresters.		C.J.B. and E.B.M.	1898
	Finch, Charles Hugh, 2nd Lieut. I.A.R.O.		G.T.H.	1885
	Finch, Philip Gerard, Capt. Northumberland Fus.	**M.C. D.**	F.M.I.	1915
W.	Finney, Arthur John, Capt. R. Dublin Fus.		C.J.S.C.	1903
	Finny, Charles Morgan, Capt. R.A.M.C.	**D.**	C.J.S.C.	1905
W.	Firth, Denis Gordon, Capt. Hants Regt.		S.H.	1908
	Firth, Francis George, 2nd Lieut. R.A.O.D.		A.F.C.	1894
	Firth, Francis John Waller, Capt. K.E.O. Cavalry, I.A.		S.H.	1910
	Fisher, Walter Robert Fitzgibbon, 2nd Lieut. R.F.A.		F.T.P.	1916
	Fitzgibbon, Allen Fitzgerald, 2nd Lieut. I.A.		E.B.M.	1907
	Fitzherbert, Humphrey Beresford, Lieut. R.A.F.		E.B.M.	1895
	Fitz-Hugh, Godfrey, Major, Denbighshire Yeo.		C.J.S.C.	1890
	Fitzmaurice, John Herbert, 2nd Lieut. K.S.L.I.		J.B.O.	1916
	Flackfield, Alfred Edward, Lieut. R.E.		C.J.B.	1913
W.	Fleming-Brown, Gerald Francis, Capt. Beds. Regt.		W.D.H.	1912
	Fletcher, Walter George, 2nd Lieut. Intelligence Corps.	**D.**	Former Master	
W.	Flinn, Oswald Sterndale, Lieut. R.W. Surrey Regt. Staff.		C.J.S.C.	1902
	Foldys, William Robert, Pte. R. Fus.		W.S.I. and W.D.H.	1904
	Foot, William, M.B., Major, R.A.M.C.	**M.C. (Bar). D.**	W.D.H.	1907
W²	Forbes, Ellert Webster, Major, R. Warwicks. Regt. and R.A.F.	**M.C.**	C.J.B.	1913
W.	Forbes, Leslie Frederick, Major, R.A.F.	**M.C.**	C.J.B.	1909
	Forbes, Stanley Williams, Capt. R. Warwicks. Regt.	**D.**	F.E.B.	1904
	Fordyce, Charles Elphinstone, Lieut. Seaforth Highlanders.		W.D.H.	1917
	Forman, Arthur Temple, Capt. R.A.O.D.	**D.**	F.E.B.	1900

For explanations and abbreviations, see page 4.

	Forman, Edward Hugh,		F.E.B.	1899
	L./Corporal, Somerset L.I.			
W.P.	Forman, Humphrey,		F.E.B. and	
	Lieut. S. Wales Borderers.		C.J.B.	1907
	Forman, John Francis Robert,		F.T.P.	1916
	2nd Lieut. Gurkha Rifles.			
	Forman, Richard Steuart,		F.E.B.	1898
	Lieut. R.A.S.C.			
	Forman, Thomas Pears Gordon, The Rev.		F.E.B. and	
	Chaplain to the Forces		Master	1904
	Foster, Augustus Vere,		T.A.B. and	
	Lieut. R.A.S.C.		S.H.	1888
	Foster, Basil le Neve,		G.T.H.	1898
	Lieut. Cheshire Vol. Regt.			
	Foster, Fermian le Neve, **D²**		W.D.H.	1905
	Capt. Inns of Court O.T.C.			
	Foster, Heaton,		J.B.O.	1916
	Lieut. E. Yorks Regt.			
	Foster, John Vere, **O.B.E.**		A.F.C.	1898
	Major, Remount Depot.			
	Foster, Reginald Guy,		A.F.C.	1893
	Lieut. London Regt. and M.G.C.			
	Foster, Reginald le Neve,		G.T.H.	1894
	Sergt., Cheshire Vol. Regt.			
	Foster-Jackson, Stanley,		C.J.S.C.	1904
	Capt. Manchester Regt.			
	Fowle, Sir Henry Walter Hamilton, **K.B.E. C.B.E.**		C.J.S.C.	1890
	Col., S. African Forces.			
	Fox, Arthur, **M.C.**		S.H.	1915
	Capt. K.S.L.I.			
	Fraser, Arthur Leslie,		F.S. and	
	Lieut. R.G.A.		C.J.S.C.	1906
W.	Freeman, Charles Henry,		F.M.I.	1914
	Lieut. R. Irish Regt.			
	French, Charles Stockley,		C.J.S.C.	1910
	Lieut. R. Dublin Fus.			
	French, Claude Alexander,		C.J.S.C.	1899
	Capt. R. Irish Regt.			
W.²	French, Edward Noel, **D²**		A.F.C.	1897
	Lt.-Col. Lincolns. Regt.			
W.	French, Thomas Nathaniel,		A.F.C.	1898
	Major, R.A.			
	Fruhe-Sutcliffe, Reginald, **D.**		W.D.H.	1909
	Major, R.E.			
	Furley, Guy Mainwaring,		G.T.H.	1896
	Lieut. R. Welch Fus.			
	Furley, Edward Hugh Mainwaring,		F.S.	1901
	Corporal, E. African Mounted Rifles.			
	Gabb, Henry Secretan, M.B.,		D.B.	1896
	Capt. R.A.M.C.			
W.	Gadsby, Henry,		E.B.M.	1908
	Capt. E. Surrey Regt.			
W.	Galt, Charles MacDonald,		S.H.	1910
	Lieut. R.G.A.			
	Gamble, Arthur Mellor		C.J.B.	1917
	Lieut. R.E.			
	Gamble, Sir David, Bart.,		F.E.B.	1895
	Capt. Denbighshire Vol. Regt.			

For explanations and abbreviations, see page 4.

	Name		Code	Year
	Garden, Archibald Ross Harvey, Lt.-Col., I.A.	D.	S.H.	1885
	Gardner, Eric, Hon. Capt. Cheshire Vol. Regt.		·S.H.	1907
W.	Gardner, William Alexander, Lt.-Col. Canadian A.M.C.		W.D.H.	1894
	Garnons-Williams, Harold Penry, 2nd Lieut. R. Welch Fus.		W.S.I. and S.H.	1915
	Garrett, Henry Grimshaw, Sub.-Lieut. R.N.V.R.		E.B.M.	1897
W.	Gaskell, Clive Hunter, Major, Wilts. Regt.	M.C., Chevalier de l'Ordre de Merite Agricole.	A.F.C.	1905
	Gaskell, Holbrook Lance, Sub-Lieut. R.N.A.S.		A.F.C.	1916
	Gaskell, Sidney, 2nd Lieut. R.A.F.		A.F.C.	1917
W.	Gaskell, William Rawstorne, Capt. K.O.S.B., T.M.B.		A.F.C.	1902
	Gaye, Ambrose, Lieut. Tank Corps.		S.H.	1896
	Gee, Lawrence, The Rev. Chaplain to the Forces.	D.	S.H.	1880
	Gell, James Bainton Stowell, 2nd Lieut. R.F.A.		F.T.P.	1916
P.	Gemmel, Henry James, 2nd Lieut. R.A.F.		C.J.B.	1917
	Geoghegan, Frederick William, Lieut.-Commander, R.N.V.R. and R.N.A.S.	D.	E.B.M.	1902
W.	Gethen, Ronald, Lt.-Col. Norfolk Regt.	M.C. D.²	W.D.H.	1913
	Gething, Burton William Ellis, Major, Northumberland Fus. Staff Capt.	D.	C.J.S.C.	1898
	Gething, Stanley, 2nd Lieut. R.F.A.		F.E.B. and C.J.B.	1906
	Getty, James Houghton, Capt. W. Yorks Regt. Staff Capt.	D.	C.J.S.C.	1907
	Gibbons, John Reginald, Capt. R.A.O.C.		F.E.B.	1902
	Gibbs, Bernard, 2nd Lieut. Rifle Brigade.	M.C. D.²	D.B. and F.T.P.	1912
W.	Gibson, Donald Grant, Major, R. Fus.	M.C. (Bar).	E.B.M.	1910
W.	Gibson, Frederick Almond, Lieut., K. Liverpool Regt.		F.T.P.	1916
	Gibson, Godfrey Marsden, Capt. R.A.S.C.		S.H.	1896
	Gillett, Richard Francis, Pte. R.A.S.C.		E.B.M.	1907
	Gillett, Basil Montgomery, Pte. R.A.S.C.		E.B.M.	1908
	Cidden, John Arthur, Lieut. I.A.		C.J.S.C. and T.E.P.	1911
	Gidden, Thomas, 2nd Lieut. Cameron Highlanders.		C.J.S.C. and T.E.P.	1911
	Gilbert, John Ernest, The Rev. Chaplain to the Forces.		S.H.	1873

For explanations and abbreviations, see page 4.

28

	Gillibrand, Thomas Percival, Capt. Lancs. Motor Corps, Vol. Force.		C.J.S.C. 1903
	Gilliland, William Miller Major, Lieut. R. Innis. Fus.		S.H. 1912
	Gilmour, William Santon, 2nd Lieut. R.F.A.		F.M.I. 1915
	Gilpin-Brown, Robert Dundas, 2nd Lieut. R.A.F.		S.H. 1916
	Gisby, Hugh Marshall, Sergeant, R.A.S.C.		G.T.H. 1897
	Givan, Harry Cooke, Lieut. R. Warwicks. Regt.		A.F.C. 1912
W.	Gleeson, Edward James Gerald Herbert Maloney, Lieut, R.F.A.		C.J.B. 1910
	Glover, Walter Clegg, Capt. K. Liverpool Regt. R.E. K.O.S.B.	Chevalier de l'Ordre de Leopold avec Croix de Guerre.	E.B.M. 1892
	Glyn, John William Westray, Pte. R.A.M.C. (Cambridge).		T.E.P. 1915
	Godber, Hugh Gerald. Capt. Northumberland Fus.		S.H. 1907
	Godson, Herbert George, Lieut. R.A.		E.B.M. 1909
W.	Goldie, Alec St Leger, Major, E. Lancs. Regt. G.S.O.		E.B.M. 1899
	Goldie, Alexander Barré, Cadet R.N.A.S.		A.F.C. 1918
	Goldie, Barré Algernon Highmore, Hon. Major, Herts Yeo.		G.T.H. 1886
	Goode, William Winter, Major, Somersets. L.I.		G.T.H. 1888
	Goodman, Geoffrey Garland, Hon. Capt. Vol. Bn. Cambridgeshire Reg.		F.E.B. 1893
	Goodman, Robert Fox, Lieut. Yeo.		A.F.C. 1901
	Goodrick-Clarke, Owen, Lieut. Worcs. Regt. W. African Regt.		W.D.H. 1914
	Goold, Edward Meredyth, 2nd Lieut. Liverpool Regt.		C.J.B. 1914
	Goolden, Donald Charles, 2nd Lieut. R. Fus.		W.D.H. 1914
W.	Goolden, Hugh Joseph, 2nd Lieut. R. Berks. Regt.		W.D.H. 1912
	Gorton, Norman W., Pte., K.S.L.I.		S.H. 1910
	Gough, Norman, Lieut. Worcs. Regt.		C.J.S.C. and T.E.P. 1911
	Gould, Philip, Major, R. Irish Fus.	**D.S.O. D.**	G.T.H. 1886
	Gouldbourn, John Banks, Corporal, Shropshire Vol. Regt.		D.B. 1892
	Gouldsmith, Charles Cecil, Major, R.F.A. and T.F.R.		S.H and F.E.B. 1893
	Graham, George, Lieut. R.A.F.		F.E.B. 1891
	Graham, George W. Major, Cork R.G.A.		E.B.M. 1902

	Name / Rank	Award	Code	Year
	Grainger, Arthur Claude, Lieut. R.A.S.C.		G.T.H.	1899
	Grainger, Edward Hastings, Major, Worcs. Regt.		E.B.M.	1892
	Grant, Albyn Evan Powell, 2nd Lieut. R. Welch Fus.		A.F.C.	1912
	Grant, Archibald Sturge, 2nd Lieut. R.G.A.	**O.B.E.**	D.B.	1891
	Grant, Bertram Dickinson, Capt. R.A.S.C.		C.J.S.C.	1900
W.	Grantham-Hill, Clermont, Lieut. King's Own Hussars.		D.B. and E.B.M.	1909
	Gray, Archibald Reynolds, Lieut. Gurkha Rifles, I.A.		F.M.I.	1916
W.	Gray, Charles Edward, Lieut. Gurkha Rifles, I.A.		F.M.I.	1915
	Gray, Cyril Seaton, 2nd Lieut. Wilts. Regt.		S.H.	1912
	Gray. Herbert Edward, 2nd Lieut. R.A.M.C.		C.J.S.C.	1890
	Gray, Vivian Seaton, Major, R.A.S.C. (M.T.)	**D.²**	A.F.C.	1910
W.	Grazebrook, Christopher John, 2nd Lieut. Worcs. Regt., M.G.C.		W.D.H.	1916
W.²	Grazebrook, Robert Michael, Capt. Glos. Regt., G.S.O.	**M.C. D.**	W.D.H.	1911
W³.	Green, Arthur Llewellyn Baldwin, Major, Herefords. Regt.	**D.S.O. D².**	C.J.S.C.	1892
W.	Green, Edward Alphonse, Capt. Somerset Yeo. A.D.C.		C.J.S.C.	1899
	Green, Ralph Beauchamp, Capt. Somerset Yeo. M.G.C.	**M.C.**	C.J.S.C.	1900
	Green, Robert Donald, Capt. Durham L.I. T.M.B.	**M.C.**	D.B.	1914
	Green, William Stewart Mial, Lt.-Commander, R.N. Div.		E.B.M.	1898
	Green-Price, Geoffrey Cecil, Capt. and Adjt., R. Guernsey Militia.		D.B.	1892
	Green-Price, James Llewellyn, 2nd Lieut. S. Wales Borderers.		D.B.	1897
	Green-Price, Sir Robert Henry, Bart., Major, Montgomeryshire Yeo., D.A.Q.M.G.		D.B.	1889
	Greenwood, George, Capt. K.O.Y.L.I.		C.J.S.C.	1908
W.	Greenwood, John, Lieut. K. Liverpool Regt.		S.H.	1904
W.P.	Greenwood, Oliver, Capt. Yorks. Regt. and M.G.C.		F.S.	1908
	Gregson, Edward Maurice, Capt. L.N. Lancs. Regt.		E.B.M.	1906
W.²	Gregson, George Arthur, Capt. R.E.		E.B.M.	1906
	Griffith, Edward Ernest, 2nd Lieut. R.F.A.		A.F.C.	1918
W.	Griffith, Francis Llewelyn, Lieut. R.F.A.		J.B.O.	1915
W.	Griffith, Gronwy Robert, Capt. R. Welch Fus.		W.D.H.	1900

	Griffith-Roberts, Thomas William, Corporal R.E.		D.B.	1899
W.	Grose, Edward, Capt., I.A.		E.B.M.	1900
	Grose, James, Lt.-Col., R.G.A.	Croix de Guerre. Ordre de l'Étoile Noir	S.H.	1891
	Grossmith, Lawrence Randall, Lieut. Recruiting Duties.		S.H.	1893
	Grove, George Frederick, Lieut., Glos. Regt.		C.J.B.	1910
	Groves, William Hall, 2nd Lieut. R.A.S.C.		G.T.H.	1900
	Grundy, Charles, Pte. Canadian Infantry.		W.D.H.	1897
	Grundy, Francis, Lieut. Manchester Regt.		W.D.H.	1898
	Gunson, John Farquhar, Pte. R.A.S.C.		W.S.I. and C.J.B.	1914
	Gurdon, Philip Norman, Capt., I.A.		S.H.	1910
	Gutch, Edward Henry Blakesley, Gunner, R.F.A.		G.T.H. and W.D.H.	1902
	Gwatkin, Willoughby Garnons, Major-General.	C.B., K.C.M.G., D², Order of St. Sava, Commander, Ordre de la Couronne.	S.H.	1897
	Gwatkin-Graves, Edward Arthur, 2nd Lieut. M.G.C.		S.H.	1897
	Hack, Matthew Starmer, Q.M.S. Artists' Rifles, London Regt. (attached),	D.	A.F.C.	1888
	Haggard, Edward Arthur, Major, Res. of Officers.		S.H.	1879
	Hair, Donald Campbell, 2nd Lieut. K.S.L.I.		S.H.	1915
W²	Hale, Ernest Nathaniel, Capt. R. Highlanders	T.D. Croix de Guerre avec Palme (French).	C.J.S.C.	1889
	Hall, James, 2nd Lieut. M.G.C.		S.H.	1916
	Hall, Robert Sinclair, Lieut. R.N.V.R.		G.T.H.	1904
W.	Hall, Henry Sydney Hofman, Capt. R. Fus.	D.S.O. D.	E.B.M.	1903
	Hallowes, Francis Brabazon, Capt. R.A.S.C.		D.B.	1912
	Halstead, Arthur Frederic, Lieut. Rifle Brigade, attchd. R. Dublin Fus.		E.B.M. and F.T.P.	1912
	Hamer, Harold, Lieut. L.N. Lancs. Regt. and R.A.F.	Air Force Cross.	F.M.I. F.S.	1910
	Hamer, Joseph Lieut. R.A.S.C.		W.D.H.	1905
	Hamer, James Edward, Pte., Sherwood Foresters.	D.	W.D.H. and F.S.	1902
	Hamer, John Lawton Parry Capt. K.S.L.I. attchd. Cheshire Reg.		D.B. and S.H.	1898

	Hamilton, Archibald Hamilton, Capt. R. Irish Rifles.		G.T.H.	1893
W.	Hamilton, George, Capt. K.S.L.I.		C.J.B.	1914
	Hamlyn, Harold James, Capt. W. Yorks Regt.		F.E.B.	1901
	Hammill, John, Capt. S. Lancs. Regt.		C.J.S.C.	1903
	Hammill, Norman, Pte., Victoria B.C. Fus.		C.J.S.C.	1899
	Hammond Fisher, Gerald Learoyd, 2nd Lieut. K. Liverpool Regt. and M.G.C.		E.B.M. and F.T.P.	1912
	Hampson, Thomas Seddon, Lieut. R.A.S.C.		T.E.P.	1913
	Hanmer, Arthur Richard, Lieut. R. Welch Fus.		S.H.	1917
W.	Hanmer, Robert Hugh, Lieut. R. Welch Fus. and R.A.F.	**M.C.**	S.H.	1915
W.	Hanmer-Jones, Eric Ingleby, Capt. R. Welch Fus.		C.J.S.C.	1898
	Hanscombe, Hugh James, Capt. S. Lancs. Regt.		W.D.H.	1896
	Harding, John Bernard, Lieut. K.S.L.I.		D.B.	1903
	Hardy, Francis Kyle, Major, York and Lancaster Regt.	**D.S.O.**	F.E.B.	
	Hargreaves, Charles Kerrison, I.F.S., I.A.R.O. (Infantry Branch).		A.F.C.	1908
W.	**Hargreaves, Ralph Walter,** Lieut. Welsh Guards.		A.F.C.	1910
	Hargreaves, Oliver, Lieut. R.A.S.C.		F.S.	1904
	Harman, Cecil Rochfort, 2nd Lieut. Glos. Regt.		S.H.	1916
	Harper, Percy, Lieut. R.G.A.		F.E.B.	1895
	Harries, Ernest Charles, The Rev. Capt. Devon County School O.T.C.		D.B.	1886
	Harries, Archie Wilkin de Winton, Pte., Penang Rifles.		G.T.H. and W.D.H.	1900
	Harries, Nelson George, Capt. S. Staffs. Regt.		D.B.	1886
	Harris, Gavin Muir, Lieut. R. Monmouths. R.E.		W.D.H.	1915
	Harris, John Ferguson, Pte., Officer Cadet Unit.		F.T.P.	1917
	Harris, Kenneth Edwin, Pte. Manchester University O.T.C.		T.E.P.	1918
	Harris, Tom Cyril Freer, Capt. Worcs. Regt.	**M.C. (Bar). D.**	W.D.H.	1910
	Harris, William Leslie Freer, 2nd Lieut. Worcs. Regt.		A.F.C.	1913
	Harrison, Brian, 2nd Lieut. R. Welch Fus.		W.D.H.	1910
	Harrison, Ernest, Signaller, Northumberland Fus.		F.S. and F.M.I.	1910

For explanations and abbreviations, see page 4.

	Harrison, George Rowland Devereux, Major, Montgomeryshire Yeo.	**T.D.**	C.J.S.C.	1896
	Harrison, James Murray Robert, Bt. Lt.-Col. R.F.A., D.A.A.G.	**D.S.O. Croix de Guerre. D**[7]	C.J.S.C.	1898
	Harrison, John German, Capt. R.F.A.		W.D.H.	1909
	Harrison, Lawrence, Capt. & Adjt. Lincolns. Regt.	**D.**	A.F.C. and C.J.S.C.	1889
W.	Hartcup, John Archibald, Capt. E. Yorks Regt. and R.A.F.		W.D.H.	1908
	Hartcup, William Richard Monyns, Major, Durham L.I. Brigade Major.	**O.B.E. D.**	G.T.H.	1900
	Hartley, George Pickup, Capt. R.F.A.	**M.C.**	E.B.M.	1910
	Hartley, James Harold, 2nd Lieut. R. Munster Fus. & R.A.F.		F.T.P.	1915
W.	Hartley, Robert, Capt. R.G.A.	**M.C. D. Croix de Guerre. Ordre de l'Etoile Noir.**	E.B.M. and F.T.P.	1912
	Harvey, Alfred Ernest, Lieut. Tank Corps.		S.H.	1906
	Harvey, Bernard Nowlan, Pte., Canadian Grenadier Guards.		C.J.S.C.	1902
	Harvey, Reginald Simpson, M.B., Captain, R.A.M.C.		C.J.S.C.	1904
	Harvey, Richard, Capt. Norfolk Regt.		F.E.B.	1903
	Harvey, William Geoffrey, M.D. Major, R.A.M.C.		C.J.S.C.	1895
	Harvey, Vivian Dacre, Capt. R.E.	**D.C.M. D.**	C.J.S.C.	1908
	Harvey, Lionel Bartley, 2nd Lieut. Derby Regt. (Vol. Force).		C.J.S.C.	1901
	Harvey-James, Arthur Keedwell, Capt. E. Kent Regt.		A.F.C.	1888
	Harwood, Henry Cecil, Lieut. Suffolk Regt.		W.S.I.	1912
W.P.	Haseler, Geoffrey Frank Lieut. R.W. Surrey Regt. & R.A.F.		W.D.H.	1912
	Haseler, Maxwell Ryland, 2nd Lieut. R.A.F.		C.J.B.	1914
	Haseler, Thomas Ryland, Capt. Tank Corps.		C.J.B.	1909
	Haseler, William Hereward, Capt. Tank Corps.		C.J.B.	1910
	Haslam, Charles Stanley, Capt. Hussars, attchd. W. Yorks Regt.	**D.**	F.E.B.	1899
W.	Haslam, Robert Humphrey, Capt. Cheshire Regt.		F.E.B.	1910
	Haslam, Sidney Bertram, Capt. R.E.		A.F.C.	1897
W.	Haslewood, Guy Harrop, Lieut. Worcs. Regt.		E.B.M.	1896
	Hatch, William Leonard Ringrose, Lieut. R. Irish Fus.		S.H.	1907
	Hatt-Cook, George, Major, Cheshire Regt.		S.H.	1901

	Havers, Henry Leslie, Major, R.F.A.				S.H.	1890
W.	Hawkes, Francis Samuel, Capt. Devon Regt. Staff. attchd. Lancaster Regt.				S.H.	1887
W.	Hawkins, Elyot Sydney, Major, K.S.L.I.	**T.D.**			C.J.S.C.	1894
	Hawksley, John Plunkett Verney, Lt.-Col. R.F.A.	**D.S.O.**	**D²**		S.H.	1894
W.	Hawley, Leslie Harry, Lieut. County of London Regt.				C.J.B.	1916
	Hay, George Lennox, Lt.-Col. R.A.O.D.	**D.S.O.**	**C.B.E.**	**D³**	C.J.S.C.	1885
	Hay, Kenneth Sydney, Paymaster-Commander, R.N.				E.B.M.	1886
W²	Haynes, Alan Henry, Major, R.F.A.	**D.**			F.S. and F.M.I.	1910
	Heald, Douglas, 2nd Lieut. Rifle Brigade.				A.F.C.	1909
W.	Heald, Thomas Claypole Lane, Capt. Cheshire Regt. G.S.O.	**M.C.**	**D²**		C.J.S.C.	1908
	Healey, Edward Stanley, Capt. & Adjutant, L.N. Lancs. Regt.				W.D.H.	1905
	Hearn, Reginald John, M.B., Capt. R.A.M.C. and R.A.F.	**D.**			F.S.	1908
	Heath, Graham Douglas, 2nd Lieut. R.G.A.				J.B.O.	1918
	Heaton, Philip Ralph, Lieut. E. African Rifles.	**D.C.M.**	**D.**		C.J.S.C. and T.E.P.	1911
	Hedley, Oswald William Edward, Lieut. R.E.				S.H.	1901
	Hemphill, Fitzroy, The Hon. Capt. K.O.S.B. Lond. T.F.A.				S.H.	1877
	Henderson, Henry Wallace, 2nd Lieut. R.A.S.C.				C.J.S.C.	1899
	Henderson, John Gibbons, Sub-Lieut. R.N.				F.M.I.	1916
	Hellyer, William E. Pte., Hampshire Regt.				F.T.P.	1918
	Henstock, Frederick Thomas, Col. Res. of Off., G.S.O., A.A. and Q.M.G.				S.H.	1879
W.	Henry, Robert Ferguson, Lieut. and Adjutant, R.F.A., A.D.C.				E.B.M. and F.T.P.	1913
	Hepton, William, Lieut. Dragoon Guards. Res. of Cavalry.				W.D.H. and E.B.M.	1903
W.	Hern, John Reginald Brock, 2nd Lieut. R.F.A.				J.B.O.	1915
W.	Heselton, John Lister, Lt.-Col. Worcs. Regt. Herts. Regt.	**D.S.O.**	**M.C.**	**D³**	S.H.	1909
	Heurtley, Archibald Charles, The Rev., Chaplain to the Forces.	**D³**			C.J.S.C.	1890
	Hibbert, Cyril Gordon Reuss, Capt. L.N. Lancs. Regt.				A.F.C.	1905
	Hibbert, John Percy Maghull, Major, R.F.A.	**M.C.**			E.B.M.	1903

W.P.	Hibbert, Oswald Yates, Major, R.W. Kent Regt. Brigade Major.	**D.S.O. M.C. D³**	E.B.M.	1899
	Hibbert, Percy John, Late Major, Border Regt. Member of Westmorland T.F.A.		J.R.	1869
	Hickman, Thomas Haighton Trevor, Pte. Auckland Mounted Rifles.		D.B.	1893
W.	Hickson, Cuthbert Gollan, 2nd Lieut. E. Lancs. Regt.		S.H.	1909
	Hide, John Seymour, Major, R.E.		S.H.	1908
	Higgins, Harold Lea, Pte., K. Liverpool Regt.		F.M.I.	1911
W.	Higgins, Warner Richard Clinton, Capt. and Adjutant, Lincolns. Regt.		S.H.	1914
W²	Highet, William Thompson Lt.-Col. R.F.A.	**M.C. D⁴**	A.F.C.	1900
	Hildyard, Frederick William, Pte. Central London Regt. (Vol. Force)		C.J.S.C.	1880
W.	Hill, Archibald Christopher, 2nd Lieut. K.S.L.I.		J.B.O.	1917
	Hill, John Arthur, Lt.-Col. R.A.S.C.	**O.B.E. D³**	C.J.S.C.	1901
	Hill, Kenneth Bransby, Lieut. R.M.		F.T.P.	1918
	Hills, George Gregory, Capt. I.A.R.O.	**M.C.**	D.B.	1898
	Hills, Percival George; 2nd Lieut. Cheshire Regt.		G.T.H. and W.D.H.	1900
	Hill-James, William, Lt.-Col. G.S.O.		D.B.	1854
W.P.	Hilton, Cecil Kirkham, Trooper, E. African Mounted Rifles.		S.H.	1903
	Hinde, Stanley Norman, Lieut. Cheshire Regt. and M.G.C.		J.B.O.	1913
	Hinkson, Giles Aylmer, Lieut. R. Dublin Fus.		C.J.B.	1915
W³	Hinmers, John Reid, Major, K.S.L.I.	**M.C. Croix de Guerre** **(French).**	E.B.M. and F.T.P.	1914
W.	Hinmers, William, Capt. K. Liverpool Regt.	**M.C.**	E.B.M. and F.T.P.	1912
	Hipkins, Frederick Wystan, Capt. Sherwood Foresters.	**M.C.**	C.J.S.C.	1904
	Hirsch, John Gauntlett, Lieut. Cape Corps, S. Africa.		S.H.	1901
W⁴	Hobbs, Arthur Radley Maurice, Lieut. Connaught Rangers.	**M.C. (Bar).**	S.H.	1905
	Hoffman, Geoffrey Arthur, Capt. R.A.M.C.		F.E.B.	1906
	Hoffman, Reginald Herbert, Capt. Northumberland Fus. G.S.O.		C.J.B.	1907
	Holberton, Philip Vaughan, Bt. Lt.-Col. Lancs. Fus.	**Serbian Order of** **White Eagle. D⁴**	D.B.	1898
	Holberton, Thomas Edmund, Capt., R.H.A.	**M.C. (Bar). D.**	D.B.	1901

For explanations and abbreviations, see page 4.

	Holcroft, Frederick, Major, T.F.R.		S.H.	1881
	Holden, Ronald Temple, Cadet Unit R.E.		D.B.	1918
	Holdroyd, Frank Victor, Lieut. K.O.Y.L.I.		W.D.H.	1903
	Holgate-Shaw, Richard, 2nd Lieut. Seaforth Highlanders.		F.T.P.	1916
	Holland, Richard Charles, Pte. City of London Nat. Guard Vols.		S.H.	1879
	Holt, Ancell Ball, Lieut. Army Pay Corps.		F.E.B. and C.J.B.	1899
	Holt, Eustace Addison, L./Corpl. K. Liverpool Regt.		D.B.	1902
	Holt, George Selwyn, Lieut. R. Welch Fus.		D.B.	1900
	Holt, John Stanley 2nd Lieut. R.A.S.C.		C.J.B. and W.D.H.	1900
	Holt, Lancelot Vere, 2nd Lieut. R. Jersey Militia		F.S. and F.M.I	1910
W.	Holt, Lionel Stephan, Lieut. Dorset Regt. and R. Berks Regt.		D.B.	1911
W²	Holt, Louis, Major, R.G.A.	Croix de Guerre (Belgian).	A.F.C.	1907
	Home, Frederick Cecil Morton, Capt. Welsh Regt.		S.H.	1911
	Hooper, Charles Gordon, Lieut. London Regt.		S.H.	1900
	Hooper, Herbert Studdy. S.S.M., R.A.S.C.	**M.C.**	S.H.	1897
	Hope, Adrian John, Lieut. R.M.A.		J.B.O.	1917
	Hope, Norman Hague, 2nd Lieut. S. Lancs. Regt.		A.F.C.	1896
W.	Hope, Ralph Walter, Capt. K. Edward's Horse.		G.T.H.	1894
W.P.	Hopkins, John Ackland Stuart, Capt. R. Innis. Fus.		T.E.P.	1913
	Hore, Charles Beauman, Major, R. Welch Fus.		D.B.	1896
	Horlick, Oliver Peter Thompson, Lieut. Ox. and Bucks Vol. Regt.		C.J.S.C.	1904
W.	Hornby, Montague Leyland, F.R.G.S., Bt. Col. and Brig.-Gen. York and Lancaster Regt., late I.A.	**C.M.G. D.S.O. D⁴**	D.B. and S.H.	1887
	Horne, Benjamin Worthy, Sergeant, H.A.C.		F.E.B.	1894
	Horne, Lancelot Worthy, Major, R.E.		F.E.B.	1892
	Horner, Eric Thornburgh, Major, Norfolk Regt.	**M.C. D.**	A.F.C.	1902
W.	Horton, Cedric Michael Gilbert, Lieut. R.F.A.		T.E.P.	1915
	Horton, Edward Victor, Capt. and Adjutant, R.F.A.	**M.C. D.**	F.M.I.	1915
	Horton, Robert Charles, Capt. and Adjutant, R.A.S.C.		F.E.B.	1892

36

	Name / Rank	Medals	Abbr.	Year
	Horton, Wilfred Winnall, M.D. Capt. R.A.M.C.		D.B.	1875
	Hotchkin, Stafford Vere, Capt. and Adjutant, R.H.A.	M.C.	G.T.H.	1892
	Household, Henry Barrows, Bt. Lt.-Col. Staff Paymaster.	D²	S.H.	1888
	Hovey, Ernest Leslie, Lieut. R.E.	M.C.	S.H.	1909
	Howard, J. P. 2nd Lieut. Hants Regt.		Former Master	
	Howard-McLean, John Robert, Lt.-Col. K.S.L.I. Hon. Col. T.F.R.	D.	S.H.	1879
	Hough, Arthur Roy, Cadet, I.A.		W.D.H.	1918
W.	Hough, William Samuel, 2nd Lieut. K.S.L.I. attchd Cheshire Regt.		C.J.B.	1914
	Howarth, Edward Goldie, Lieut. Oxfordshire Hussars Yeo.	D.	A.F.C.	1898
	Howarth, Walter Goldie, F.R.C.S., Capt. R.A.M.C.		A.F.C	1897
	Howe, Francis Herbert, Bt. Major, Welsh Regt.		S.H.	1885
	Howe, Randall Lionel Bentham, Superintendent, Church Army Hut, Belgium.		A.F.C.	1907
	Howell, Arthur Anthony, Brig.-Gen. R. Fus.	**C.M.G. T.D. D³** **Cross of Order of** **St. Anne.**	C.J.S.C.	1878
	Howell, Joseph Matthew, late Capt. S.W.B. Member of Merioneth T.F. Association.		S.H.	1878
	Howson, Hugh Edmund Elliott, Lieut. Shrewsbury School O.T.C.		Former Master	
	Howson, John Aspden, Capt. E. Lancs. Regt.		F.S.	1906
	Howson, Thomas Aspden, Capt. R.F.A.	D.	W.D.H. and F.S.	1903
W.	Hoyle, Harry, Bombadier, R.G.A. Q.M.S. Gold Coast Regt.		W.D.H. and A.F.C.	1896
	Hudson, Charles Arthur Norman, Cadet, R.M.C., Sandhurst.		A.F.C.	1918
	Hudson, Ernest Walter, Lieut. R.F.A.		S.H.	1896
W²	Hudson, Philip James, Lieut. K.S.L.I.	M.C.	F.T.P.	1916
	Hudson-Kinahan, Cecil Barton, Lieut. K. African Rifles.		F.E.B.	1900
	Hughes, Brian Holland, Capt. London Regt. and M.G.C.		S.H.	1914
	Hughes, Christopher Tatham Devey, Pte., K.S.L.I.		C.J.B.	1913
	Hughes, Henry Halcomb, C.M.M. R.N.V.R.		W.D.H.	1906
	Hughes, Richard Leslie, Paymaster-Lieut. R.N.V.R.		S.H.	1913

37

	Name	Honours			Award	Year
	Hughes-Games, Joshua Bower, Capt. Durham L.I. A.D.C.	**M.C.**			S.H.	1907
W.	Hughes-Games, William Bower, Pte. Canadian Infantry.				F.S.	1906
	Hughes Parry, Thomas Richard Jonathan Hughes, Lieut. Welsh Horse,				S.H.	1891
	Hugh-Jones, Thomas Whitley, Lieut. R. Welch Fus.				W.D.H.	1912
	Humphrys, Francis Henry, Major, I.A. and R.A.F.	**D.**			S.H.	1898
W.P.	Hunt, Benedict Gerald Philip Lieut. Flight Commander R.A.F.				E.B.M. and F.T.P.	1912
	Hurtley, Robert John, Mechanic, R.A.F.				E.B.M. and F.T.P.	1914
	Hutchinson, Geoffrey, Lieut. R.A.S.C.				W.D.H.	1904
	Hutchinson, Noel Wilfrid, Capt. and Adjutant, R.A.S.C.	**D.**			A.F.C.	1906
	Huxley, George Arthur, Major, R.E.				A.F.C.	1905
	Illingworth, Wilfrid Law, Capt. and Adjutant, R.E.				F.E.B.	1895
	Inglis, Claude Cavendish, 2nd Lieut. R.E.				S.H.	1900
	Inglis, James Malcolm, 2nd Lieut. R. Irish Fus.				A.F.C.	1917
	Ingram, Francis Manning, Major, O.C. Shrewsbury School O.T.C.	**T.D.**	**O.B.E.**	**D.**	Master.	
	Ingrams, Leonard Sinclair, 2nd Lieut. Coldstream Guards.				T.E.P.	1918
W.	Ingrams, William Harold, Capt. K.S.L.I.				W.S.I. and S.H.,	1914
W.	Irvine, Hugh Colley, 2nd Lieut. R.F.A.				C.J.B.	1917
W²	Ivens, Harold Thomason Carew, Lt.-Col. I.A.				E.B.M.	1899
	Izod, Kevan William, Bt. Major, L.N. Lancs. Regt.	**D³**			S.H.	1904
	Jackson, Cyril, 2nd Lieut. R.G.A.				D.B.	1901
	Jackson, Sir Frederick John, late Governor and Commander-in-Chief, Uganda.	**K.C.M.G.** **C.B.** Grand Officer of the Order of Leopold (Belgian).			S.H.	1878
	Jackson, Herbert, Corpl., R. Warwicks. Regt.				D.B.	1895
	Jackson, John Owen, Pte., Artists' Rifles.				D.B.	1896
W²	Jackson, Mark Keith, Capt. R. Warwicks. Regt.	**M.C. (Bar).**			E.B.M.	1911
	Jackson, Norman, Lieut. Upper Burmah Vol. Rifles,				C.J.S.C.	1909
	Jackson, Ralph, 2nd Lieut. I.A.R.O.				D.B.	1905
	Jackson, Robert Melville, Capt. Suffolk Regt.				S.H.	1896
W.	Jackson, Robert Dunnett, Capt. K.S.L.I.	**M.C. (Bar).**			A.F.C.	1911

For explanations and abbreviations, see page 4.

Jackson, William Douglas, Capt. R.A.F.	**D.F.C.**	E.B.M. and F.T.P.	1915
Jagger, Arthur Humphrey, Capt. R. Warwicks. Regt.		F.M.I.	1913
Jagger, Francis Field Cunningham, M.B. Capt. R.A.M.C.		G.T.H.	1893
James, Charles Edward, Corporal, Middlesex Regt.		C.J.B. and S.H.	1900

W. James, Clement, **M.C. D²** C.J.S.C. 1906
Pte. Sherwood Foresters, Lieut.
R.G.A.

James, David William, Capt. S. African Infantry.		A.F.C.	1890
James, Ernest Hodson, Pte., K.S.L.I.		A.F.C.	1908
Jebb, Reginald Douglas, Capt. R. Sussex Regt. Staff Capt.	**M.C. D.**	G.T.H. and W.D.H	.1903
Jeffcock, Robert Salisbury, Capt. S. Staffs. Regt.		C.J.S.C.	1894
Jeffreys, Jeffrey Rhys Powell, Cadet, R.M.C. Sandhurst.		A.F.C.	1918
Jepson, Rowland Walter, Lieut. Cheshire Regt. Dulwich College O.T.C.		D.B.	1907

W. Jerome, John Samuel, **M.C.** W.D.H. 1914
Lieut. Rifle Brigade,

Jessop, John William, S.H. 1879
Lt.-Col. Lincolns. Regt.

Johnson, Gilbert Ernest, Croix de Guerre D.B. 1907
Capt., Army Cyclist Corps. (Belgian) **D.**

W. Johnson, Herbert Stone, S.H. 1898
Capt. R.F.A.

Johnson, Philip, Major, R.A.O.D.		W.D.H.	1898
Johnston, John Alexander Weir, Major, R.A.O.D.		S.H.	1898
Johnstone, John, Capt. Leinster Regt.		D.B. and C.J.S.C.	1906
Johnson, Marcus Labron, Lieut. S. Lancs. Regt,		A.F.C.	1904
Johnston, Robert Christopher, Pte. Artists' Rifles. Innis. Fus.		T.E.P.	1914
Jollands, Brettle Evans, Lieut. Pembrokeshire Yeo.		A.F.C.	1888

Jones, Evan Bowen, G.T.H. 1887
Hon. Lt.-Col. Merioneth. Vol. Force.

Jones, Dallas Gordon Donnell Johnson, C.J.S.C. 1885
Capt. R. Welch Fus.

Jones, Daryl St Aubyn, Lieut. R.A.M.C.		S.H.	1899
Jones, Edmund George, Lt.-Col. Pembrokeshire Yeo. and M.G.C.	**T.D.**	F.E.B. and G.T.H.	1897
Jones, Edward James, Capt. Lancs. Fus.		G.T.H.	1902
Jones, Henry Alan Reid, 2nd Lieut. Devon Regt.		F.M.I.	1913

W.	Jones, Henry Herbert, 2nd Lieut. R. Welch Fus.		W.D.H.	**1910**
	Jones, Lewis Austin, Lieut. K.O. R. Lancaster Regt.		C.J.S.C.	**1895**
	Jones, Richard Laurence, Capt. R. Welch Fus.		F.S. and F.M.I.	**1909**
	Jones, Ronald Potter, Major, R.A.O.D.		S.H.	**1893**
W.	Jones, Thomas Cecil, Lieut. R. Fus.		C.J.S.C.	**1893**
	Joyce, James Leonard, F.R.C.S., Bt. Major, R.A.M.C.		C.J.S.C.	**1901**
	Judson, Joseph Edward, Capt. R.A.M.C.		G.T.H.	**1893**
W.	Jourdier, Max J. A. Bt. Major, E. Surrey Regt. Brigade Major. G.S.O.	**D.S.O. D.**	E.B.M.	**1902**
	Keatinge, Eustace Gabriel Lawrence, Lieut. Northumberland Fus.		A.F.C .and D.B.	**1911**
W.	Keitley, Cyril Humby, Capt. Manchester Regt.	**M.B.E. D.**	C.J.S.C. and T.E.P.	**1910**
	Kelly, Robert Stewart, Capt. R. Welch Fus.		F.E.B.	**1891**
	Kemble, Reginald Siddons, Lieut. K. Liverpool Regt.		W.S.I.	**1915**
	Kempson, Eric William Edward, Major, R.E.	**M.C. D²**	C.J.S.C. and W.D.H.	**1895**
	Kendall, Edward Hext, Lt. D.C.L.I. Flight Sub-Lieut., R.N.A.S.		S.H.	**1911**
	Kendall, Hugh Berenger, Capt. and Adjutant, R.F.A.	**D.**	S.H.	**1904**
	Kendall, Henry Ewing, The Rev., Chaplain to the Forces. R.N.	**O.B.E.**	S.H.	**1907**
W³	Kendall, Henry John, Lieut. K.S.L.I.		S.H.	**1909**
P.	Kendall, William James, Capt. K. Liverpool Regt. and M.G.C.		S.H.	**1907**
	Kenyon, Harold Margerison, Major, R.A.S.C.		C.J.S.C.	**1897**
W.	Kershaw, Philip Southwell, Lieut. R.A.F. Balloon Commdr.		A.F.C. and C.J.S.C.	**1892**
	Keysell, Folliott Sandford, The Rev. Chaplain to the Forces.		C.J.S.C.	**1890**
	Kinchin-Smith, Austin Edward, Captain, K.S.L.I.	**M.C. D.**	J.B.O.	**1916**
W.P.	Kinchin-Smith, Francis John, Lieut. K.S.L.I.		E.B.M. and F.T.P.	**1914**
	King, Jefford, Capt. and Adjutant, R.F.A.		T.E.P.	**1916**
	King, Lionel James, Lieut., Yeo.		F.T.P.	**1916**
W.	Kirkpatrick, Yvone Eustace Sutton, Lieut. R.A.F.		A.F.C.	**1916**
	Kitchin, Anthony Walter Brook, 2nd Lieut. R.W. Surrey Regt.		S.H.	**1914**
	Kitchin, Arthur Everard, Capt., Shrewsbury School O.T.C.		Master	

Kitching, John,		F.M.I.	1917
Cadet Edinburgh Univ. O.T.C.			
Kitson, Charles Henry,	D.	G.T.H.	1889
Lieut. R.A.S.C.			
Kittermaster, Digby Bliss, The Rev.	M.C. D.	D.B. and	
Chaplain to the Forces.		S.H.	1896
Knight-Eaton, Norman Davis Usel			
Henry Mason,		S.H.	1881
Major, Beds. Regt.			
Knapton, John Roylance Bernard,		S.H.	1918
2nd Lieut. K.S.L.I.			
Knighton, George Francis,		S.H.	1907
Capt. Sherwood Foresters.			
Knowles, John Lyndon,		S.H.	1915
Lieut. Rifle Brigade.			

W. Knox, Robert Kyle,   M.C.   W.D.H. 1914

2nd Lieut. R. Irish Rifles.

Kyle, James,		D.B.	1907
Lieut. Artists' Rifles.			
R.A.F. (Medical Branch).			
La Brooy, Mynert Victor Theodore Johnston,		S.H.	1912
Lieut. R.G.A.			
Lancaster, Arthur Noel,		G.T.H.	1899
Lieut. K. Liverpool Regt.			
Lancaster, Cyril Pearson,		G.T.H. and	
Lieut. R. Scots Fus.		W.D.H.	1900
Lancaster, Gerald William,	M.C.	C.J.S.C.	1906
Capt. Monmouthshire Regt. attchd.			
Welsh Regt.			
Lancaster, James.		C.J.S.C.	1896
Capt. Monmouthshire Regt.			
Lancaster, Wilfrid Drake, A.M.I.E.C.,	D²	G.T.H. and	
Lt.-Col. R.E. Inspector of Works.		W.D.H.	1901

W. Lander, Thomas Offley.   E.B.M. 1908

Pte., R. Fus.

Langford, Charles William Stenhouse,		F.T.P.	1917
2nd Lieut. K.S.L.I.			

W. Lane, Frank Bernard,   W.D.H. 1897

Major, Bengal Lancers, I.A.

D.A.A.G.

Langford James, Richard Lloyd, D.D., The Rev.		S.H.	1892
Chaplain, Calcutta Port Defence Vols,			
Langford James, John Wynn Lloyd,		S.H.	1898
Pte., Calcutta Vol. Rifles.			
Langley, Cyril Owen,	D.	C.J.S.C.	1898
Capt. S. Staffs. Regt. Adjutant			
and Brigade Major.			
Lasbrey, Percy Urwick, The Rev.	D.	C.J.S.C.	1884
Chaplain to the Forces.			
Lascelles, Lionel,		E.B.M.	1912
Lieut. R.A.S.C.			
Last, Ernest Courthope,		D.B.	1902
Major, R.E. Port Construction.			
La Touche, Denis Digges,		F.M.I.	1914
Capt. Welsh Regt.			
Launder, William Gordon,		W.D.H. and	
Lieut. R.F.A.		F.S.	1902

Law, Abraham Archibald,
    2nd Lieut. Cheshire Regt. — F.S. and S.H. 1902

Law, Harrington Robley,
    2nd Lieut. Tank Corps. — S.H. 1916

W. Law, Hugh Francis d'A. Stuart, **M.C.** — S.H. 1914
    Capt. Irish Guards. A.D.C.

Law, Robert Redman, — D.B. 1884
    Capt. R.A.M.C.

Lawder, Cecil Edward, **O.B.E.** — D.B. and A.F.C. 1894
    Lt.-Col. R.F.A. & R.A.F. S.O.

W. Lawrence, Alan, — W.D.H. 1908
    2nd Lieut. S. Staffs. Regt.

Lawrence, Charles Trevor, **D.** — C.J.S.C. 1897
    Major, Hants. Regt. and W. Africa Frontier Force.

Lawrence, Henry Hansen, — F.M.I. 1918
    Gunner, R.F.A.

Lawrence, Peter,   ·   S.H. 1901
    Pte. K. Liverpool Regt.

Lawson, Eustace Charles, **M.C.** — D.B. 1895
    Capt. Middlesex Regt.

W. Lea, Percy Lister Zair, **M.C.** — F.M.I. 1913
    Lieut. R.F.A.

Lea, John Douglas, — F.M.I. 1917
    Lieut. R.F.A.

Leadbitter, Eric Cyril Egerton, — E.B.M. 1908
    Paymaster-Lieut. R.N.R.

Leadbitter, Francis John Graham, — E.B.M. 1899
    2nd Lieut. K.R.R.C. (attchd.).

Leake, Charles Ferguson, — E.B.M. 1902
    Capt. K.S.L.I.

Leake, Harold John, **M.C.** — W.D.H. 1911
    Major, Shropshire R.H.A.

Leake, Kennedy Whitford, — E.B.M. 1909
    Gunner, R.F.A.

W. Leake, Victor George, — W.D.H. 1906'
    2nd Lieut. K.S.L.I.

Leather, Arthur Bowring, — C.J.S.C. 1898
    2nd Lieut. R.G.A.

Lee, Edward George, — E.B.M. 1909
    Lieut. R.A.S.C.

W.P. Lee, James Lyell, **M.C.** — E.B.M. 1911
    Capt. Lancs. Fus.

W. Lee, Richard Francis, — E.B.M. and F.T.P. 1912
    Capt. E. Lancs. Regt. and R.A.F.

Lee, Stephen Grosvenor, — S.H. 1908
    Capt. Rifle Brigade.

Lee. Wilfrid Millsom, — F.M.I. 1916
    Lieut. K. Liverpool Regt. and I.A.

Leech, Robert Edward Holt, — C.J.B. 1911
    2nd Lieut. K.S.L.I.

Leedam, Richard Walter, — C.J.B. and S.H. 1904
    2nd Lieut. R. Warwicks. Regt.

W. Leggett, Harold Ackworth, — S.H. 1892
    Major, Sherwood Foresters.

W. Leggett, Robert Anthony Cleghorn Linington, **D.S.O. O.B.E. D³** A.F.C. and S.H. 1893
    Lt.-Col. Worcs. Regt.

For explanations and abbreviations, see page 4.

Leslie, John Henry		S.H.	1872
Major, R.A. (ret.)			
Lester, Hugh Lewis Pingo,		S.H.	1918
Flight Sub.-Lieut. R.A.F.			
Levy, Kenneth Adolph.		T.E.P.	1913
Lieut. R.F.A.			
Lewis, Bernard,		S.H.	1874
Hon. Major, R. Welch Fus. and R.D.C.			
Lewis, Cecil Ernest Millington, M.D.		T.A.B.	1885
Commandant, Bickley Red Cross Hospital.			
Lewis, Gilbert Cecil Gaunt,		S.H.	1917
2nd Lieut. I.A.			
P. Lewis, Harry Gethin,		F.M.I.	1918
2nd Lieut. R.A.F.			
Lewis, John Dunning Gaunt,		S.H. and	
Lieut. K.S.L.I.		D.B.	1911
Lewis, Nevill Graham Newcome Hart,		F.S. and	
Capt. Mon. Regt. Att. R. Sussex Regt.		F.M.I.	1910
Lewis-Morgan, Walter Vyvyan,	**M.C.**	F.M.I.	1912
Lieut. R.G.A.			
Leyson, William Aubrey.		A.F.C. and	
Glamorgan Red Cross Hospital.		S.H.	1904
Lindop, Thomas Evans,		T.E.P.	1918
Prob. Flight Sub-Lieut. R.A.F.			
Lingeman, Eric Ralph,		J.B.O.	1916
2nd Lieut. I.A.			
Lipscomb, William Temple,		G.T.H.	1899
Major, Yorks. Dragoons. A.D.C.			
Litt, John Percy, M.D.	Cavalier of the Order	F.E.B.	1904
Major, R.A.M.C.	of the Redeemer (Greek).		
W. Litt, William George,	**T.D.**	D.B.	1895
Major, K.S.L.I.			
Littler, Hilary Vaughan,		D.B.	1907
Lieut. Central Ontario Regt.			
Livesey, Geoffrey H.		A.F.C.	1891
Recruiting Staff.			
Livingstone, Frank Darley,		E.B.M.	1904
Capt. R.A.S.C.			
Livingstone-Learmonth, David,		S.H.	1916
Cadet, R.M.A., Woolwich.			
Llandaff, The Right Rev. The Lord Bishop of,		S.H.	1886
Chaplain to the Forces. R.F.A.			
Lloyd, Charles Evan,		A.F.C.	1893
Lieut. Oxfordshire Vol. Regt.			
Lloyd, Charles Patterson,		S.H.	1877
Major, E. Kent Regt.			
Lloyd, Ernest Robert Vivian,	**M.C.**	A.F.C.	1907
Capt. Canadian Infantry.			
Lloyd, Ernest Thomas.		D.B. and	
Major, R.D.C.		S.H.	1879
Lloyd, Gilbert Kingsley,		S.H.	1899
2nd Lieut. K.S.L.I.			
Lloyd, Humphrey,		J.B.O.	1917
Pte. R. Fusiliers			
Lloyd, John Daniel Stuart,	**M.C. O.B.E. D². **	S.H.	1896
Major, Welsh Horse (Yeo.)	**Croix de Guerre (French).**		
	Order of Leopold. Croix		
	de Guerre (Belgian).		

For explanations and abbreviations, see page 4.

43

	Lloyd, Reginald John, 2nd Lieut. Labour Corps.			W.D.H. and D.B. 1910
W.	Lloyd, Wilfrid Lewis, Capt. Kumaon Rifles, I.A.	**M.C.**		D.B. and J.B.O. 1913
	Lloyd-Jones, Arthur, 2nd Lieut. R.F.A.			C.J.B. 1912
W²	Lloyd-Jones, Charles Henry, Lieut. R. Welch Fus.			F.M.I. 1915
	Lloyd-Jones, Newcombe, Capt. R.D.C.			G.T.H. 1888
	Lloyd-Jones, Hubert, 2nd Lieut. R. Welch Fus.	**D.**		G.T.H. 1896
	Lloyd-Williams, Kelyth Pierce, 2nd Lieut. Welsh Regt.			S.H. 1912
	Locket, Eimer George, 2nd Lieut. Suffolk Regt.			S.H. 1907
	Longworth, Eustace Counsellor, Capt. Lancs. Fus.			E.B.M. 1908
	Longworth, Frank, Lieut. Cheshire Regt.			E.B.M. 1906
	Longrigg, William Fallowfield, Pte. Kent Vol. Regt.			S.H. 1894
	Loveday, David Goodwin, 2nd Lieut. Ox. and Bucks L.I.			E.B.M. and F.T.P. 1915
	Low, John, Lieut. R.F.A.			J.B.O. 1912
	Low, Walter Percival, The Rev. Chaplain to the Forces (S. Africa).	**D.**		C.J.B. and S.H. 1895
	Lowe, Frederick Arthur, Capt. R.E. Inland Waterways and Docks.			F.E.B. 1897
	Lowe, Henry St Alban, Capt. Radley College O.T.C.			G.T.H. 1894
	Lowe, William Douglas, D.Litt. Lt.-Col. Durham L.I.	**D.S.O. M.C.**	**D⁴**	G.T.H. 1898
	Lowe, William, 2nd Lieut. R.E.			F.E.B. 1897
	Lowndes, Richard Charles, Lieut. I.A.			F.E.B. 1904
	Lucas, Robert Beart, Lieut. Res. Regts. of Cavalry.	**D.**		S.H. 1893
	Lutener, Richard Arthur Maurice, 2nd Lieut. K.S.L.I.			S.H. 1914
W²	Lyle, Sydney James, Capt. R. Irish Rifles and R.A.S.C.	**M.C. D.**		C.J.S.C. 1890
	Lyon (formerly Schwind), Charles Arthur Lieut. R.M.A.			S.H. 1917
	Lyon (formerly Schwind), Frederic Lambert, 2nd Lieut. R.N.			S.H. 1918
W.P.	Lyster, Philip Graves, Major, R.A.			C.J.S.C. 1893
W.	Macan, Arthur Vernon, Lieut. Canadian Infantry.			C.J.B. and A.F.C. 1899
	Macaulay, Horace, Lieut. Seaforth Highlanders.			F.M.I. 1912
W.	Macaulay, Frederic Robert Harms. Lieut. R. Dublin Fus.			J.B.O. 1916

For explanations and abbreviations, see page 4.

	Macaulay, Richard Hugh Harms, Cadet, R.M.C., Sandhurst.		J.B.O.	1918
	Macbeth, Allan, Capt. Ry. Transport Officer. Staff Lieut.		W.D.H.	1900
W.	Mackenzie, Allan Victor, Lieut. K.S.L.I.	**M.C.**	S.H.	1915
	MacClellan, Gordon Ponsonby, Bt. Lt.-Col. R.G.A.	**D.S.O. (Bar). D⁴.** **Croix de Guerre** **(French).**	F.E.B.	1897
W.	MacClellan, John Ponsonby, Sergeant, London Scottish.		C.J.B. and F.E.B.	1901
	MacCreery, William Michael, 2nd Lieut. I.A.		A.J.W.	1917
	Maclaran, Malcolm Sandford, Major, R.F.A.	**D.**	E.B.M.	1907
	Maclean, Gordon Forbes, Capt. Argyll and Sutherland High'rs.	**M.C.**	S.H.	1914
	MacLeod, Evan Cameron, Lt.-Col. I.M.S.		D.B.	1885
	MacMahon, John Aquila, Lieut. R.A.M.C.		A.F.C.	1907
	MacRobert, Norman Murie, 2nd Lieut. Rifle Brigade.		F.M.I.	1917
	Maddox, Cecil Richard, Capt. I.A.		S.H. and W.D.H.	1901
	Maddison, Lionel Frederick, 2nd Lieut. Durham L.I. attd. R.A.F.		J.B.O.	1917
W.	Malone, Richard Maurice Fitz Gerald, Capt. Norfolk Regt.		T.E.P.	1914
	McClintock, Lawson Tait, Capt. Norfolk Medical Corps.		G.T.H.	1895
W²	McConnan, Charles Walter, Capt. Border Regt.	**M.C.**	W.D.H.	1903
	McConnan, George, Capt. K. Liverpool Regt.		G.T.H. and W.D.H.	1901
	McDonald, James Ratcliff, Major, London Regt. and T.F.R.	**Order of the Nile,** **4th Class.**	G.T.H. and W.D.H.	1900
	McDonald, Ronald Bruce, Lieut. R.A.S.C.	**D.**	G.T.H. and W.D.H.	1903
	McEwan, Alan Grandage, Lieut. R.N.		W.D.H.	1913
	McFerran, George Cecil, 2nd Lieut. Argyll and Sutherland Highlanders.		S.H.	1916 ·
W.	McFerran, John Rowan Addison, Capt. R. Irish Rifles.		F.M.I.	1914
	McFerran, Maurice Anderdon, 2nd Lieut. R. Irish Rifles.		S.H.	1915
W.	MacIver, Alan Squarey, Capt. Lancs. Fus.	**M.C.**	E.B.M and F.T.P.	1913
	McIver, Reginald Squarey, Lieut. Lancs. Fus.		E.B.M.	1911
	McClymont, Crawford James, 2nd Lieut. K. School, Warwick O.T.C.		W.D.H.	1907
	McLaren, James, Lieut. M.G.C.		A.F.C.	1911

	Manby, Charles William Lane, Lieut. R.N.V.R.		E.B.M.	1896
	Manby, George Lyndsay Hardinge. **D.** Major, Sherwood Foresters, Brigade Major.		E.B.M.	1896
W.	Manly, Lawrence Arthur, **M.C.** Lieut. Lancs. Fus.		F.T.P.	1916
	Mann, Hector Campbell, Hon. Lieut. R.A.S.C.		D.B.	1904
	Mansergh, Wilmsdorff George, Capt. Manchester Regt.		D.B.	1896
	Marriner, Kenneth Dalrymple, M.B., Lieut. R.A.M.C.		F.E.B.	1903
W.	Marsh, Conrad Richard Creswell, Lieut. K.S.L.I.		C.J.B.	1911
	Marsh, Frank Douglas, **M.C.** Major, R.A.M.C.		F.E.B. and C.J.B.	1907
	Marshall, Herbert John Owen, 2nd Lieut. R.M.		S.H.	1918
	Marshall, Roger Charles, Lieut. R.F.A.		S.H.	1907
	Marston, Edward Richard, 2nd Lieut. Shropshire Regt. (Vols.)		C.J.S.C.	1884
	Martin, Henry Stuart, Capt. D.C.L.I.		G.T.H.	1890
	Martin-Sperry (formerly Richter) Cecil Gustav, Capt. British Guiana Militia.		S.H.	1901
	Martin-Sperry (formerly Richter) Frederic Harold, Lieut. R.A.S.C. (M.T.)		S.H.	1905
	Martyn, Rutter Barry, Lt.-Col. R.A.F.	**M.C. D².** Order of St. Anne with Swords.	C.J.B. and S.H.	1904
W.	Mason, J. L. 2nd Lieut. I.A.		W.D.H.	1917
W.	Massey, Bernard Wilfrid Arbuthnot, Capt. R.F.A.		S.H.	1903
	Mathews, Arnold, **D.** Lieut. Cheshire Regt.		C.J.B.	1913
	Mathews, Arnold Burnett, Sub-Lieut. R.N.V.R.		W.D.H.	1916
	Matthews, Robert Stanley, Pte. H.A.C.		S.H.	1907
	Maule, Geoffrey Lamb, Capt. R.A.M.C.		W.D.H.	1909
	Maunsell, Richard Lucius Dixie, Cadet, R.A.F.		F.M.I.	1918
	Maurice, Lawrence Colley, **O.B.E. D.** Lt.-Col. R.E. Assist. to Engineer-in-Chief.		S.H.	1898
	Maund, John Anthony Hansby, Lieut. I.A.		F.M.I.	1916
W.	Maw, Allan, Capt. Manchester Regt.		F.S.	1908
	Mein, Owen Coore, Capt. R.E.		C.J.S.C.	1904

For explanations and abbreviations, see page 4.

Melland, Edward Guy, — A.F.C. 1908
Lieut. Cheshire Regt.

W.P. Meredith, Herbert Thomas Douallier, — W.S.I. and
Lieut. K. Liverpool Regt. — C.J.B. 1910

Meredith, Hugh Owen, — C.J.S.C. 1897
Lieut. Queen's Coll., Belfast O.T.C.

W. Meredith, John Henry Mervyn, — D.B. 1912
Lieut. E. Surrey Regt.

Metcalfe, George Christopher, — W.D.H. 1906
Capt. R.A.M.C.

Miles, Bevis Lipscomb, **M.C. D²** W.D.H. 1903
Capt. London Regt.

Miles, Harold Philip, — S.H. 1917
2nd Lieut. K.S.L.I.

Miles, Henry Robert, — S.H. 1885
2nd Lieut. Connaught Rangers.

Miles, Philip John, F.R.G.S., **C.M.G. C.B. D².** S.H. 1883
Brig.-General I.A.

Miles, Richard, — S.H. 1917
Pte. Inns of Court O.T.C.

Miles, Hubert Elfric, — W.D.H. 1896
Lieut. R.A.S.C.

Miller, Edwin Swainson, M.D., — C.J.S.C. 1886
Fleet Surgeon, R.N.

W² Miller, Gerald William, **D.S.O. M.C. D³** W.D.H. 1913
Capt. and Adjutant, K. Liverpool **Chevalier of the**
Regt. Brigade Major.' **Order of Leopold**
and Croix de Guerre.

Miller, Kenneth Leven, — F.M.I. 1912
Capt. R. Highlanders.

W.P. Miller, Reginald Taverner, **D.** W.D.H. 1912
Capt. and Adjutant, Manchester Regt.

Milligan, William, **D.** W.D.H. 1910
Capt. R.F.A. Staff Capt.

W. Milward, Douglas Sutherland, — D.B. 1911
Capt. Worcs. Regt. and
Labour Corps.

Milward, Henry Charles Rutherford, — D.B. 1911
Lieut. Shropshire R.H.A. & R.A.F.

Milward, Victor Graham, **D.** D.B. 1882
Major, Warwicks. Regt. (Vol. Bn.)

Minor, Hugo Walford, — G.T.H. and
Pte. (Signaller) S. Lancs. Regt. — W.D.H. 1901

Mitchell, Alfred Sherrington, **D²** C.J.S.C. 1895
Capt. R. Warwicks. Regt.
Staff Capt.

Mitchell, Edward Grose Harper, — S.H. 1902
Capt. Rifle Brigade,

Mitchell, George Mathew Guy, — D.B. 1891
Pte. Shropshire Vol. Regt.

W. Mitchell, Robert Gordon, — J.B.O. 1916
2nd Lieut. R.A.F.

Mitchell, Tom Illingworth, — S.H. 1903
Major, Yorks Regt.

Mitford, Cuthbert William, — Master.
2nd Lieut. Shrewsbury School
O.T.C.

W.	Moir, James Adolph. Lieut. R.A.F.		C.J.B.	1915
	Monro, David Henry Carmichael, Lieut. Canadian Infantry.		S.H.	1903
	Moon, Jasper, Capt. K. Liverpool Regt.	**O.B.E. D³.** **Chevalier of the** **Order of Aviz (Portuguese).**	G.T.H.	1899
W.	Moore, Joseph Roger, Capt. R. Irish Rifles.		S.H.	1912
	Moore, John Sugden, Lieut. R.A.O.C.	**D.**	S.H.	1910
	Moore, Richard, 2nd Lieut. W. Yorks Regt.		S.H.	1915
	Moreton, John Patrick, Lieut. Dragoon Guards.	**M.C.**	S.H.	1914
	Morgan, Claude Ellis, Capt. Hants Regt.	**D.**	E.B.M.	1900
	Morgan, Eric Elton, Flight Officer, R.A.F.		D.B.	1917
	Morgan, George Sydney, Lieut. Dorset Regt.		D.B.	1913
	Morgan, Hugh Penrith, Major, R.F.A.	**M.C.**	D.B.	·1911
W.	Morgan, Spencer Fleming, Capt. & Adjutant, Cheshire Regt.	**D.**	C.J.S.C.	1908
	Morgan-Owen, Llewellyn Isaac Gethin, Bt. Lt.-Col. S.W.B. G.S.O.	**C.M.G. D.S.O. D⁶**	G.T.H.	1896
W²	Morgan-Owen, Morgan Maddox, Lt.-Col. Essex Regt. and Rifle Bde.	**D.S.O. D²**	G.T.H.	1896
W³	Morley, Reginald Mills, Lieut. Lancs. Fus.		T.E.P.	1914
	Morris, Allan McLean, Capt. K. Liverpool Regt.	**D.**	S.H.	1910
	Morris, Cyril Walter Montague, 2nd Lieut. I.A.		T.E.P.	1918
	Morris, Ernest Edwin, The Rev. Canon, Chaplain to the Forces.	**T.D.**	S.H.	1873
	Morris, Clifford, Major, R.F.A.	**M.C. (Bar). D.**	A.F.C.	1907
	Morris, Gordon McQueen, Lieut. K. Liverpool Regt.		A.F.C.	1912
	Moser, George Reginald, Lt.-Col. R.A.F. S.O.		E.B.M.	1896
	Moser, Herbert Guy, Surgeon, R.N.		E.B.M.	1908
	Moser, John, Sapper, Canadian Engineers (France). Capt. Army Pay Corps, Canada.		E.B.M.	1907
	Moser, Richard, Capt. R.A.M.C.		E.B.M.	1909
	Mosley, John William Paget, Capt. R.F.A. Staff.		D.B. and C.J.S.C.	1890
	Mudford, Arthur Cecil, Pte. New Zealand Infantry.		S.H.	1912
	Mountford, Cecil, Lieut. R.A.S.C. (M.T.)		F.S.	1908
	Mudford, Sandy, Pte. York and Lancaster Regt.		T.E.P.	1912

For explanations and abbreviations, see page 4.

W.	Muir, John Gordon, Lieut. K. Liverpool Regt.	**M.C.**	F.M.I.	1916
	Muirhead, Albert William, Lieut. R.A.S.C.		F.S.	1911
	Muirhead, Thomas Geoffrey, Pte. R.A.O.C.		S.H.	1908
	Muirhead, Thomas Arthur, 2nd Lieut. K.O.S.B.		A.F.C.	1892
	Murdoch, Hugh Campbell, Commander, R.N.	**O.B.E.**	F.E.B.	1898
	Murray, Walter Godfrey Patrick, Lt.-Col. I.A. A.Q.M.G.	**D.S.O. D.**	S.H.	1891
	Musson, Sydney Ashhurst, Lieut. R.A.S.C.		S.H.	1891
	Mylius, John Kingsford, Lieut. K.S.L.I.	**D.**	S.H.	1914
	Nadin, Trafford, Capt. & Adjt., Sherwood Foresters.		E.B.M.	1896
	Nalder, Frank Shirley, Capt. K.S.L.I.		S.H. and J.B.O.	1914
	Nadin, Joseph, 2nd Lieut. Labour Corps.		S.H.	1904
	Napper, William Henry, Major, R.A.S.C.	**D.**	G.T.H.	1900
W.	Neale, Roland Hayward, Capt. Lincolns. Regt. and M.G.C.		S.H.	1914
	Nelson, George Herbert, Major. R.F.A.	**D.**	A.F.C.	1907
	Nelson, John Walton, Major, R.G.A.	**M.C. D.**	F.M.I.	1914
	Nelson, Richard Owen, Capt. R.A.S.C. (M.T.)		A.F.C.	1904
	Neville, Henry Seymour, Capt. R.A.F. Staff Officer.		J.B.O.	1914
	Nevett, Thomas Alfred, L./Corporal, K.S.L.I.		W.S.I.	1913
	Nevinson, Henry Woodd, War Correspondent—France, Salonika, Egypt, Germany.		S.H.	1875
	Newill, Harry Strick, Lieut. K.S.L.I.		W.D.H.	1911
	Newill, Robert Daniel, Capt. R.H.A.		F.S.	1908
	Newland, Sir Foster Reuss, M.D., (Hon.) Surgeon-General, R.A.M.C.	**K.C.M.G. C.M.G. C.B. D⁵. Croce di Guerra.**	S.H.	1880
	Newman, Kingsley, Pte. R. Sussex Regt.		G.T.H.	1893
	Newton, John William, 2nd Lieut. Hussars Yeo.		S.H.	1906
	Nicholas, William Llewellyn, The Rev. Canon. Chaplain to the Forces.		S.H.	1868
	Nichols, Frederick Peter, M.B., Lt.-Col. R.A.M.C.	**D²**	S.H.	1875
	Nicholson, Robert Leonard St Clare, Capt. T.F.R.		C.J.S.C.	1891
	Nicholson, Ronald Scholfield, Lieut. Recruiting Duties.		C.J.S.C.	1889

For explanations and abbreviations, see page 4.

	Nicholson, Walter Adams, Lt.-Col. R.A. (Res. of Officers).		G.T.H.	1884
W.	Nickson, John Edgar, 2nd Lieut. R. Welch Fus.	M.C. (Bar).	T.E.P.	1917
	Norman, Duncan, Capt. R.E.	M.C. Chevalier of the Order of Leo-pold. Croix de Guerre.	E.B.M.	1908
	Norris, William Forbes, Lieut. Norfolk Regt. (Cyclist Co.)		A.F.C.	1912
W.	Norton, David George, Major, Lancs. Fus.		C.J.B. and E.B.M.	1904
	Norton, David Barton Moon, Cadet, R.M.C., Sandhurst.		F.T.P.	1916
	Norton, Gilbert Paul, Lt.-Col. W. Riding Regt.	D.S.O. T.D. D³.	E.B.M.	1899
W.	Nugent, Arthur Charles, Capt. R. Irish Lancers.		S.H.	1911
	Oakes, Geoffrey Marriott, Major, R.F.A.		C.J.S.C.	1906
	O'Callaghan, Charles, Lieut. R.N.	D.S.C.	C.J.B.	1913
W.P.	O'Callaghan, Cornelius Edward Alexander, Lieut. R. Munster Fus.		J.B.O.	1915
	Oakden, Ralph, Major, Rifle Brigade.		F.E.B.	1892
	O'Carroll, Francis Brendan Ely, 2nd Lieut. R. Dublin Fus.		F.M.I.	1913
	Ogle, John Wilfrid, Lieut. N. Western Ry. Bn., I.A.		W.D.H.	1907
	Oldham, Frederick Hugh Langston, Bt. Lt.-Col. R.A.	D.S.O. D⁶. Cavalier of the Order of SS. Maurice and Lazarus.	E.B.M.	1895
	Oldham, James Basil, 2nd Lieut. Shrewsbury School O.T.C.		E.B.M.	1901
	Oliver, James Scott, Cadet, Edinburgh Univ. O.T.C.		F.M.I.	1917
	Oliver, Richard Edward Deane, Lieut. R.E.		C.J.S.C.	1907
	Ommaney, George Gascoigne, Major, R.E. and R.N.A.S.		D.B.	1907
	O'Neill, Samuel, Lieut. Lancs. Fus.		E.B.M.	1911
	Onslow, Thomas, 2nd Lieut. K.S.L.I.		S.H.	1916
	Orme, Edward Leslie, Lieut. R. Welch Fus.		W.D.H.	1914
	Orme, Francis Reginald, Lieut. R. Welch Fus.		W.D.H.	1911
	Ormrod, Garfield, M.D., Bt. Lt.-Col. R.A.M.C.	D.	F.E.B.	1898
	Ormrod, Herbert, Capt. Lancs. Fus. and K. Liverpool Regt.	D.	F.E.B.	1899
	Osborne, Alan Fell, Pte., London Field Ambulance.		S.H.	1899

For explanations and abbreviations, see page 4.

W.	Oswell, Harold Lloyd, Lieut. N. Staffs. Regt.		S.H.	1913
	Overton, Reginald Ernest, Lieut. R.F.A.	**D.**	W.D.H.	1911
	Owen, Arthur Banks, 2nd Lieut. K.S.L.I.		S.H.	1917
	Owen, Geoffrey Livy, Lieut. R.A., Bimbashi, Egyptian Army.		S.H.	1909
	Owen, Humphrey Francis, Lieut. R. Welch Fus.		^ F.C.	1903
	Owen, James Loftus, Pte. County of London Regt. (Vol.), Chief Engineer to War Office, Admiralty and R.A.F.		D.B.	1877
	Owen, Percival Wilcox, 2nd Lieut. K.S.L.I.		W.D.H.	1907
W.	Owen, Philip Richard Tudor, Lieut. E. Kent Regt.		S.H.	1905
W.	Owen, Robert Charles Dorsett, Capt. R. Welch Fus.		A.F.C.	1906
	Owen, William Churchill, Lieut. R. Welch Fus.		S.H.	1904
	Owen, William Henry Kenrick, Capt. Welsh Regt		S.H.	1913
	Owtram, Henry Cary, 2nd Lieut. R.M.		A.F.C.	1918
	Padmore, Alan Reynolds, 2nd Lieut. R.A.F.		C.J.B.	1917
	Padmore, James Leslie, Capt. and Adjutant, R. Warwicks Regt.	**M.C. D.**	C.J.B.	1914
W³	Paget, Bernard Charles Tolver, Bt. Major, Ox. and Bucks L.I. Brigade Major.	**D.S.O. M.C. D⁴** **Order of the Crown** **of Italy. Silver** **Medal for Military** **Valour.**	C.J.S.C.	1905
	Paget, Edward Francis, The Rev. Chaplain to the Forces, S. Africa.	**M.C.**	C.J.S.C.	1904
W.	Paget, Richard James, Capt. Manitoba Regt., Canadian Infantry. A.D.C.		C.J.S.C.	1902
	Palin, Henry William Bourne, Pte., New Zealand Infantry.		S.H.	1900
W²	Palmer, Geoffrey James Head, Lieut. R. Irish Regt. (attchd. R. Irish Rifles).		F.M.I.	1915
	Parker, George Alexander, 2nd Lieut. R. Welch Fus.		J.B.O.	1916
W.P.	Parkes, Gerard Allport Hickling, Lieut. R.A.F.		W.D.H.	1915
	Parkin, Alfred, Lieut. R.A.S.C. (M.T.)		F.S. and F.M.I.	1910
	Partridge, James Adams Penell de Woodston, Pte., Canadian Infantry.		W.D.H.	1909
	Parr, Cecil Robert Morrall, Lieut. R.A.S.C. (M.T.)		F.E.B.	1899

	Parrott, William Sydney,		C.J.S.C.	1905
	Lieut. R.A.S.C.			
	Parry, John Humphreys,		E.B.M.	1909
	2nd Lieut. E. Kent Regt. and R.A.F.			
	Parry. Lionel Dalton,		A.F.C.	1895
	1st Class Stoker, R.N.			
	Parsons, Alfred Henry,		S.H.	1900
	Capt., I.A.			
	Paterson, James,	**M.C. D².**	C.J.B. and	
	Major, London Scottish Regt.		S.H.	1902
	A.Q.M.G.			
W.	Paterson, John William Mayne,		J.B.O.	1915
	Lieut. Highland L.I.			
	Paterson, Leslie Arnott,		S.H.	1908
	2nd Lieut. Essex Regt.			
	Pattinson, John Herbert,		C.J.S.C.	1896
	Capt. Durham L.I.			
	Pearson, Noel Murray,	**M.C. (Bar).**	S.H.	1901
	Capt. & Adjt., Yeo. Brigade Major.			
W.	Pearson, Philip Walter,	**M.C.**	W.D.H.	1915
	Lieut. K.S.L.I.			
	Pearson, Robert Thomas,		S.H.	1891
	Capt. R.A.S.C. and R.A.F.			
	Pearson, Robert Stanley,	**O.B.E. D.**	A.F.C.	1892
	Major, Hussars (Yeo.) Brigade Major.			
	Peck, Kenneth,		A.F.C.	1903
	2nd Lieut. K. Liverpool Regt.			
W.	Peele. Joshua John.		G.T.H.	1896
	Capt. Nigeria Regt. R.A. (Reserve			
	of Officers).			
	Peele, Leonard Cresswell,		D.B.	1887
	Lieut. R.D.C.			
	Pegge, Arthur Vernon,	**M.C.**	A.F.C.	1911
	Capt. R.A.M.C.			
	Pemberton, Guy,		A.F.C.	1901
	Capt. and Adjutant, E. Kent Regt.			
W.	Pendlebury, Henry Maurice von Monté,		D.B.	1912
	Capt. K.S.L.I.			
	Pendlebury, William Johann von Monté,		D.B.	1909
	Major, R.F.A. Staff Captain.			
	Penn, Charles Edward,		D.B.	1890 ,
	Pte. London Regt.			
	Perrin, Eugène Courtenay,	**O.B.E.**	F.E.B.	1905
	Major & Adjutant, R.A.F. S.O.			
	Perrin, Michael,	**M.C.**	F.E.B. and	
	Capt. L. N. Lancs. Regt.		C.J.B.	1908
	Percy-Smith, Hubert Kendall,		J.B.O.	1916
	Lieut. 40th Pathans I.A.			
	Perry, Harold Mowbray,		S.H.	1898
	Lieut. R.E.			
	Petrie, Sir Edward Lindsay Haddon,		S.H.	1899
	Lieut. R.A.S.C.			
	Petrie, James Arnold,		F.E.B.	1897
	Divl. Commander, W. Riding Special			
	Constabulary.			
	Philips, Henry Vaughan,	**M.B.E.**	A.F.C.	1899
	Capt. Northumberland Fus.			
	Ministry of Nat. Service.			

For explanations and abbreviations, see page 4.

	Phillips, Reginald Maurice, Lieut. Welsh Regt.		A.F.C.	1915
W²	Philp, John de Riemer, Capt. R. Warwicks. Regt.		S.H.	1907
	Pickering, Atkinson, Lieut. W. Riding Vol. Regt.		S.H.	1875
W.	Pigott, Alan John Keefe Pemberton, Lieut. and Adjutant, R. Irish Regt. attchd. Cheshire Regt.		D.B.	1911
	Pigott, Eric John Keefe Pemberton, 2nd Lieut. R. Irish Regt.		D.B.	1912
	Pigott, Noel Frederick Pemberton, Capt. R.E.		D.B.	1905
	Pilcher, Alan Humphrey, Lieut. R.F.A.	**M.C.**	W.D.H.	1916
	Pilkington, Richard Austin, 2nd Lieut. E. Lancs. Regt. & T.F.R.		S.H.	1889
	Pilling, John Lawrence, Lieut. R.F.A.	**M.C.**	W.D.H.	1916
	Pipe, John Clifford, Sub.-Lieut. R.N.V.R.		C.J.S.C.	1906
	Pitcairn-Jones, Edward, 2nd Lieut. Rifle Brigade.		S.H.	1915
	Platnauer, Maurice, Capt. and Adjutant, R.G.A.		W.D.H.	1906
	Plowden, Humphrey Roger, Capt., Lancers.		F.S.	1906
	Plummer, John Humphreys, 2nd Lieut. Gordon Highlanders.		F.E.B.	1902
W²	Pollitt, Fred Septimus, Lieut. R.F.A.	**D.**	W.D.H.	1908
	Pollock, Arthur William Alsager, Lt.-Col. Yorks L.I. Staff.	**D².**	S.H.	1872
	Ponsford, James William Prior, Sergeant, R. Fus.		W.D.H.	1914
	Ponsonby, Reginald Gordon, Lt.-Col. R.E.		E.B.M.	1894
	Porritt, Charles Herbert, Lieut. Yorks L.I. attchd. R. Welch Fus.		F.E.B.	1895
	Porritt, Sydney Sherwood, Capt. R.A.S.C.		C.J.S.C.	1906
	Porter, John Stansfield, Major, E. Yorks Regt. and W. African Regt.		A.F.C.	1905
	Porter, Harry Michael Stansfield, Major, R.G.A. and R.E.	**M.C. (Bar).**	A.F.C.	1900
	Potts, Harold Garnock, L/ Corporal, R.A.S.C.		D.B. and C.J.S.C.	1901
	Pouncey, George Ronald, Lieut. I.A.		S.H.	1916
	Pound, John Russell, Capt. K.S.L.I.		Master.	
	Powell, Arthur Edward, Major, R.E.		E.B.M.	1899
	Powell, Charles Noel, 2nd Lieut. E. Surrey Regt. attchd. K.R.R.C.		G.T.H.	1899

For explanations and abbreviations, see page 4.

	Powell, Matthew Alexander,			G.T.H. and	
	Trooper, K. Edward's Horse.			W.D.H.	1901
	Powell, Sydney Price,			W.D.H. and	
	2nd Lieut. R.A.F.			E.B.M.	1899
	Powell, Thomas Clark,			F.M.I.	1916
	2nd Lieut. R.G.A.				
	Powell, Walter S.			W.D.H.	1903
	Lieut. K.E.O. Cavalry, I.A.				
	Pownall, Henry,			F.M.I.	1912
	Lieut. H.A.C.				
W.	Poyser, Kenneth Ellaston,	**D.S.O.**	**D³**	S.H.	1900
	Lt.-Col. K.O. Yorks L.I.				
	Pratt, Ernest Percival,			F.M.I.	1917
	Wireless Telegraphist, R.N.V.R.				
	Preece, Denis Edward Goodwin,			D.B.	1913
	Capt. I.A.R.O.				
	Price, John David,			S.H.	1900
	P.S. Bn. London Regt.				
	Price, Herbert Davise,			F.S.	1903
	Lieut. M.G.C.				
	Priestley, Francis John Lloyd,			A.F.C. and	
	Lt.-Col. Hussars (Yeo.)			S.H.	1893
	Priestley, Percival Thomas, M.B.,			E.B.M.	1906
	Major, R.A.M.C.				
W²	Prince, Peregrine,	**D.S.O.**	**D²**	E.B.M.	1899
	Lt.-Col. K.S.L.I.				
	Comt. T.M. Training Centre.				
	Prince, Peregrine Charles,			E.B.M.	1890
	Capt. R.A.M.C.				
W.	Prince, William Howard,			A.F.C.	1910
	Capt. Lancs. Fus.				
	Prichard, Richard Francis,			F.T.P.	1915
	Lieut. R. Monmouth R.E.				
	Pritchard, Alan Bulmer,			D.B.	1915
	Pte. H.A.C.				
	Pritchard, Fred Eills,			F.T.P.	1917
	Lieut. R.M.A. Howitzer Bde.				
	Pritchard, Harry Bayldon,			T.E.P.	1916
	Lieut. R.F.A.				
	Prior, Charles Geoffrey,			W.D.H.	1915
	Capt. Baluchistan L.I., I.A.				
	Proctor, Charles Edward,			S.H.	1888
	2nd Lieut. R.F.A.				
	Pryce, Thomas Tannatt,	**V.C. M.C. (Bar). D.**		A.F.C.	1904
	Capt. Grenadier Guards.				
	Pryce Jones, Albert Westhead,	**O.B.E. T.D. D.**		E.B.M.	1889
	Col. Saskatchewan Regt., Canadian				
	Infantry.				
	Pugh, John Edwin,			F.T.P.	1916
	Lieut. R.A.F.				
	Pullen, John Edward,			R.J.D. and	
	Capt. R.E.			A.F.C.	1902
	Pullen, Richard Standiford,	**D²**		W.D.H.	1900
	Lieut. S. Staffs. Regt.				
	Pybus, Gilbert Douglas,			W.D.H.	1915
	Capt. I.A., attchd. Rattray's Sikhs.				
W.	Quiggin, Percy Milcrest,	**M.C.**		S.H.	1906
	Major, R.G.A.				

For explanations and abbreviations, see page 4.

54

W.	Rabone, Eric Lawrence, Capt. Worcs. Regt. Brigade Major.	**M.C.**	**D.**		W.D.H.	1907
	Ractivand, Demetri, Lieut. K.S.L.I.	**M.C.**			W.D.H.	1916
	Rae, Charles Edward Leathart, Lieut. R.N.V.R.				E.B.M.	1902
	Raikes, Arthur Francis Morgan, Capt. York and Lancaster Regt.	**D.**			A.F.C.	1915
W.P.	Raikes, Jack Francis Cochrane, Capt. Monmouths Regt.				A.F.C.	1910
W.	Raikes, Kenneth Cochrane, Major, Monmouths Regt.	**O.B.E.**	**D²**		A.F.C.	1908
	Raikes, Marcus Hamilton, Capt. Border Regt. and I.A.R.O.		.		S.H.	1907
	Raikes, Robert Morgan, Lieut. R.F.A.				A.F.C.	1915
W³	Rambaut, Gerrard Marlande, Major, R.F.A. (T.)	**D.S.O.**	**D.**		Master.	
	Ramsbotham, Richard Bury, Capt. Rattray's Sikhs, I.A. Staff.	**M.B.E.**			S.H.	1899
	Ransome, Charles Edward Cedric, Prob. Lieut. R.M.				J.B.O.	1918
	Ratliff, Edward Francis, Capt. Rifle Brigade.	**M.C.**			W.D.H.	1914
W.	Raven, Geoffrey Earle, Lieut. W. Yorks Regt.	**M.C.**			E.B.M. and F.T.P.	1912
	Ravenscroft, Douglas, Capt. R.F.A.	**M.C.**			F.E.B.	1898
	Ravenscroft, Leslie, Lieut. R.A.S.C.	**M.C.**			W.D.H.	1904
	Rawcliffe, Allan Sumner, Pte., S. African Infantry.				W.D.H.	1905
	Rawlinson, William Gray, Lieut. D.C.L.I.				E.B.M.	1906
W.	Rawstorne, James Oscar, Capt. R. Welch Fus. Staff.				W.D.H.	1910
	Rayner, William Hartree, M.R.C.S., Capt. R.A.M.C.				C.J.S.C.	1898
	Rees, Alexander Armstrong, M.B., Capt. R.A.M.C.				A.F.C.	1902
	Rees, John Trevor, 2nd Lieut. R. Welch Fus.				A.F.C.	1911
	Rendall, Philip Stanley, Lieut. K.S.L.I. Staff Lieut.				W.D.H.	1914
	Reynolds, Alfred Brian Challen, Lieut. Coldstream Guards.				W.D.H.	1918
	Reynolds, Victor Eustace, Capt. W. Yorks Regt.				S.H.	1896
W.	Rhys, Hubert Ralph John, Lieut. R.G.A.				T.E.P.	1916
	Rhys, Watkin Leoline Tom, 2nd Lieut. Rifle Brigade.				S.H.	1908
	Richards, Arthur Pierre, Capt. Durham L.I.				G.T.H.	1900
W²	Richards, Darcy John Rigby, Major and Adjutant, R.G.A.	**D.S.O.**	**M.C.**	**D.**	F.S. and F.M.I.	1908

Richards, Evan Ivor Glasbrook, Capt. and Adjutant, Welsh Regt.			S.H.	1908
Richards, John Francis Chatterton, Lieut. R.E. Cable Section.	**D.**		S.H.	1916
Richardson, Alan Joseph Macdonald, Capt. Somerset Yeo.			T.E.P.	1913
Richardson, Joseph Herbert, Engineer Sub-Lieut. R.N.V.R.			E.B.M.	1896
Richardson, William Quintus Newsum, 2nd Lieut. R.A.F.			F.M.I.	1916
Richmond, Harry, Pte. Shropshire Vol. Regt.			Master.	
Richmond, Maurice Hope, The Rev. Chaplain, Church Army, Egypt.			D.B.	1904
Rider, James Sidney Dundas, The Rev., Chaplain to the Forces.	**M.C.**		G.T.H. and W.D.H.	1901
Ridgway, Thomas, Lt.-Col. S. Lancs. Regt.	**D.S.O. M.C.(Bar).D²**		E.B.M.	1899
Ridpath, Harold, Capt. Ry. Transport Officer. Staff.			E.B.M.	1892
Rigby, John Ashton, Major and Adjutant, Lancs. Motor Vol. Corps.			S.H.	1892
Rigby, Reginald Ashton, Bt. Major, R. Welch Fus.			A.F.C.	1892
Rigg, Samuel Edward, Capt. R.A.M.C.	**D.**		D.B.	1889
Rigg, William Horrocks, Capt. Lancs. Vol. Regt.			F.E.B.	1899
Riley, Henry Davison, Capt. E. Lancs. Regt.			W.D.H. and A.F.C.	1898
Ritson, Eustace Blackburne, 2nd Lieut. M.G.C.			W.D.H. and S.H.	1901
Roberts, Astley Carrington, Lt.-Col. R.F.A.	**T.D.**		D.B.	1881
Roberts, Cyril Edward, Lt. Yeo.			D.B.	1902
Roberts, Cyril John, Lieut. R. Welch Fus.			J.B.O.	1915
Roberts, Douglas Walkden, Major, R.A. G.S.O.			G.T.H.	1893
Roberts, Frederick William, Major, Northants. Regt.			C.J.S.C.	1904
Roberts, George Gerald, Lieut. S. Staffs. Regt.			D.B.	1914
W. Roberts, Hugh Oliver, Capt. Rifle Brigade, attchd. Middlesex Regt.	**D.**		A.F.C.	1898
W. Roberts, John William Nelson, M.D., Capt. R.A.M.C.			E.B.M.	1899
Roberts, Noel Humphreys, 2nd Lieut. K.O.S.B.			D.B.	1910
Roberts, Oswald Dale, Lieut. Durham L.I. and Labour Corps.			D.B.	1904
Roberts, Wilfrid Hugh, Sub-Lieut. R.N.V.R.			D.B.	1918
Robertson, Wilfrid Edmond, Lieut. S.W.B. and M.G.C.			S.H.	1895

Robertson-Eustace, Robert William **D.S.O.**   E.B.M. 1889
    Barrington,
    Major, Unattached List. Superin-
    tendent of Police, E. Africa.

Robinson, Humphrey John,   C.J.B. and
    Capt. S. African Bde. R.E.   E.B.M. 1897

Robinson, Hugh Muschamp,   E.B.M. 1901
    Lt. R.N.D. Hawke Bn.

Robson, Arthur Preston Rynyon,   F.S. 1907
    Capt. W. Yorks Regt.

Rochdale, The Rt. Hon. The Lord,   S.H. and
    Hon. Col. Lancs. Fus.   G.T.H. 1884

Rodney, William Francis, The Hon.,   S.H. 1914
    2nd Lieut. Rifle Brigade.

Rogers, Arthur Sidney,   F.S. 1903
    Major, R. Welch Fus.

Rogers, Eric Norman Showell,   C.J.S.C. 1909
    Lieut. Lancers. A.D.C.

Rope, Frederick Michael,   D.B. 1905
    Capt. R.A.F.

Rogers, Esmond Hallewell,   F.E.B. and
    2nd Lieut. R. Warwicks. Regt.   C.J.B. 1909

Rose, Edmund Frederick,   A.F.C. 1893
    Capt. R.A.M.C.

Rose, Thomas Allen,   **D.S.O.**   D.B. 1891
    Capt. R. Scots Fus.

Ross, Archibald Hugh Houston,   S.H. 1915
    Lieut. R.E., attchd. Tyne E.E

W. Routh, Charles Richard Nairne,   S.H. 1915
    Lieut. Rifle Brigade.

Rowland, Stanley Jackson,   A.F.C. 1913
    Lieut. R. Welch Fus. attchd.
    K. Liverpool Regt.

Rowland-Hughes, Hubert Idrian,   F.E.B. and
    Lieut. R.A.S.C.   C.J.B. 1908

W² Rowlands, Albert Victor Parish,   C.J.B. 1915
    Lieut. Worcs. Regt.

Rowley, Cecil Gerald Alured,   D.B. and
    2nd Lieut. Dorset Regt.   T.E.P. 1918

Rudd, Kenneth Sutherland,   C.J.B. 1913
    Capt. and Adjutant, W. Yorks Regt.

Rugg, Reginald Francis,   S.H. 1909
    Capt. R. Welch Fus.

Rushton, William Frederick,   C.J.S.C. 1904
    Lieut. K. Liverpool Regt. and
    Devon Regt.

Russell, John Bernard,   E.B.M. 1902
    Corporal. Air Mechanic, R.N.A.S.
    and R.A.F.

W. Russell, John Malcolm,   C.J.S.C. 1904
    2nd Lieut. Art. & Inf. Coopn. School.

Russell, William Sydney Kemp,   **O.B.E. D.**   F.M.I. 1914
    Capt. R. Sussex Regt. & K.R.R.C.
    Staff.

Ruston, Joseph Seward,   **T.D. D.**   S.H. 1888
    Lt.-Col. Lincoln Co. Terrl. Assocn.

W. Ruston, William,   S.H. 1892
    Major, Lincolns. Regt. and N. Devon Yeo.

For explanations and abbreviations, see page 4.

Rutley, Maurice Dennett, Pte. Penang Rifles.		C.J.S.C.	1905
Rutter, Donald Campbell, Capt. R.A.F.	**M.C.**	F.T.P.	1914
Rutter, Eric Charles Victor, Capt. and Adjt., Cheshire Regt.	**D.**	T.E.P.	1916
Ruxton, William Stewart Mitchell, Capt. Border Regt.	**M.C.**	W.D.H.	1915
Ryder, Frank Eatock, Lieut. Canadian Artillery.		F.E.B.	1904
Rylands, Harry Randall, Lieut. R.D.C.		C.J.S.C.	1897
Rylands, Reginald Victor, 2nd Lieut. Manchester Regt.		W.D.H.	1908
Sabin, John Howard, Capt. R. Welch Fus.		F.E.B. and C.J.B.	1911
Salaman, Nevil Charles, 2nd Lieut. R.F.A.		S.H.	1907
Sale, Richard, Capt. K.S.L.I. and Shrewsbury School O.T.C.		Master.	
Salt, Charles Edward Fozbrooke, M.R.C.S. Capt. R.A.M.C.		F.E.B.	1899
Salt, Harold Geoffrey, Pte. The Buffs, and 2nd Lieut. R.A.S.C.		D.B.	1897
Salt, Hubert Henry Lieut. Shropshire Vol. Regt.		D.B.	1880
Salt, Reginald Nowell, Pte. Shropshire Vol. Regt.		D.B.	1885
Salt, Walter Petit, Capt. Lancs. Fus.	**D.**	G.T.H.	1897
Salt, Wilfrid Ernest, Pte., The Buffs, and 2nd Lieut. R.A.S.C.		D.B.	1892
Salt, W. H. 2nd Lieut. S. Staffs. Regt.		D.B.	1917
Sampson, Cecil Arthur, Lieut. R.A.M.C.		G.T.H.	1897
Sampson, John de la Haye, Capt. Welsh Regt.	**M.C.**	S.H.	1907
Sampson, Richard Harry, J.P., Lieut. Glamorgan Vol. Regt.		S.H.	1873
Sampson, Richard Harry, Lieut. Welch Regt. Brigade Intelligence Officer.		S.H.	1907
Sampson, Tom Burton, Lieut. K.S.L.I.		C.J.S.C.	1907
Samuelson, William Denys, Capt. R.G.A.	**D.**	F.M.I.	1913
Sandford, George Calrow, M.D., Major, R.A.M.C.		D.B.	1879
Sandie, John Gray, Capt. L.N. Lancs. Regt. and Tank Corps.	**M.C.**	A.F.C.	1915
Sanger, Gerald Fountaine, Lieut. R.M.A. (Howitzer Bde.)		A.F.C.	1916

W. Sabin; W. Sandie (marginal W.)

	Sargeaunt, George Montague, Lieut. Marlborough College O.T.C.		F.E.B., F.S. and S.H.	1901
	Saunderson, Harry Vincent, Lieut. R.F.A. and R.A.F.		J.B.O.	1915
	Savage-Armstrong, Francis Savage Nesbitt, D.S.O. D⁴ Lt.-Col. S. Staffs. Regt., Essex Regt. Rifle Brigade and R. Warwicks. Regt.		S.H.	1899
W.	Savage-Armstrong, John Raymond Savage, Capt. and Adjutant, Leinster Regt.		S.H.	1900
	Saville, Robert Charles, Bt. Lt.-Col. Dur. L.I. and D.A.Q.M.G.		C.J.S.C.	1887
	Sawyer, James Edward, Hill, M.D., **D.** Bt. Lt.-Col. R.A.M.C.		A.F.C.	1893
	Scholefield, Charles Bingley, Lieut. R.N.V.R.		S.H.	1901
	Schute, Alec Wilfrid, **D²** Major, R.A.S.C.		F.E.B.	1904
	Schute, Reginald Gordon, Capt. and Adjutant, R.A.S.C.		F.E.B.	1902
	Scott-James, Edward, Capt. R.F.A.		E.B.M.	1889
	Scott, Percy Eliot, Lieut. R.G.A.		D.B.	1896
	Scott-Deakin, Reginald, Lieut. R.F.A.		D.B.	1912
	Seaman, Sir Owen, D. Litt., Lieut. County of London Vol. Regt. Inns of Court Companies.		S.H.	1880
	Searle, Arthur Mackenzie, **M.B.E.** Capt. R.E. Staff Lieut.		C.J.S.C.	1910
	Seed, William, 2nd Lieut. R.A.F.		C.J.S.C.	1910
	Segner, Frank John Alexander, 2nd Lieut. R.A.F.		S.H.	1915
W.	Sergeant, Frederick Walter Beatie, Capt. Manchester Regt.		F.S.	1908
	Sergeant, John Furlow McConnell, Pte. Canadian Infantry.		F.S. and F.M.I.	1910
	Shackles, Kenneth George, 2nd Lieut. E. Yorks Regt.		S.H.	1913
	Shackles, Ronald Guy, M.C. 2nd Lieut. K.S.L.I.		S.H.	1917
	Sharp, Harold Withers, Major, Leicesters. Regt.		E.B.M.	1904
	Sharp, Mi'ton, **M.C.** Lieut. R.F.A.		S.H.	1899
	Sharpe, Edgar Ravenhill, Corporal, County of London Vol. Regt.		D.B.	1892
	Sharples, Frank Deeks, **O.B.E. D²** Capt. and Adjutant, R.A.S.C.		C.J.S.C.	1907
	Shaw, Harold Edwin, Capt. Rifle Brigade.		G.T.H.	1896
	Shaw, Robert, Capt. K. Liverpool Regt.		E.B.M.	1909
	Shaw, Thomas, Transport Officer, R.A.M.C.		C.J.B. and G.T.H.	1898
	Shaw, Robert Gould, 2nd Lieut. R. Horse Guards.		S.H.	1916

W.	Shaw, Walter Ledgard, Capt. (Signals) Rifle Bde. and R.E.		A.F.C. 1915
P.W.	Shawcross, Eric Leonard, Lieut. W. Yorks Regt.		A.F.C. 1907
W.	Shawcross, Roger Raines, Capt. and Adjutant, Sherwood Foresters. Brigade Staff Capt.		F.S. and W.D.H. 1906
	Shawe, James Whylock, Major, R.E.		A.F.C. 1898
	Sheffield, Arthur Digby,	**D.**	S.H. 1915
	Lieut. K.S.L.I.		
	Sheldon, Thomas William, Capt. and Adjutant, R.A.M.C.		F.S. 1906
	Shepherd, Thomas Dowker, Capt. Border Regt. (Vol. Force).		S.H. 1900
	Sherrington, Carl Ely Rose, Lieut. Ox. and Bucks L.I. Staff Lieut.	**M.C.**	F.M.I. 1915
	Shimwell, Humphrey, Capt. London Regt.	**D.**	E.B.M. 1903
	Shimwell, Oliver, Capt. London Regt.		E.B.M. 1904
	Shorland-Ball, Leslie, 2nd Lieut. R. Irish Fus.		G.T.H. 1899
	Short, Norman Dudley, Lieut. Cheshire Regt.		F.E.B. 1900
	Shuttleworth, Henry Lee Hadwen, I.C.S., F.R.G.S. Trooper Punjab Light Horse (Vols.)		C.J.B. and G.T.H. and W.D.H. 1901
	Shutt, John Eric, 2nd Lieut. R.A.S.C.		F.M.I. 1914
	Sidebottom, Colin Howard, Midshipman, R.N.		T.E.P. 1914
	Sidebottom, Herbert, Capt., District Remount Officer.		G.T.H. 1889
	Sidebotham, John Frith, Lieut. K.S.L.I.		S.H. 1910
	Sidebottom, Russell, Capt. Staffs. Yeo.	**D.**	W.D.H. 1909
	Sidebottom, Samuel Richards, Lieut. R.F.A.		J.B.O. and T.E.P. 1914
	Sillar, Ernest Gemmel, 2nd Lieut. Indian Labour Corps.		D.B. 1885
	Simms, John Basil Pulling, 2nd Lieut. Northumberland Fus. and R.A.F.		A.F.C. 1916
	Simonis, Hans, Lieut. R.A.F.		F.M.I. 1912
	Simonis, Rudolf, 2nd Lieut. R.A.S.C.		W.D.H. 1912
	Simpson, Palgrave, Pte. Penang Rifles.		E.B.M. 1899
	Simpson, Thomas Clifton, Capt. W. Lancs. Div. Engineeers, R.E.	**M.C.**	A.F.C. 1904
	Sims, Reginald Jack, 2nd Lieut. R.G.A.		D.B. 1907
	Sinclair, Robert, Major, R.M.L.I. G.S.O.		G.T.H. and W.D.H. 1901
W³	Sinnett, John Lionel Maurice, Lieut. R.F.A.	**M.C.**	W.D.H. 1916

W.	Skelton, Alan John, 2nd Lieut. R.F.A.		T.E.P.	1917
W.	Skelton, Dudley Sheridan, Lt.-Col. R.A.M.C.	**D.S.O. D²**	S.H.	1897
	Skelton, Eric George, Major, West India Regt. D.A.A.G.	**D.**	S.H.	1898
	Slaney, Edward, Major, Recruiting Duties.		J.R.	1872
W.	Sleigh, John Harold, Lieut. D.C.L.I.		E.B.M.	1910
	Smale, Leslie Crozier, Pte., K.S.L.I.		C.J.B.	1914
	Skipwith, Robert Grey, Pte. Hants Carabiniers Yeo. and York Hussars.		S.H.	1914
	Smalley, Skelton, Lieut. Cambridgeshire Regt. Capt. I.A.		C.J.B.	1912
W.P.	Smart, Frederick Linnington, Sapper, R.E. Despatch Rider,		W.D.H.	1909
	Smart, George Orme, 2nd Lieut. R.A.F.		S.H.	1903
	Smart, Godfrey Eric Sutton, Staff Car Driver, R.A.S.C.		W.D.H.	1909
	Smart, Norman, Lieut. Lancs. Fus. and M.G.C.		W.D.H.	1909
	Smedley, Ralph Davies, M.D. Capt. R.A.M.C.		S.H.	1895
W.	Smith, Archibald William, Capt., Glos. Regt.		S.H.	1915
	Smith, Charles Ledward, 2nd Lieut. R.F.A.		G.T.H.	1898
	Smith, Crowther, Lieut. Hong Kong Vol. Art. Gunner R.G.A.		G.T.H. and W.D.H.	1902
	Smith, Frederick Hargreaves, Major, R.A.S.C.	**O.B.E. D.**	E.B.M.	1887
	Smith, George Rainier de Herriez, Major, I.A. and Remount Service.	**O.B.E. D.**	D.B.	1883
	Smith, Hugh Stewart, Capt. Arg. and Suthld. Highlanders.		C.J.S.C.	1908
	Smith, John Adams, 2nd Lieut. Northumberland Fus.	**M.C. D.**	F.M.I.	1913
	Smith, John Turner, Mechanic, R.A.F.		S.H.	1912
	Smith, Robert Charles Standring, M.D., Capt. R.A.M.C.		S.H.	1897
	Smith, Roland Winn, Lieut. Welsh Guards.		W.D.H.	1917
W.	Smith, Ronald Herbert, Capt. Beds. Regt.	**D.**	E.B.M.	1900
	Smith, William Reginald Sturston, 2nd Lieut. R.A.F.		J.B.O.	1916
W⁴	*Smyth, Gerald Brice Ferguson, Brig.-General, Bt. Major and Bt. Lt.- Col. R.E. Brigade Commander	**D.S.O. (Bar). D⁵.** Croix de Guerre. Legion d'Honneur	S.H.	1901
	Snushall, Edward Donald, Lieut. R.F.A.		C.J.B.	1911

Snushall, Guy Francis, Lieut. Northants Regt.		C.J.B.	1913
Smyly, William Cecil, Sub-Lieut. R.N.R.		G.T.H.	1900
Sopwith, Sydney Shelford, 2nd Lieut. Shrewsbury School O.T.C.		Master.	
Southcomb, Edward Hamilton, 2nd Lieut. Manchester Regt.		T.E.P.	1912
Southam, Arthur Henry Ridgway, Lt.-Col. Cadet Bn. London Regt.	**Order of St. John of Jerusalem.**	D.B.	1893
Southam, Lionel Arthur Clement, Lt.-Col. R.F.A.	**D.S.O. D. Croix de Guerre (Belgian)**	D.B.	1889
Southwell, Evelyn Herbert Lightfoot, Lieut. Rifle Brigade.		Master.	
Sparrow, Arthur, Capt. R.A.F.		D.B.	1912
Sparrow, Cyril Wellesley, Lieut. Middlesex Regt.		G.T.H.	1900
Spencer, Arthur Max, 2nd Lieut. Rifle Brigade.		F.T.P.	1915
Spencer, Robert Hopwood, Capt. R.A.F.		C.J.B. and A.F.C.	1899
Spencer, Thomas Charlton, L./Corporal, H.A.C.		E.B.M. and F.T.P.	1914
Sprott, Frederick William, Lieut. I.A.		E.B.M.	1906
Spurrier, Reginald Stretton, Major, Dragoon Guards.	**D.**	S.H.	1900
W² Stallard, Richard Henry, Capt. Worcs. Regt.	**M.C. (Bar).**	W.D.H.	1911
Stanfield, Charles Cecil, Capt. E. Kent Regt.		S.H.	1901
Starkie, Walter F. Y.M.C.A. Worker (Italy).		E.B.M. and F.T.P.	1910
Stanwell, William, Lieut. R.A.M.C.		D.B.	1876
Stavert, Robert FitzRoy, Pte. Cadet Unit O.T.C., R.A.S.C.		A.F.C.	1906
Steedman, Charles Dawes, Lieut. R.F.A.		G.T.H.	1886
Steedman, James William, Pte. Samoa Relief Force.		G.T.H.	1891
Steer, Edward Pemberton, Capt. Monmouths. Regt.		A.F.C.	1900
Steer, Gordon Pemberton, Capt. Somerset L.I.		A.F.C.	1903
Stevenson-Jones, Ralph Buckley, Red Cross Motor Ambulance Driver.	**Croix de Guerre (French).**	C.J.B. and A.F.C.	1903
Stewart, Archibald Balfour, Lieut. Cheshire Regt.		T.E.P.	1915
Stewart, Douglas Martin, Capt. Welsh Regt.		S.H.	1904
W. Stewart, James Baildon, Lieut. R. Highlanders.		J.B.O.	1914
Stokes, Aleyn Whitley, Lt.-Col. R.E.	**D.S.O. M.C. D³**	S.H.	1897
Stokes, Geoffrey Calcott, 2nd Lieut. R. Bucks Hussars Yeo.		C.J.B.	1917

	Stokes, John Dalrymple, 2nd Lieut. E. Surrey Regt.		D.B.	1894
	Stokes, Josiah, Lieut. Herefords. Regt.		G.T.H.	1900
	Stokes, Robert Stanley, 2nd Lieut. R. W. Kent Regt.		W.D.H.	1903
W.	Stones, Hubert Boys, Capt. R. Lancaster Regt.	**D.**	S.H.	1914
W²	Stones, Richard Boys, Capt. and Adjutant, Durham L.I. G.S.O. Brigade Major.	**M.C. (Bar). D.** **Croix de Guerre** **(French).**	A.F.C.	1912
	Storr, Morton Harry John, Lieut. T.F.R.		S.H.	1896
	Stranaghan, Cyril Patrick Andrew, M.B. **D.** Capt. R.A.M.C.		S.H.	1896
	Stranaghan, John Stephens, Major, H.A.C. Staff Captain.	**M.C. D.**	A.F.C.	1903
	Stretch, Michael John, Private. (Regiment not known).		S.H.	1906
	Stott, Basil, Pte. R. Fus.		W.D.H.	1904
	Strange, Geoffrey Lionel, Major, R.E.		D.B.	1903
	Strong, Gervase Noel Edward, Lieut. Sherwood Foresters.		S.H.	1907
	Stuart, Alexander George, Bt. Lt.-Col. I.A. G.S.O.	**D.**	C.J.S.C.	1890
	Stuart, Cyril Adolphus, L./Corpl., K.S.L.I.		W.S.I.	1914
	Stuart, Charles Lancelot Alfonso, Sergt., British West Indies Regt.		W.S.I.	1911
	Stuart, Viscount, Lieut. R. Scots Fus.		S.H.	1899
	Sulivan, Gerald Henry, Capt. R.M.L.I.		S.H.	1901
	Summers, Gerald, Lieut. R.A.S.C.		C.J.B. and E.B.M.	1904
	Summerson, Thomas Philip Sanderson, 2nd Lieut. R.A.F.		J.B.O.	1916
	Surridge, Charles Ernest North, 2nd Lieut. R.M.		S.H.	1918
	Sutton, Ralph, 2nd Lieut. R.G.A.		S.H.	1899
	Swainson, George Houghton, Capt. R.F.A.		F.S.	1901
	Swainson, Joseph Leonard, Lt.-Col. D.C.L.I.	**D.S.O. D²**	E.B.M.	1896
	Swan, Frederick George, Capt. Tonbridge School O.T.C.		F.E.B.	1906
	Swettenham, James Parry, Major, R.E.		D.B.	1889
	Swettenham, William Alexander Why- bault, Lt.-Col. R.G.A. G.S.O.	**C.B.E. D²**	D.B.	1887
	Symes, Glascott Henry, Trooper, Yeo.		W.S.I.	1914
	Swifte, Ernest Godwin Meade, Major, R.A. and Tank Corps.	**Order of St. Vladimir**	S.H.	1889

W² Swifte, Frank William,   F.E.B. 1893
Major, R. Fus.

Sympson, Edward Mansel, M.D.,   S.H. 1879
Lt.-Col. R.A.M.C.

Synge, Mark,   **D.S.O. C.I.E. D³** C.J.S.C. 1889
Lt.-Col. S.T. Corps, I.A.

Tallents, Francis Prŷs,   W.D.H. 1916
Lieut. K. Liverpool Regt.

W³ Tarleton, Francis Roland,   **D.S.O. D². Legion** A.F.C. 1894
Lt.-Col. R. Highlanders. Brigade **of Honour. Croix**
Major.   **de Guerre.**

Tate, Sir Robert William,   **K.B.E.**   C.J.S.C. 1891
Major, Trin. Coll. Dublin O.T.C.

Taylor, Arthur Ainsworth,   **M.C.**   E.B.M. 1902
Lieut. Worcs. Regt.

Taylor, Charles Edgar,   C.J.S.C. 1904
Capt. Westmorland and Cumberland Yeo.

Taylor, Frank Walter,   T.E.P. 1914
Lieut. R.F.A.

Taylor, Geoffrey Lyon,   E.B.M. and
Capt. K. Liverpool Regt. and M.G.C.   F.T.P. 1912

Taylor, George Alfred,   F.S. and
Mechanic, R.A.F.   F.M.I. 1911

Taylor, Henry Dyson,   W.D.H. 1905
Lieut. R.A.S.C.

Taylor, James George, M.D.,   C.J.S.C. 1893
Capt. R.A.M.C.

Taylor, John Reginald,   C.J.S.C. 1896
2nd Lieut. Northumberland Fus.

Taylor, Joseph Thomas,   F.M.I. 1912
Mechanic, R.A.F.

W. Taylor, Robert Emery,   **M.C. D.**   E.B.M. 1899
Capt. Middlesex Regt. Staff Capt.

Taylor, Thomas Mountford,   S.H. 1903
2nd Lieut. R.G.A.

Taylor, William Hamilton Hepburn,   F.T.P. 1917
2nd Lieut. R.G.A.

Taylor, William Roughead,   S.H. 1918
2nd Lieut. K.S.L.I.

W. Tennant, Edward,   E.B.M. 1886
Lt.-Col. I.A.

Terry, Edward Ernest Gregory,   E.B.M. 1897
2nd Lieut. R.A.S.C.

Terry, Sidney Guy,   S.H. 1909
Pte. R.A.M.C.

Terry, William Gregory,   E.B.M. 1900
Capt. Lancs. Fus.

Tetley, Maxwell,   A.F.C. 1891
2nd Lieut. R.A.S.C.

Thomas, Frank Silvers Williams,   **T.D. D.S.O. M.C.** W.D.H. 1897
Major, Yeo.

Thomas, Hubert Alan Spence,   W.D.H. 1917
2nd Lieut. Welsh Guards.

Thomas, James Hugh, M.B.,   **D.S.O. D²**   S.H. 1895
Lt.-Col. R.A.M.C.

Thomas, Oliver Glegge,   T.E.P. 1913
Lieut. R.A.F.

For explanations and abbreviations, see page 4.

	Thomas, Sir William Beach, War Correspondent, France.	**K.B.E.**	S.H.	1887
	Thomas, Thomas Griffith Brockholes, Capt. R. Jersey Militia.		E.B.M.	1890
	Thomson, Angus James, 2nd Lieut. R.F.A.		T.E.P.	1917
	Thomson, Douglas Stoker Brownlie, M.B. **D.** Major, R.A.M.C.		S.H.	1898
	*****Thom son, Edward Brudenell,** Lieut. R.F.A.		T.E.P.	1914
	Thompson, Arthur Edgar, 2nd Lieut. R.G.A.		G.T.H. and W.D.H.	1903
	Thompson, Brian Bell, Capt. R.E.		F.M.I.	1916
	Thompson, Charles Brodrick, Lieut. Assist. Political Officer, E. Africa.		S.H.	1908
	Thompson, D'Arcy Percival Pelham, 2nd Lieut. K.S.L.I.		J.B.O.	1918
W.	Thompson, Joseph Lowes, Capt. W. Yorks Regt.	**D.**	W.D.H.	1905
	Thompson, Stephen Edwin Wright, Major, Remount Service.	**D²**	A.F.C.	1894
	Thompson, William Guy Duncan, Paymaster Lieut. R.N.R.		D.B.	1903
W.	Thompstone, Eric Westbury, Capt. K.S.L.I. attchd. Glos. Regt.	**M.C. Italian Silver Medal for Military Valour.**	W.D.H.	1915
W.	Thompstone, Ralph, Lieut. S. Staffs. Regt.		W.D.H.	1914
	Thorburn, Jack Walter Ashton, 2nd Lieut. Labour Corps.		J.B.O.	1916
	Thorn-Pudsey, Alfred Henry, Capt. Recruiting Duties.		S.H.	1882
	Thorne, Foster Newton, Lt.-Col. R. Sussex Regt.		A.F.C.	1898
	Thornes, William George Downes, Capt. Manchester Regt.		D.B.	1890
	Thornton, Claude Frederick, Major, Wilts Regt. Brigade Major.	**D.**	S.H.	1894
W.	Thornton, William Brooke, Bt. Lt.-Col. Brig.-General. Sherwood Foresters.	**D.S.O. D.**	S.H.	1893
	Thursfield, John Hunt, Major, R.F.A.	**D.**	W.D.H.	1911
	Thursfield, William Reginald Proud, Pte. Hongkong Volunteers.		E.B.M.	1897
	Thwaites, Daniel, Lieut. Res. Regt. of Cavalry.		C.J.S.C.	1892
	Tickell, George Warren, Lieut. Arg. and Sutherland High- landers and I.A.		F.M.I.	1913
	Tinker, Henry William Cossart, Lieut. R.N.V.R.	**O.B.E.**	F.E.B.	1903
	Tippet, Alexander Arnold, 2nd Lieut. K.S.L.I.		F.M.I.	1912
	Tippet, John Aylmer, Capt. R.A.M.C.	**M.C.**	E.B.M.	1910

	Tombling, John Henry,				Master.	
	Lieut. Shrewsbury School O.T.C.					
	Treadgold, Cecil Hallworth, M.D.,				E.B.M.	1899
	Capt. R.A.M.C.					
	Tongtor, Mom Chow,	•			T.E.P.	1912
	Interpreter, Siamese Force.					
	Treasure, Charles Edgar,				D.B.	1897
	Lt.-Col. R.F.A.					
	Treasure, James Herbert,	**D.**			D.B.	1891
	Major, R.G.A.					
	Treasure, John Percy, The Rev.,				D.B.	1886
	Lieut. R.N.V.R.					
	Tripp, Cyril Claude Howard,				A.F.C.	1914
	2nd Lieut. L.N. Lancs. Regt.					
	Tudor, Alan Roper,				W.D.H.	1908
	2nd Lieut. Seaforth Highlanders.					
	Tudor-Owen, Cyril,				S.H.	1896
	Capt. Border Regt.					
W.	Tudor-Owen, Herbert Francis Gordon,	**D.**			S.H.	1904
	Capt. Rifle Brigade. Staff Capt.					
	Tudor-Owen, William Courtney, I.C.S.,				S.H.	1896
	2nd Lieut. I.A.R.O. (Cav. Branch).					
	Turner, Herbert Samuel Alston,				F.T.P.	1915
	2nd Lieut. Yorks. Regt.					
	Twentyman, Harold Edward, M.I.M.E.,				C.J.S.C.	1887
	Lt.-Col. S. Staffs. Regt. and					
	Lincolns. Regt.					
	Twidell, Thomas Leslie,				S.H.	1918
	2nd Lieut. Shropshire Yeo.					
	Twiss, Arthur Montague,				E.B.M.	1898
	Capt. R.E. Sappers and Miners.					
P.	Twiss, Clifford Charles Horace,	**D.S.O.**	**D.**		E.B.M.	1898
	Lt.-Col. E. Yorks. Regt.					
	Twist, Thomas Kenyon,	**M.C.**	**D²**		T.E.P.	1914
	Capt. (Flight Group Comdr.) R.A.F.					
	Urwick, Reginald H., M.D.,				School Med.	
	Capt. R.A.M.C.				Officer.	
	Unwin, Harold Arthur Robert Edmond,				G.T.H.	1899
	Capt. R.A.M.C.					
W⁴	Unwin, Joseph Daniel,	**M.C.**	**D.**		W.S.I.	1914
	Capt. Northants Regt. and Tank Corps.					
	Unwin, Stephen Ralph,		**D.**		G.T.H.	1895
	Capt. Devon Regt. (attchd.) In-					
	structor School of Musketry.					
	Usher, Robert Howell Craster,	**M.C.**			D.B. and	
	Capt. Wilts Regt. Flight Com-				C.J.B.	1914
	mander R.A.F.					
	Vachell, Frank Tanfield,	**M.C.**			S.H.	1908
	Major, R.A.					
	Vaisey, Roland Maddison,				S.H.	1903
	Capt. and Adjutant, R.F.A.					
	Valérie, John, M.R.C.S.,				D.B.	1884
	Capt. R.A.F.					
	Vardy, Albert Theodore,				S.H.	1907
	2nd Lieut. R. Warwicks. Regt.					
	Vaughan-Williams, Francis,				S.H.	1872
	Major, Ox. and Bucks L.I.					

For explanations and abbreviations, see page 4.

	Vaughan-Williams, Reinalt, Major, Yeo. Staff Capt.	**Order of the Nile,** **4th Class. D²**	S.H.	1906
W.	Veitch, James Jarman Morgan, Lieut. Grenadier Guards.		S.H.	1916
	Vernon, Alan Frederick Maule, • Lieut. R.N.V.R. Intelligence Staff.		F.E.B.	1895
	Vernon, Sydney Rutty, Capt. Ox. and Bucks L.I. and Rifle Brigade.	**T.D.**	A.F.C. and G.T.H.	1889
W²	Vince, William Bernard, Lt.-Col. London Regt.	**D.S.O. M.C. D²**	S.H.	1908
	Viner, George Arthur, Lieut. R.M.		F.T.P.	1918
	Vint, Edward John Cyril, Lieut. London Regt. and T.M.B.		S.H.	1912
	Vint, Wilfrid George, Pte. W. Riding Regt.		S.H.	1904
W.P.	Voelcker, Francis William, Lieut. K.S.L.I.	**M.C.**	S.H.	1914
	Wace, Geoffrey George, Capt. and Adjutant, K.S.L.I.		D.B.	1898
	Wace, Michael Henry, Lieut. Baluchistan L.I., I.A.		E.B.M. and F.T.P.	1915
	*Wace, Stephen Charles, Lt.-Col., Bt. Major, R.M.A. Staff, Admiralty.	**C.B.E. Chevalier of the Legion of Honour and Crown of Italy.**	D.B.	1900
	Wade, George Nugent, Lieut. Worcs. Regt.		D.B.	1912
	Wade, Gerald Darnton, 2nd Lieut. Rifle Brigade.		F.M.I.	1917
W.	Wade, Henry John Edward, Lieut. Cheshire Regt.		A.F.C.	1912
	Wale, Eric Harry, Capt. R.E.	**M.C. D.**	D.B.	1910
W.P.	Wallis, John Dunstane, Lieut. Yeo.		W.D.H.	1907
W.	Walker, Angus Campbell, Lt.-Col. R.F.A.	**M.C.**	W.D.H.	1911
	Walker, Clifford Stanley, C.Q.M.S., R.A.S.C. (M.T.)		S.H.	1898
	Walker, Edward Robinson, Sergeant, London Regt.		T.E.P.	1916
W.	Walker, Frederick Winn, 2nd Lieut. Australian Infantry.		S.H.	1892
W.	Walker, George Frank Douglas, Capt. W. Yorks. Regt.		J.B.O.	1915
	Walker, Gerald King, Capt. and Adjutant, R.E.	**M.C. D.**	F.T.P.	1913
W³	Walker, Sir Harold Bridgwood, Major-General, I.A.	**K.C.M.G. K.C.B.** **D⁵ Croix de Guerre** **Legion d'Honneur.** **Officer of the Mili-** **tary Order of Savoy.** **Croce di Guerra.**	D.B. and G.T.H.	1880
	Walker, Hugh Reginald Oriel, Major, Punjabis, I.A.		D.B.	1902

	Walker, Harold Elliot, Lieut. R.G.A.		W.D.H.	1917
	Walker, John Allsop, F.I.C., Capt. M.G.C.		S.H.	1891
	Walker, John Arthur, Capt. R. Welch Fus.		E.B.M.	1909
	Walker, John Bury, Capt. R.E. Staff Capt.		S.H.	1897
	Walker, Lawrence Edward, Major, R.F.A.	.	S.H.	1890
	Walker, Reginald Fydell, 2nd Lieut. Manchester Regt.		F.M.I.	1913
	Walker, Robert Hugh, **D.** Lieut. Seaforth Highlanders.		A.F.C. and S.H.	1891
	Walker, Thomas Ramsbotham, The Rev. Chaplain to the Forces,		S.H.	1900
W.	Walker, Victor Kynaston, Rifleman, London Rifle Brigade.		E.B.M.	1911
	Wall, George Lynton, Qmr., R.F.A.		W.D.H.	1918
	Wallace, Arthur Williams Baillie, **D.** Bt. Lt.-Col. Durham L.I. D.A.A.G.		C.J.S.C.	1894
W.	Wallace, Quintin Vaughan Brooke, M.D. **M.C. D.** Capt. R.A.M.C.		C.J.S.C.	1908
	Walmsley, John Banks, **D.F.C.** Flight Lieut. R.A.F. and I.A.		E.B.M. and F.T.P.	1915
W.	Walmsley, Leonard Peel, Capt. S. Lancs. Regt.		F.E.B. and C.J.B.	1907
	Walton-Brown, Stanley, Capt. R.A.S.C.		S.H.	1904
	Walton-Evans, David Saxon, Pte. Australian Infantry.		A.F.C.	1894
	Walton-Evans, Herbert Wynne, Pte. Australian Infantry.		F.E.B.	1892
W²	Ward, Charles Eaton, Capt. K.S.L.I. and K. African Rifles.		D.B.	1898
	Ward, Humphrey Plowden, 2nd Lieut. R.F.A.		S.H.	1917
	Wardle, John Leek, 2nd Lieut. Deccan Horse, I.A.		S.H.	1917
	Waterfield, Arthur Cyril, **M.C. D.** Capt. and Adjutant, K.S.L.I., T.M.B.		S.H.	1911
	Waters, Arthur, Hon. Major, late V.B. K.S.L.I. R.D.C.		D.B.	1874
	Watkins, Charles Rowlatt, **C.I.E. D.** Imperial Customs Department.		A.F.C.	1901
	Watkins, John Charles, 2nd Lieut. E. Lancs. Regt.		A.F.C.	1899
	Watkinson, Frank, Worker in Red Cross Hospital.		C.J.S.C.	1886
	Watmough, Cyril William, 2nd Lieut. R.A.S.C.		S.H.	1902
	Watson, George Mann, 2nd Lieut. R.E.		C.J.B.	1917
	Watson, Henry Sinclair, **D.** Major, R.E. Dep. Chief Electrical Engineer.		E.B.M.	1895

For explanations and abbreviations, see page 4.

	Watts, William Anderton, Capt. R.A.S.C.		E.B.M.	1887
	Waugh, William Lawrence, The Rev. Chaplain to the Forces.		C.J.S.C.	1889
	Wayne, Herman George Wellington, Major, W. Riding Regt.		C.J.S.C.	1885
	Weaver, John Yardley, Capt. R.A.S.C. and I.A.	**M.C.**	F.E.B. and C.J.B. F.M.I.	1908 1912
	Webb, Henry Stanley, . 2nd Lieut. E. Surrey Regt.			
W.	Webb, Lawrence Herbert, Lieut. E. Surrey Regt.	**M.C.**	W.S.I. and S.H.	1914
	Weller, Arthur Julius, 2nd Lieut. Shrewsbury School O.T.C.		Master.	
	Wells, Frank, Major K. Liverpool Regt. Staff Capt.		F.E.B.	1894
	Wells, Norman Lancaster, Lieut. L.N. Lancs. Regt.		F.E.B.	1906
W.	West, John Milns, Capt. and Adjutant, Rifle Brigade.		F.M.I.	1914
	West, Gilbert Witter, Major, K.O. R. Lancaster Regt.		S.H.	1890
	West, Thomas Temple, Hon. Capt. Northants Regt. Vol. Force.		A.F.C.	1892
W.	Westby, Henry Edmund Porter, Lieut. R. Welch Fus.		A.F.C.	1896
W.	Western, Oswald, Lieut. R.G.A.		C.J.S.C.	1907
	Westlake, Albert Neave, Lieut. N. Staffs. Regt. and R.A.F.	**M.C.**	S.H.	1912
	Wethered, Leslie William Temple, Lieut. R.F.A.	**Croix de Guerre (Belgian).**	F.M.I.	1916
	Whale, Arthur, Pte. R. Fus.		C.J.S.C.	1907
	Whale, George, Major, R.A.F. Staff Officer.	**D.**	C.J.S.C.	1902
	Wheatley, Arthur Nevin, Major, W. Riding Regt.		F.E.B.	1905
	Wheatley, Richard Nevin, Corpl., Arg. & Suthld. Highlanders.	**D.**	F.E.B.	1896
W.	Whinfield, Henry Charles, Major (Bt. Lt.-Col.) R. W. Surrey Regt.	**D.**	A.F.C. and C.J.S.C.	1889
	Whishaw, Alexander Yeames, Major, R.F.A. Staff Lieut.		C.J.S.C.	1886
	Whishaw, Edward Richard, Lt.-Col. Manchester Regt. D.A.A.G.		T.A.B. and C.J.S.C.	1889
	White, Geoffrey Lloyd, 2nd Lieut. R.F.A.		A.F.C.	1917
	White, Malcolm Graham, Lieut. Rifle Brigade.		Master.	
	Whitehead, Alfred Gordon, Capt. W. Yorks Regt. and R.A.F. (Flight Commander).		C.J.S.C. and T.E.P.	1911
	Whitehead, Geoffrey Nield, 2nd Lieut. R.A.F.		C.J.S.C.	1907

Whitehead, George Robert Beetham, Lieut. R.A.S.C.			S.H.	1914
Whitehead, John William St John, Cadet, R.M.C. Sandhurst.			S.H.	1917
Whiteley, John Percy, Lieut. R.H.A.			F.T.P.	1915
Whitfield, John Osborn, Capt. Shrewsbury School O.T.C.			Master.	
Whitworth, Arthur, Pte. Central London Regt. (Vols.)			S.H.	1894
Whitworth, Dysart Edward, Capt. Lancers, I.A.	M.C.	D.	S.H.	1907
Whytehead, Hugh Holtom, 2nd Lieut. N. Staffs. Regt. and R.A.F.			W.D.H.	1912
Wilcox, Basil Syres, Lieut. R.A.F.	D.F.C.		C.J.B.	1916
Wild, Henry Cecil, Cadet, R.A.F.			F.T.P.	1918
Wild, Walter Leslie, 2nd Lieut. Tank Corps.			F.T.P.	1914
Wilde, Gaston Francis, Cadet, R.A.F.			F.M.I.	1918
Wilding, Harry, 2nd Lieut. A.G's. and Q.M.G.'s Staff.			S.H.	1897
Wildridge, Ricardo Jack, Capt. R.A.S.C.			S.H.	1907
Wilkinson, Charles Leyburn, Major, R.F.A.	D.S.O.	D.	S.H.	1904
Wilkinson, Ernest Wightman, 2nd Lieut. W. Riding Regt.			D.B.	1896
W. Wilkinson, George Edward, Major, Northumberland Fus. and M.G.C.	M.C.	D.	S.H.	1899
Wilkinson, Joseph Harold, Lieut. Lancers, I.A. A.D.C.			J.B.O.	1915
W. Williams, Alfred Gregson, Surgeon, R.N.	O.B.E. Croix de Guerre (French)		S.H.	1907
W. Williams, Charles Reginald, Lt.-Col. R. Munster Fus.	D.S.O. M.C. D²		S.H.	1898
Williams, Edward Kynaston, Lieut. R.A.M.C.			A.F.C.	1896
Williams, Frederick John Gregson Capt. R.E.			S.H.	1903
Williams, John Kynaston, Hon. Major, R.E. I.A.R.O.			A.F.C.	1893
Williams, Mervyn Granville, Lieut. R.A.S.C.			C.J.B. and W.D.H.	1897
W. Williams, Rupert, M.V.O., Capt. R.E.			G.T.H. and W.D.H.	1901
Williams, Thomas Reinalt, Capt. R. Welch Fus.	M.C.		W.D.H.	1907
Williams, William Charles Bamford, Major, R. Welch Fus.	M.C.	D.	F.E.B.	1904
Williams, William Reginald, Lieut. County of London Regt. Vol. Force.			A.F.C. and C.J.S.C	1891
Williams, William Thomas, Pte., Shropshire Vol. Regt.			D.B.	1887

For explanations and abbreviations, see page 4.

Williams, Victor Owen, Lieut. and Adjutant, Welsh Regt.			A.F.C.	1916
Williams-Vaughan, Edward Anthony, 2nd Lieut. K.S.L.I.			W.S.I.	1915
Willoughby, Rowland James, Lieut. Devon Regt.			D.B.	1916
Wilson, Arthur Edward, Lieut. R. Warwicks. Regt.			F.E.B. and C.J.B.	1908
Wilson, Arthur Stafford, 2nd Lieut. Rifle Brigade.			A.F.C.	1910
Wilson, Colin Buchanan, 2nd Lieut. Lancs. Fus.			W.D.H.	1906
Wilson, Keith Alexander Buchanan, Cadet, R.N.A.S.			W.D.H.	1917
Wilson, Samuel, Capt. Somerset L.I.			W.D.H.	1914
Winder, Alexander Stuart Monck, M.B., Capt. R.A.M.C.			S.H.	1902
Winton, Harold Barkley, 2nd Lieut. R.A.F.			A.F.C.	1912
W³ Withers, Kenneth Sheldon, Capt. Cheshire Regt.	**D.**		E.B.M.	1909
Withers, Noel Harrison Eley, Pte., R.A.S.C.			D.B.	1908
Withers, Walter Norman, Major, R. Welch Fus.			G.T.H.	1890
Wodehouse, Charles Ewart, Flight Lieut. R.N.A.S.			F.T.P.	1916
Wodehouse, Everard Hay, Lieut. R.F.A.			S.H.	1913
Wolfe-Murray, David Knightley, Lieut. R.G.A. A.D.C. to Inspector General of Artillery, India.			J.B.O.	1915
Wolfe-Murray, Philip George, Lieut. R.N.V.R.			D.B.	1909
Wood, Allan, 2nd Lieut. R.F.A.			F.E.B.	1905
Wood, Arthur Evelyn, Capt. L.N. Lancs. Regt.			C.J.B.	1899
Wood, George Ronald, Capt. Ox. and Bucks L.I.			S.H.	1888
W. Wood, Philip, Lieut. R.A.F.			D.B.	1916
W. Wood, Richard Henry, Lieut. S. Lancs. Regt.			F.E.B.	1894
W. Wood, Thomas, Lieut. K.S.L.I.			D.B.	1911
Wood, Matthew Rodney, Capt. Lancs. Fus.	**M.C.**		T.E.P.	1914
Woodhouse, Gerald Herbert, Capt. E. Riding Yeo. Staff.			F.S.	1908
Woodroffe, John Morris, 2nd Lieut. Shrewsbury School O.T.C.			Master.	
Woodroffe, Leslie, Capt. Rifle Brigade.	**M.C.**	**D.**	Master.	
Woodruff, William Leslie, Lieut. R.F.A. T.M.B.			J.B.O.	1914

Woods, William Thornley Stoker, 2nd Lieut. R.F.A.		T.E.P. 1915
Woodward, Arthur Maurice, **D²** Lieut. Gen. List. Staff Lieut.		A.F.C. 1902
Woodward, Francis Willoughby, **D.S.O. D⁵** Bt. Lt.-Col. L.N. Lancs. Regt. attchd **Croce di Guerra.** Manchester Regt. **Croix de Guerre** **(French). Order** **of the Nile. Order** **of the Medjidieh.**		C.J.S.C. 1889
Woodyatt, Nigel Gresley, **C.I.E. C.B. D.** Maj.-General I.A. Col. 7th Gurkhas.		S.H. 1879
Worthington, Thomas Shirley Scott, Pte. Inns of Court O.T.C.		S.H. 1918
Wórrall, Henry, Lieut. Cheshire Vol. Regt.		A.F.C. 1910
Worth, Thomas, 2nd Lieut. Cheshire Regt.		E.B.M. and F.T.P. 1911
Worthington, Frank, Lieut. Wilts Vol. Regt.		S.H. 1884
W. Worthington, Guy Jukes, Capt. N. Staffs. Regt. M.G.C.		S.H. 1904
Worthington, Roger Ernest, **D.S.C. D.** Paymaster-Lieut. R.N.		S.H. 1904
Wright, Alfred George William, **T.D.** Lt.-Col. R.F.A.		C.J.S.C. 1897
Wright, Edward John Miller, Pte. R.A.S.C. (M.T.)		C.J.B. 1915
Wright, Frank Leslie, Lieut. Worcs. Regt.		S.H. 1898
Wright, Harry Roland, Lieut. W. Yorks. Regt.		S.H. 1896
Wright, William Edmiston, Capt. S. Staffs. Regt. Tank Corps.		E.B.M. 1906
Wright, William Edward Bellyse, Lieut. K.O. Yorkshire L.I.		D.B. 1913
Wurtzburg, John Austin, The Rev., Hon. Chaplain to the Forces.		E.B.M. 1897
Wylie, Angus, M.B., Capt. R.A.M.C.		D.B. 1895
Wynne Jones, Llewellyn, The Very Rev. (Dean of St. Asaph), Chaplain to the Forces.		D.B. and S.H. 1877
W. Wynne-Williams, Arthur Ivor, **M.C.** Lieut. R.F.A.		A.F.C. 1913
Yates, Charles Edward, M.P., **C.S.I. C.M.G.** Col., 1st Ambulance Flotilla, Seine.		D.B. 1867
Yates, Oswald Vavasour, Lt.-Col. and Hon. Col. Recruiting Duties.		S.H. 1872
Yates, Ralph Cyril, Capt. and Adjutant, R.G.A.		W.D.H. 1917
Yeldham, Cecil Walter Francis, Lieut. R.M.		E.B.M. and F.T.P. 1913
Young, Alexander, Capt. S. Lancs. Regt. Tank Corps Staff.		T.E.P. 1914

For explanations and abbreviations, see page 4.

W.P.	Young, Eric William, Lieut. R.E. Electric Lights Cos.		D.B.	1913
	Young, Frederick Hugh, Major, R.A.M.C.	**O.B.E. D.**	C.J.S.C. and T.E.P.	1910
	Young, James Charles, Major-General. War Office.		S.H.	1871
	Young, John William Alexander, Local Capt. Egyptian Civil Service.	**Order of the Nile.** **D²**	S.H.	1892
W.	Young, Frederick David, Lieut. London Regt.		W.D.H.	1911
W.	Young, William Litton Rowland, 2nd Lieut. R. Innis. Fus.		F.T.P.	1915
	Young, Thomas, Lieut. Tank Corps.		C.J.S.C. and T.E.P.	1913
	Zeller, Walter Dillon, Major, R.E.	**M.C.**	F.E.B.	1901
	Zimmern, Norman Harold, Lieut. Lancs. Fus. Brigade Intelligence Officer.	**M.C.**	F.S.	1907

The following were interned, Ruhleben, 1914—1918.

Bock, Charles Richard	..	..	..	..	E.B.M.	1897
Eglington, Guy Cecil	..	..	..	..	S.H.	1913
Russell-Taylor, Herman	..	..	..	..	A.F.C.	1908
Worthington, Andrew Yorke,		..	..	..	S.H.	1912

73

Obituary of Old Salopians.

———◆◆———

* Denotes a Member of the Old Salopian Club.
** Denotes a Member of the General Committee.

Aug. 11, 1917.—**Harold Ackroyd,** *V.C.*, *M.C.*, Capt. R.A.M.C., killed in action, was at Shrewsbury (A.F.C.) 1891–6, Caius College, Cambridge, and Guy's Hospital, London. Although fully qualified as a doctor he never practised, but spent many years in the research laboratories at Cambridge. In Feb., 1915, he was commissioned as a temporary Lieut. in R.A.M.C., being attached to the Royal Berkshire Regt., and was promoted Captain in 1916. He was awarded the Military Cross in 1916, and was slightly wounded on July 31, but remained on duty. He won the *V.C.* for conspicuous bravery as set out in the following official particulars : " During recent operations Capt. Ackroyd displayed the greatest gallantry and devotion to duty. Utterly regardless of danger, he worked continuously for many hours up and down and in front of the line tending the wounded and saving the lives of officers and men. In so doing he had to move across the open under heavy machine-gun, rifle, and shell fire. He carried a wounded officer to a place of safety under very heavy fire. On another occasion he went some way in front of our advanced line and brought in a wounded man under continuous sniping and machine-gun fire. His heroism was the means of saving many lives and provided a magnificent example of courage, cheerfulness and determination to the fighting men in whose midst he was carrying out his splendid work. This gallant officer has since been killed in action."

Oct. —, 1918.—**George Norman Adams** was at Shrewsbury (C.J.S.C.) 1903–5, and in the Football Eleven. Leaving, he went to the Mars Ironworks, Ettingshall, being specially connected with the sheet-iron department. On the outbreak of war he was gazetted Lieutenant in Sept., 1914, in the South Staffordshire Territorials. After serving for some time in France he was invalided home with rheumatic fever, but recovered, and went to the front again in 1916. In the Somme battle he was severely wounded in the leg at Gomme-court on July 1, 1916, and with difficulty crawled to safety. On recovery, Lieut. ADAMS was gazetted Captain in February, 1917, and attached to a reserve battalion of the South Staffords for training work. While in the 4th Northern General Hospital, Lincoln, for slight indisposition, acute pneumonia suddenly supervened, and he succumbed to the disease.

May 16–17, 1915, aged 28.—*Lawrence Kingston Adams,
Lieut., 7th Bn. the King's Liverpool Regt. (T.F.) ; at Shrewsbury
(A.F.C.) May, 1901–July, 1903. He took 1st Class Honours in the
Architectural School at Liverpool University in 1906, then studied at
Oxford, Paris and Rouen, eventually becoming an Associate of the
Royal Institute of British Architects. Immediately on the outbreak
of the War he joined the Liverpool Regt., and was shot through the
heart while leading his platoon in a night attack on a German
trench.

May 3, 1917.—James Carlton Addy, *M.C.*, Capt. East Yorks
Regt. Missing May 3, 1917, he is now reported killed in action on
that date. At Shrewsbury (C.J.S.C. and T.E.P.) 1905–1910, and
Trinity College, Cambridge, and was granted a commission Aug., 1914.

Oct. 1916.—*Andrew Leslie Aitchison, 2nd Lieut. King's Own
Scottish Borderers. Of wounds received near the Somme. He
was at Shrewsbury (T.E.P.) 1910–5, and afterwards at Sandhurst,
receiving his commission 19 July, 1916.

March 27, 1918.—Charles Derek Alltree, Lieut., reported
wounded and missing March 23, during the German offensive on
the Cambrai front, is now reported by the International Red Cross
Society, Geneva, as having died on March 27, in a German hospital,
from the effects of his wounds. Lieut. ALLTREE, who was at
Shrewsbury (D.B.) 1912–13, and then entered the service of the
Capital and Counties Bank at Dovercourt, was gazetted to the 12th
(Service) Batt. South Lancashire Regt., in Nov., 1915, was transferred to the R.W.F. in Sept., 1916, and had been in France about
three months. In the course of his training at a corps school in
France he was awarded a medal for riding efficiency.

Oct. —, 1918.—Ernest Woodbourne Alltree, Acting-Lieut.
Royal Naval Reserve, died in Norway, where he had been interned
for the past three years. He was at Halifax, Nova Scotia, on the
outbreak of war, and at once came home, joining the Navy. During
his residence in Norway he married a Norwegian lady. He was at
Shrewsbury 1903–4 as a Dayboy.

Oct. 22, 1918.—Hew Graham Anderson, Lieut. British Columbia
Regiment, was wounded on Oct. 13, and died in hospital
on the 22nd. He was at Shrewsbury (S.H.) 1901–5, and Head of
his House. He passed direct from the Army class into Sandhurst,
but gave up the military for a commercial career, entering the office
of Messrs. Balfour, Williamson & Co., and later proceeding for that
firm to Seattle and Vancouver. On the outbreak of war he joined
the Canadian Forces, with a commission, and coming over with the
first contingent, he was seriously wounded near Ypres in April, 1915.

November 20, 1914.—Major **Norman Ruthven Anderson,** 130th King George's Own Baluchis, Indian Army, aged 40, was assassinated by a Mahsud Sepoy of his regiment whilst embarking at Bombay for active service. Major ANDERSON, who was born in 1874, entered the School in 1888, left in 1892, and passed into the Royal Military College, Sandhurst. He received his commission as 2nd Lieut. (unattached) in 1894 ; was gazetted to the Indian Staff Corps in 1896 ; promoted Lieut. Indian Army in 1897 ; Captain 130th Baluchis in 1903 ; and Major in 1912. He served in the operations at Mekran in 1898, taking part in the Action of Gok Parosh, and also in the China Expedition in 1900, for which he received the Medal.

Aug. —, 1918.—**Henry Wynne Apperley,** Lieut.-Col., who died at Rajghat, Beltiah, Chumparun, India, at the age of 67, was the youngest son of the late Col. W. W. APPERLEY (Bengal Army), of Morben, Machynlleth. He was at Shrewsbury 1867–8, left to become a planter in Bengal, and received his first commission in 1873, in the Behar Light Horse, retiring after 40 years' service. He served in the Afghan War of 1878–80, and was present with the Bazar Valley Expedition as a volunteer, taking part in the affair at Jagi Thana, near Shutargarden Pass, the Battle of Charasiab, the action at Kabul, and the march from Kabul to Kandahar. He was twice mentioned in despatches, and received the medal and clasps, as well as the bronze star and the brevet of Major.

Aug. 11, 1916.—Of wounds received in action, **Oliver Vaughton Arnold,** 2nd Lieut. 6th Bn. (S.R.) (attached 2nd Bn.) Worcestershire Regt. At Shrewsbury 1902–5, he rowed in his House Boat (Haydon's), which won the Challenge Oars, and went Head of the River. A solicitor in Birmingham, he enlisted in the Public Schools Bn., in Aug., 1914, and was gazetted to the 6th Worcesters, 27 Jan., 1915, with whom he served in Gallipoli. Invalided home, he was on recovery attached to the 2nd Bn., and sent to France, where he was seriously wounded in High Wood, on July 11, and died a month later.

, 1918.—**Frederick Adolph Aron** (G.T.H. and W.D.H., 1900–6), reported killed in action, left in the Upper VI., and was gazetted Temp. 2nd Lieut. in the 10th (Service) Batt. South Lancs. Regt., being promoted Lieut. Dec. 16, 1915.

July 31, 1915, aged 48.—****Frederic Marriner Aston,** Capt., 6th (Service) Bn. Duke of Cornwall's L.I., who was at Shrewsbury (S.H.) from Easter, 1880–July 1886. He won the Senior Steeplechase, the Half-Mile and the Two Miles in 1885, and the Quarter Mile and Cricket Ball in 1886 ; was in the Cricket XI. in 1885 and 1886, and the Football in 1883, 84 and 85, being Capt. in the Easter

Term of 1886. Going up to Pembroke College, Cambridge, Aston gained his " Soccer " Blue and was in his College Cricket XI. After taking his degree he played for the Crusaders when they won the London Charity Cup, and, coming to Shrewsbury to study Law, he captained the Town Football Team which won the Welsh and Shropshire Cups. He was admitted a solicitor in 1902. Capt. ASTON had commanded the Wade Bridge Volunteers for five years, but had retired before the War broke out. He, however, rejoined a Service Bn. and was killed in action in Flanders.

Aug. 2, 1916.—*Gerald Lovell Backhouse, 2nd Lieut. Norfolk Regt., attached Royal Flying Corps. A member of Pickering's 1910-4, he left for Sandhurst, and was gazetted to the Norfolk Regt., 12 May, 1915, being only 17 when he gained his commission. Transferred to the R.F.C., he quickly gained promotion, and was chosen to fly the Scout machine in the 46th Flying Squadron. Under orders for the front in France, he was killed instantaneously, while flying at Hendon.

June 16, 1915.—*Leonard Vale Bagshawe, Capt., King's Own Scottish Borderers (attached to 1st Northumberland Fusiliers), (E.B.M., 1892-6). After taking his degree at Ch. Ch., Oxford, he went out to Burmah as one of the Forest Managers of the Bombay Burmah Trading Corporation. At home on leave when the war broke out, he was gazetted Lieut. in the 3rd (Reserve) Bn. of the K.O.S.B., Nov. 9, 1914, was attached for service to the Northumbrians, going to the front with them in December, and was promoted Capt. shortly before he fell in action, near Ypres, aged 38.

March 24, 1918.—Walter Arthur Francis Bailey, 2nd Lieut. 2nd Oxford and Bucks Light Infantry, reported "missing" on March 24, 1918, now officially presumed killed on that date, was at Shrewsbury (Prior's), where he was a house-monitor, and passed into the Sixth Form in Michaelmas Term, 1915. While at School, he was one of the contributors to " V.B." He volunteered for service, and entered Sandhurst as a prize cadet at the age of 17, passing out in October, 1916. He went to the front in November, 1917.

Sept. 18, 1918.—Philip Gillespie Bainbrigge, 2nd Lieut. Lancashire Fusiliers, attached Welsh Regiment, was killed in action on September 18. He went to Eton as a King's Scholar, and there won the Newcastle Medal and many other prizes, then to Trinity, Cambridge, with a Scholarship, and afterwards took the Bell University Scholarship and a First Class in both parts of the Classical Tripos, taking his degree in 1914. The Rev. C. A. Alington, who had been his master in college and Eton, then invited him to join his staff with the particular purpose of upholding the great classical traditions of Shrewsbury, where he was from September, 1914, to March 1917. After training with the Inns of Court O.T.C.

he was gazetted to the Welsh Regiment and served with it to the last, although he had obtained his transfer to the Lancashire Fusiliers (the old 20th Regiment) on account of family associations. He had taken over from his company commander, who was wounded early in the assault, " led on his men who thoroughly trusted him, captured the objective, anf then during consolidation, in anticipation of counter-attack, courageously led a patrol to reconnoitre a sunken road suspected of holding the enemy in force in his front."

Sept. 6, 1916.—**Leslie Shorland Ball,** 2nd Lieut. 3rd Bn. (S.R.) Royal Irish Fusiliers, attached 8th (Service) Bn. At Shrewsbury 1898-9 (G.T.H.) he was in his House Cricket XI, and, after leaving, was Secretary and Treasurer of the Aberdovey Golf Club. Joining the Inns of Court O.T.C. in March, 1915, he was gazetted to the 3rd Bn. R.I.F. on Oct. 7 following, and was sent to France in July, 1916, attached to the 8th Bn. On Sept. 6 he volunteered to drive some Germans out of Leuze Wood, and safely accomplished the work ; but immediately afterwards was struck by a shell and instantaneously killed.

June 22, 1916.—**Arthur Chaplin Banks,** 2nd Lieut. 2nd Bn. Royal Welsh Fusiliers, was at Shrewsbury 1911-4, Head of his House (T.E.P.), and in the School Football XI., leaving for Sandhurst. His commanding officer wrote : " I have lost one of my most gallant officers, and a born soldier. The enemy blew an enormous mine, followed by a terrific bombardment. They lifted their barrage, and made a strong infantry attack. They got a real bad beating. Banks had his platoon up, and went for them. He killed four Germans himself before he was killed, and they were all lying together."

September 12, 1918.—**Allæn Noel Birkett-Barker** (S.H. 1907–10), Sergeant, 66th Brigade, R.G.A., reported killed in action.

.—**Harry Loftus Barlow,** Temp. 2nd Lieut. R.E. (F.E.B. 1903–5), reported killed in action.

Sept. 23, 1917.—**John Lancashire Barlow,** who was killed in action on Sept. 23, 1917, at the age of 18, entered Mr. Oldham's House in Sept. 1912. On the day that war was declared in the first week of the holidays, he enlisted in the 8th Essex Cyclist Corps at the age of 15. He served in this corps till Dec., 1914, when, being much too young for active service, and being keenly interested in aviation and aeroplane engines, he went to the Bournemouth Aviation School and took his pilot's certificate, after which he acquired further knowledge of the subject by joining the Wells Aviation Factory. When old enough he obtained a commission in the R.F.C., gaining his wings in April, 1917, and going out to France immediately afterwards took part in the Battle of Messines and other engagements. At the time of his death, though a 2nd Lieut., he was acting as Flight-Commander.

March 26, 1917.—**Thomas Bate,** Lieut. R.W.F. (T.). Lieut. BATE was killed on March 26, 1917, at Gaza, aged 27. He was at Shrewsbury (E.B.M. 1904–8), and shortly before the war joined the Royal Welsh Fusiliers, and served with them in Gallipoli. He rowed in the School crew and was one of the finest swimmers that the School has ever produced : he won the Up-river Swimming Cup in no less than four successive years, 1905, 1906, 1907, 1908, on the first occasion when barely 15 years old. On leaving School in 1908 he went to Assam as a tea-planter but returned to England on the death of his father, Mr. THOMAS BATE, of Kesterton, Flint, whom he succeeded.

December 22, 1915.—*****John Euel Witherden Bath,** Temp. Lieut., 5th (Service) Bn. Royal Berks Regt. (S.H., 1906–12), a Præpostor, Choregus, and a Gentleman of the Runs. He gained a Bible Clerkship at All Souls' College, Oxford, and represented his University against Cambridge in cross-country running, being also a member of the Thames Hare and Hounds, and on joining the Service took part in many Army cross-country races. He was gazetted from a Cadet of the O.T.C. to be a Temporary 2nd Lieut. on August 29, 1914, was subsequently posted to the 5th Royal Berks Regt. and was killed by a shell when going round the trenches with his Colonel.

July 7, 1915.—*****Philip Heacock Baynes,** Sergeant, 1st Rifle Brigade (S.H. 1892–7). He was Capt. of the Boats, and rowed in the crew of 1897, the first Eight to represent Shrewsbury against another school (and in which were six members who afterwards served in the South African War, three of whom have now passed away—viz., MARTEN, killed in action in South Africa ; HALHED, fatally mauled by a lion in the Soudan ; and BAYNES). He served with the Shropshire I.Y. in the Boer War, being offered a commission but declining it, and gaining the Medal with three Clasps. On returning from active service Baynes, as an artist " won a wide reputation and his strong fresh work was familiar in *Punch* " (*Punch Roll of Honour*, Oct. 6, 1915.) He enlisted in the Rifle Brigade as a Private, went to the front in October, 1914, was at first reported " missing," but is now " believed to have been killed."

Sept. 21, 1918.—**John Edward Becker,** aged 30, was at Shrewsbury (C.J.S.C.) 1902–6. In the years 1911–13, he held a commission in the Royal Engineers (T.) Signal Company, Leeds. At the end of that period he went out to Uganda, coffee-planting, and on August 5, 1914, joined the Uganda Defence Force as a despatch-rider on the German and Belgian Congo borders. He came home in 1915, and abtained a commission in the Royal Engineers, 1st London Divisional Signal Co. He was sent to Gallipoli and after the evacuation on December 20, 1915, was in charge of a wireless station near Salonica until May, 1916, when he was sent to East Africa. He took part in the marvellous trek across the wilds of German East Africa, suffered much from hardship, fever, and privation, and died at Dar-es-Salaam on September 21, 1918.

September 29, 1915.—*Eric Herbert Belk, Private, 4th Bn. The Cameronians (Scottish Rifles, T.F.), was at Shrewsbury (E.B.M.) May, 1908–July, 1911. On leaving he studied Law, but when war was declared enlisted as a private, and after eight months' uninterrupted service at the front, was killed by a shell while working his machine gun during the action at Vermelles, in France.

April 7, 1918.—Benedict Godfrey Allen Bell, 2nd Lieut. R.A.F., was killed on April 7. Born in 1891, he was at Shrewsbury (A.F.C.) 1906–8. In 1912 he went out to Singapore. After having made several unsuccessful applications for leave, he resigned his appointment, and reached home in March, 1917. He joined the R.F.C. inmediately, and went out to the front January, 1918.

Jan. —, 1918.—Arnold John Bennett was at Shrewsbury (S.H.) 1897–1900. He served for some time in the Baden-Powell Constabulary in South Africa, and later lived in Canada. He was ordained in 1908, and became Curate of Pewsey, Wilts. In 1911 he offered himself for four years to the Railway Mission, Regina, Canada, through the Archbishop's Western Canada Appeal. In 1916 he volunteered as a temporary Army Chaplain, and served with the Royal Warwickshire Regt., winning the *M.C.* in July. In 1917 he was transferred to Egypt and Palestine, where he contracted the fever from which he died.

August 21, 1915.—*George Robert Bennett, Temp. 2nd Lt., 5th Bn. Connaught Rangers (T.E.P., 1911–14) and winner of the Senior Steeplechase He was one of the many O.SS. who enlisted in the ranks of the 5th K.S.L.I. in September, 1914, and was given a commission after some months' service. He was instantaneously killed in action in Gallipoli while leading his men in a charge on the Turkish trenches, being shot through the heart, aged 21.

October 13, 1915.—*John William Bennett, Lieut., 3rd Bn. Royal Munster Fusiliers (S.R.), (S.H., 1904–8), fell in action in France, aged 25. He was in business with his father at Ballinacurra, Co. Cork, was gazetted to the 3rd Munsters in November, 1914. promoted Lieut. in May, 1915, and went out to the front in August attached to the 2nd Bn.

October 7, 1915.—In hospital in France, of wounds received September 25, *Harry Pynson Bennitt, Capt., 7th (Service) Bn. Seaforth Highlanders, aged 46. He was at Shrewsbury (C.J.S.C). 1885-7. Won the 100 yards and half mile in 1886, and was in the Football XI for two years. He went up to B.N.C., Oxon., and subsequently joined the Devon R.F.A. (S.R.). He was seconded to the 2nd King's African Rifles, and saw active service in Somaliland and in the expedition up the Gambia in 1901 (Medal, three Clasps). He was a Captain in the Reserve of Officers when he was called up on the outbreak of hostilities and posted to the Seaforths. He had also been wounded in July.

July, 15, 1916.—*Raymond Bevir, Temp. 2nd Lieut. 10th (Service) Bn. Royal Fusiliers, aged 28. He was at Shrewsbury (S.H.) 1902-7, left for Oxford as an Exhibitioner of Hertford, was Captain of his College Boat Club, and kept goal for the Football XI. In 1910 BEVIR was elected Librarian of the Union, and in 1911 President, was called to the Bar (Inner Temple) 1914, enlisted in the Royal Fusiliers at the outbreak of the war, gained his commission 15 Jan., 1915, and was killed in action while leading his men in a charge.

—, 1916.—Alexander Macpherson Blair, Capt. Ceylon Planters' Rifle Corps, and Temp. Capt. 2nd Bn. South Lancs. Regt. At Shrewsbury (G.T.H.), 1888-90, he went to the front with the Overseas Contingent of the Ceylon Planters' Rifles (in which he had been a Captain since 26 Sept., 1912), and was on 7 May, 1915, transferred to a temporary commission in the South Lancs.

July 1, 1916.—*Myles Boddington, M.C., Temp. Capt. 6th (Service) Bn. King's Shropshire L.I., aged 24. At School (S.H.), 1906-10, he was Choregus, and for two years in the Football Eleven. Going up to University College, Oxford, he took his degree in 1913, and was subsequently articled to a solicitor. Gazetted to the 6th Shropshires, he became full Lieut. 22 Nov., 1914, and Capt. 31 Oct., 1915, was awarded the Military Cross for conspicuous gallantry in the field, and fell in action on the first day of the Battle of the Somme.

October 13, 1915.—*Oswald William Boddington, Lieut., 5th Bn. Prince of Wales' North Staffordshire Regt. (T.F.), who wasat Shrewsbury (E.B.M.) 1902-7, coxing his House boat to the Head of the River. He then went up to Emmanuel College, Cambridge, and subsequently entered his father's business at Stoke-on-Trent. On the declaration of war he enlisted as a private in the 5th North Staffords, getting his commission in December in that year, and falling in action near Hulluch in the great advance of October, 1915, aged 26.

March 13, 1917.—At the Pinewood Sanatorium, Wokingham (of tuberculosis aggravated by active service), the Rev. **Vincent Coke Boddington,** formerly Curate of East Ham, aged 30.   At Shrewsbury (G.T.H. and W.D.H.), 1899-1901, he graduated from St. John's Coll., Cambridge, and was appointed a Temporary Army Chaplain, Nov. 22, 1914.

May 25, 1915.—***Harry Hargreaves Bolton,** Capt., 5th Bn. East Lancashire Regt. (T.F.), at Shrewsbury (E.B.M.) 1900-4, died from wounds received in action in the Dardanelles, aged 29.

March 26, 1918.—**Maurice Baldwin Bolton,** *M.C.*, Capt., 5th East Lancashire Regt., who was reported missing on March 21, 1918, is now known to have died of wounds in a German hospital at Le Cateau on March 26, in his 27th year.   He was at Shrewsbury (E.B.M.) 1906-11, and Pembroke College, Cambridge, and graduated in 1915.   At the outbreak of the war he joined the Cambridge O.T.C., and was gazetted to the 11th Manchester Regt. on Aug. 22, 1914, being promoted Captain in May, 1915.   In July, 1915, he was transferred to the East Lancashire Regiment, and went out to France in February 1917, being attached to the 1/4th Bn. On Nov. 22 in the same year he was awarded the Military Cross for gallant conduct in the field near Nieuport.   In February, 1918, on the reorganization of divisions, he was transferred to the 4th East Lancashire Regt., 66th Division.

July 1, 1915.—**Charles Edmund Boote,** *T.D.*, Lieut.-Col., 6th North Staffordshire Regt. (T.F.), fell in action, aged 42.   At Shrewsbury (E.B.M.), 1887-91, he left to join the firm of P. and R. Boote, Burslem, Staffs., of which he became Managing Director.   He joined the 2nd V.B. North Staffords in 1892, and transferred to the 5th North Staffords (T.F.) when the Territorial Force came into being.   He served with the Volunteer Service Co. in the South African War (Hon. Capt. in the Army and Medal), went to France as Major of the 5th North Staffords and was promoted to the command of the 6th Bn. (T.F.) of the same Regiment.

Sept. 25, 1917.—**Frank Hardinge Follett Booth,** Capt. Worcestershire Regt., reported wounded and missing on Sept. 25 last, is now presumed to have been killed on that date, in his 29th year.   Capt. Booth was at Shrewsbury (W.D.H. 1903-8), Merton College, Oxford, at which he graduated, and St. Chad's Theological College, Regina, Sask., it being his intention to take Holy Orders.   On the outbreak of war, failing to get a commission at once, he enlisted as a trooper in King Edward's Horse.   From this corps he received a commission in the Worcestershire Regt. in November, 1914,   He was seriously wounded in December, 1915, rejoining his regiment after nine months at home.

June 18, 1917.—**Arthur Frederick Botham,** Lieut., R.F.A., died of wounds on June 18, 1917, aged 28. He was educated at Merchant Taylors School and Clare College, Cambridge, where he was a Wrangler in 1911 and captained his College Fifteen. Afterwards he was appointed mathematical master at Shrewsbury and later held the same post at Tonbridge School. At the outbreak of war he joined the H.A.C. Battery, and was in Egypt for a year, returning in 1915 to take up his commission. He was a keen and popular sportsman and played regularly for the Old Merchant Taylors Football Club and for Middlesex County.

June 2, 1917.—**Edwin Rhodes Bottomley,** 2nd Lieut. R.F.A., attached R.F.C., was at Shrewsbury 1909–13, and for three years a member of the O.T.C. On leaving he entered the firm of Lucien Marcan's Successors, of Bradford, but was only there a few months, as on the second day of the war he enlisted in the 4th West Riding Brigade, shortly afterwards receiving a commission in the same. He transferred to the R.F.C. in 1916, obtained his pilot's certificate and his " wings " at the beginning of this year, and was shortly afterwards sent out. He was killed while flying close to the German lines on June 2, 1917, aged 22.

May 10, 1919, as the result of injuries received in a motor collision **Bazil Edward Creswell Boucher,** Lieut. 1st Batt. Royal Welsh Fusiliers, aged 21. He was at Shrewsbury (T.E.P.) 1912–16, and joined the Army in May, 1917. He was Adjutant of his Battalion for a few weeks after the Armistice, having been promoted Lieut. earlier in the year, and had seen much service with his Regt. in France and Italy, on the latter front taking part in the decisive operations, on the Piave against the Austrians, and winning the Croce di Guerra.

Dec. 29, 1916, aged 35.—*****Charles Thurston Bowring,** Lieut. Canadian Machine Gun Corps. At Shrewsbury (C.J.S.C.), 1895-9, and in the crew for two years, he went to Lausanne University, Switzerland, where he took his degree in Electrical Engineering. He then went through the apprenticeship course with the Westinghouse Co., at Pittsburg, U.S.A., joining the State Elevator Co. at Winnipeg, Canada, in 1913. Enlisting in the Canadian Expeditionary Force at the beginning of the War, he obtained his commission in the Canadian Infantry in Jan. 1915, and became Machine Gun Officer to his Bn. Later he was transferred to the Brigade Machine Gun Company as second in command, and was killed in action.

Aug. 28, 1918.—**Frank Harvey Bowring,** Major, King's Liverpool Regt., was killed in action August 28. While at Shrewsbury (C.J.S.C., 1894-8) was in both cricket and football teams, and afterwards was a regular player in the Northern Nomads F.C. He graduated from

Christ Church, Oxford, in 1902, and subsequently qualified as a Solicitor. He was appointed a Temp. Captain in the 17th Service Battalion (1st City) Liverpool Regiment, December 2, 1914. Returning home wounded he was promoted Temp. Major and second in command of the 21st Reserve Service Battalion of the same Regiment, May 28, 1916, being subsequently re-transferred to a Battalion at the front.

—**Thomas Stratford Bradburn,** Temp. Surgeon R.N. (S.H. 1896–9), died of illness contracted on active service. He went up to Hertford College, Oxon., and then studied Medicine at Birmingham University.

—**William Robert Bridges,** Lieut. Bedfordshire Regt., killed in action (S.H. 1910–13). He had previously been wounded.

March 13, 1918.—Captain **John Lawrence Brindle,** of the 4th Loyal North Lancashire Regiment (T.F.), died at Banchory, N.B., March 13, 1918, aged 23, through illness contracted on active service in France, 1915-16. He was at Shrewsbury (W.D.H.) 1909-13, and was gazetted Captain in July, 1915.

June 26, 1915.—**Harold Broadbent,** Rifleman, Rifle Bn., Liverpool Regt. (T.F.), at Shrewsbury (S.H.), 1905-08, fell in action in the Dardanelles.

Feb. 11, 1919.—**Eric Brownlee Brodie,** Lieut. R.A.F., entered the School (F.M.I.) in May, 1912, and left in August, 1914, to take up Civil Engineering. He joined the R.A.F. at the end of 1916, and after passing through the various Schools of Instruction, was sent out to France in Nov., 1917. In the following January he was severely wounded in fighting, losing some fingers and being in hospital four months. After recovering he was posted as Instructor to Beverley and subsequently to the Doncaster Aerodrome, but returned to France in Nov., 1918, as a " Snipe Pilot," going on to Germany with the Army of Occupation after the Armistice was signed. He was killed on Feb. 11, 1919, as the result of a collision when flying, on the outskirts of Cologne.

April 23, 1917.—**Cecil Arthur Brown** was reported wounded and missing on April 23, 1917. He entered Mr. Haydon's House in 1908 and left in 1912. In 1911 he played in the winning House Cricket XI., he was in the School Football XI. in the same year and got his school colours at Cricket the following summer. He left at the end of that term ; the next two years he spent in Engineering works, and in 1914 obtained a Commission in the Sherwood Foresters.

September 25, 1915.—*__William Leonard Brown,__ Lieut. 6th Bn. The Sherwood Foresters, Notts. and Derby Regt. (T.F.) ; at Shrewsbury (W.D.H.), 1906-9 ; admitted a Solicitor, 1915 ; killed in action in France.

July 12, 1915, killed in action at Krithia, Gallipoli, __Andrew Bulman,__ Lieut. 4th Border Batt. King's Own Scottish Borderers (T.F.). He was at Shrewsbury (S.H.) 1905–7, then worked in a business office at Kelso for two years. Afterwards he entered the Edinburgh College of Science to study Architecture and Constructional Drawing. He joined the Territorial Force in 1912, and was gazetted full Lieut. Aug. 28, 1914. With his Regt. he went to Gallipoli in May, 1915, in the 52nd Division. On July 12, the Batt. suffered heavy casualties in an attack on Krithia. Among those reported missing was Lieut. A. BULMAN, and it is presumed he was killed in that action. He was an enthusiastic fisherman and yachtsman ; also a prominent member of the Kelso Rugby Football Club ; when the Scotch International Rugby Fifteen went to Paris in 1913 Bulman accompanied it, and being a famous player on the Bagpipes, dressed in full highland costume he played the Scotch side on to the field for the game.

Feb. 15, 1918, from the effects of war strain on active service.— __Geoffrey Percival Bulmer,__ *M.C.*, Lieut. in the King's Shropshire Light Infantry, attached R.F.C. He had had very exciting adventures in France. On one occasion when he was in an aeroplane his pilot collapsed and the machine fell 10,000 ft. on to some trees. (S.H. 1909–13).

Sept. 11, 1919, suddenly, at the General Hospital, Gharial, Murree, India, while on active service, __Francis William Burbury,__ Lieut.-Col. 24th Home Counties Batt. (T.F.), The Rifle Brigade, Prince Consort's Own, second son of the late SAMUEL HAWKESLEY BURBURY (O.S.), *M.A.*, *F.R.S.* Col. Burbury, who was 54, was at Shrewsbury (S.H.) 1880–4, where he was a Præpostor ; 4 years in the Cricket XI, being captain in his last year ; two years in the Football being also captain ; and senior whip. He went up to Pembroke College, Cambridge, was gazetted 2nd Lieut. in the Queen's Own Royal West Kent Regt. in 1886, and promoted Capt. in 1896. In this year he transferred to the Militia Batt. and served with it in the Mediterranean 1901-2. He was promoted Major in the 3rd (S.R.) Batt. Royal West Kents, in Sept. 1914, and was appointed to command the 24th Batt. Rifle Brigade, on Nov. 17, 1915. Col. Burbury who had served in France before he went out to India, was a partner in the firm of Messrs. Thomas Taylor and Sons, Ltd., linen manufacturers, Barnsley, and was a J.P. for the West Riding of Yorkshire. A keen athlete, he played at half back for his Regt. when it won the Inter-Regimental Cup in 1894, and regularly for the Army Association team. He also frequently assisted the Barnsley Cricket Club, after he had left the Regular Army.

September 27, 1915.—**Gilbert Edward Burney,** Temp. Lieut. 8th (Service) Bn. Gordon Highlanders, was at Shrewsbury (C.J.S.C.) 1905–10, and then went out to take up coffee planting in Ceylon. He returned to England in November, 1914, and obtained his commission. For some time he was A.D.C. to the General of his Division, was mentioned in the despatches of January 1, 1915, and died of wounds received in action in Flanders while bringing up reinforcements on September 25, aged 24.

July 27, 1916.—*John Gilchrist Burnie, Private, P.S. Bn., Royal Fusiliers, killed in action. A son of Dr. W. GILCHRIST BURNIE (O.S.), of Bradford, he was in the School House 1906–11, leaving as a Præpostor for St. John's College, Oxford, where he had won a History Exhibition. He enlisted in Sept., 1914, having previously served in both his school and University O.T.C. He was nominated by the War Office for a commission, but on a medical examination he was rejected on account of short sight. After six months' training he was again offered a commission and was strongly recommended by his colonel, but a medical board upheld the previous decision. He was offered his discharge from the Army, but declined, and had been at the front for the last nine months. His platoon officer speaks of him as a splendid soldier and one whom it will be difficult to replace.

June 17, 1918.—**Kenrick Hamond Burton** came to Shrewsbury in the Summer Term, 1910 (Pickering's) and left in July, 1914, being then a member of the Lower Sixth. On the declaration of War he was one of that gallant band (of whom there are now few living) who came back to Kingsland, and marched from School Gates to the Depot of the K.S.L.I. to serve in the ranks of the Regiment. In the course of the next year he was given a commission in the 2/6th (Rifle) Battalion of the King's Liverpool Regiment, with which he went to France. On the night of June 16–17, 1918, while scouting, he was hit at close range by a machine-gun bullet. Those who attempted to rescue him could get no reply and as nothing whatever has since been heard his friends have been obliged to give up all hope that he has survived.

July —, 1915.—*John Bury, Lieut., 5th Battery, 1st East Lancs. Brigade, R.F.A. (T.F.) (E.B.M., and F.T.P. 1907–11), fell in action in Gallipoli, aged 21. He was a cotton manufacturer at Accrington.

Sept. 20, 1918.—**Harold Butterworth,** *M.C.*, Lieut. R.F.A., killed on September 20, aged 21, was at Shrewsbury (Prior's), 1911–15, and for two years in the O.T.C. Immediately on reaching the age of 18 he left school and was given a commission in the West Lancashire R.F.A. He went out to France in April, 1916. A few months later he was attached to an anti-aircraft battery. He was awarded the Military Cross for his ability and resource in handling his section and his personal courage during several days of active operations in a critical period. His C.O. wrote :—" He thoroughly deserved the Military Cross which was given him. He always ' played the game,' and whilst in command of his section backed me up most loyally. His section is well known and has more than once been called the finest out here. He was in command of it at the time of his death."

April 23, 1917.—**Charles David Calcott,** Lieut. the King's Liverpool Regt., was killed in action in the fighting on the Western Front on April 23, 1917. Lieut. Calcott went out with the Shropshire Yeomanry in Aug., 1914. From the Yeomanry he was promoted to commission rank and posted to the King's Liverpool Regt. He was wounded in the Battle of Montauban on July 1, 1916. He returned to France last January, and had been through much severe fighting. Lieut. Calcott, who was 23, was at Shrewsbury (D.B.) 1909–10.

Nov. 18, 1916.—**Edward Campbell,** Lieut. North Staffordshire Regt., came to Shrewsbury (C.J.B.) in May, 1910, and went to Sandhurst in Jan., 1915. On Nov. 18, 1916, to meet an emergency, he volunteered to act as Bombing Officer of his Company. Two enemy trenches were taken and among many casualties he was stated to be missing. The War Office now report that he was killed in the action.

March —, 1918.—Killed in action, **Trevor Carus-Wilson,** *T.D.*, *D.S.O.*, Major Duke of Cornwall's L.I. (*T.*), who served in the South African War, winning the Queen's Medal with five clasps. He was at Shrewsbury (G.T.H.) 1885–7 ; and afterwards an engineer on the G.W. Railway.

Sept. 25, 1915.—*****George Ronald Ashburner Case,** 2nd Lieut., 3rd Bn. South Lancs. Regt. (S.R.) (E.B.M. and F.T.P. 1910-14), who rowed three years in the School crew, and then went to Pembroke Coll., Cambridge. He was killed " somewhere in Flanders," aged 19.

August 10, 1915.—*****Harold Chell,** Temp. Lieut. 8th (Service) Bn. Royal Fusiliers (A.F.C., 1904-8), died on hospital in Flanders of shell-wounds received the previous day. He was Junior Whip, 1906 ; Senior, 1907 ; and in the Football XI and the Crew. He won the

Junior Steeplechase, the Senior twice in successive years, and many events at the Sports in 1907-8, rowing also in his House boat, which won the Challenge Oars, and was Head of the River in the same year. He went up to St. John's Coll., Cambridge, and was studying Medicine at St. Mary's Hospital, London, when war broke out. Then he was gazetted from a Cadet of the O.T.C. as Temp. 2nd Lieut. on August 22, 1914, being shortly afterwards posted to the 8th R.F.

— —, 1917.—**John Victor Church,** 2nd Lieut., K.S.L.I., killed in action (S.H., 1912–15).

July 19, 1915.—*****Claude Rex Cleaver,** Capt. and Adjutant, 29th Punjabis, Indian Army ; at Shrewsbury (C.J.S.C.) 1899–1903. After passing through Sandhurst, he was appointed to the Indian Army in 1905 and early in the War went with his Regiment as Company Commander and Adjutant, to East Africa, when he was wounded in action near Taveta, and taken prisoner on July 14, dying on July 19, aged 30.

.—**Eric Arnold Cleaver,** Lieut. East Yorks. Regt., attached R.F.C. as a balloon officer, killed in action (W.D.H. 1893-6). For some time he was on the staff of the National Bank, Johannesburg, S. Africa.

Feb. 19, 1919, in London, from pneumonia following influenza, **Verschoyle Crawford Climo,** Major, late the West India and Manchester Regiments, aged 51. Major CLIMO was at Shrewsbury (D.B. and S.H.) 1880–5, Captain of the Football XI. (being elected to that position immediately he received his Colours), and a Præpostor. Going to the R.M.C., Sandhurst, he was First Queen's West India Cadet in 1887, was gazetted 2nd Lieut. in the West India Regiment 1888, Lieut. 1890, Capt. 1895 and Major 1900. He served in the Ashanti Expedition of 1895-6 (Star), and in the South African War, on the Staff of the Mounted Infantry in 1901 (Medal). He passed the Staff College in 1898, and was a first-class interpreter in modern languages. Major CLIMO transferred to the Manchester Regiment in 1905, and was appointed on the Headquarters Staff of the Indian Army in 1907. In 1914 he was in the Reserve of Officers, on retired pay, and was immediately made a General Staff Officer, 2nd Grade, which position he was holding at the time of his death. He was twice mentioned in Despatches for his services in the present and twice wounded.

.—**Owen Mostyn Conran,** Major, King's Own Royal Lancaster Regt., attached R.F.C., was killed in France when on bombing duty. He was at Shrewsbury, 1895-1896 (W.D.H.), served in the South African War, and joined the Royal Lancashire Regiment from the South Lancashire Militia in 1901. He was made Captain in July, 1907, and on July 29, 1913, was seconded for service with the Egyptian Army, becoming Major in September, 1915. At the outbreak of the war he saw active service in Egypt and the Sudan, and did a considerable amount of flying. In July, 1916, he was sent to England on sick leave, during which he obtained permission to become attached to the R.F.C. In November, 1916, he was made Flight Commander, and in April, 1917, he went to France.

Oct. —, 1918.—**John Howard Cooke** (E.B.M. 1908–10), Lieut. R.A.S.C., was in the School Cricket XI, and a dangerous fast bowler and a big hitter. On leaving he went into business, and on the outbreak of hostilities obtained a commission in the R.A.S.C. He was severely wounded in the leg in France and died in hospital at Trouville.

July 21, 1915.—**Richard Humphrey Coxon**, Rifleman, 16th Bn. The London Regt. (Queen's Westminster Rifles) (T.F.), was at Shrewsbury (E.B.M.) 1903–8. He joined the Rifles two days after the declaration of War, landed in France in Oct., 1914, and acted as Battalion Interpreter from Nov. to April, when, preferring to share the dangers of his comrades, he went back to the trenches where he was killed by a sniper's bullet a few miles north of Ypres.

Nov., 1920.—**John Craig,** *V.D.*

May 12, 1915.—*****Arthur Thomas Crawford Cree**, Lieut., 7th Bn. Durham Light Infantry (T.F.), was at Shrewsbury 1895–1900, leaving as 5th in the School for Magdalen Coll., Oxford. He gained a 2nd Class in Lit. Hum. in 1904, was called to the Bar (Inner Temple) 1905, for some years going on the N.E. Circuit, then practicing at the Chancery Bar. On Aug. 4, he joined the Inns of Court O.T.C., obtained his commission in November, left England on May 4, and met his death in action almost immediately, aged 33.

—**Denis Merville Crewe,** Lieut. Cheshire Regt. (T.), was reported " Missing, believed killed " on July 18th, 1917. He was at Shrewsbury (C.J.S.C. and T.E.P.) from 1908 to 1912.

—**Guy Henry Goad Crosfield,** 2nd Lieut. Rifle Brigade. Killed in action (A.F.C. 1911–15).

Sept. 18, 1918.—Corporal **Ernest Llewellyn Cross,** killed in action, was at the School 1894–6, as a Day boy, then qualified as a chemist and druggist, and was serving in the 7th Battn. Manchester Regt. He kept goal for the School in many matches, including the Repton, just missing his 1st XI. Football Colours.

Jan. 2, 1920, at his residence, The Hay Farm, Madeley, Salop, **Robert Singlehurst Cross,** late Lieut. 10th Batt. The King's Regiment (Liverpool Scottish), aged 30. He was at Shrewsbury (A.F.C.) 1903-6, and rowed bow of the School Crew. When the War broke out he originally joined the Inns of Court O.T.C. as a Private. He had farmed for some time in Queensland and S. Africa, and died from the effects of trench fever.

July 10, 1916.—****Sir Foster Hugh Egerton Cunliffe,** *Bt.*, Temporary Major 13th (Service) Bn., Rifle Brigade, and Member of the Governing Body of Shrewsbury School. He was educated at Eton, where he was best known as a remarkably successful left-handed bowler, and at New College, Oxford, where he was to prove himself a man of fine intellect as well as a fine cricketer. He played for the University, as he had previously played for Eton, from 1895–1898, and obtained Honours in the School of Modern History. Elected a Fellow of All Souls in 1898, his association with that college continued until his death, and he had recently become Estates Bursar. Always a close student of modern history, and possessed of a wonderful knowledge of the Napoleonic campaigns, he was appointed to be first Lecturer on Military History at Oxford in 1905, and was the author of the official history of the Boer War, which work he carried out with characteristic thoroughness and accuracy. No finer tribute to his ability in this direction could have been paid than his appointment as first editor of the *Times* history of the present war, a task he was obliged to relinquish on his acceptance of a commission in the Rifle Brigade. He had already acquired considerable experience in military training as Lieutenant of the 1st Cadet Bn. (Royal West Surrey Regt.), to which his rapid promotion in the Rifle Brigade is probably due. As the *Times* said :—" In the long list of men of high promise and much achievement who have fallen in the past two years, Sir FOSTER CUNLIFFE'S name will have a memorable place. He was a man of high character, great charm and warm friendships, a good landlord and a keen all-round sportsman in the best sense of the word. He combined an ardent love of English country life with the tastes of a student and a strong sense of public duty. It is a combination which is not too common in these days, and would have been invaluable in the time of national reconstruction which lies ahead. As a soldier he would probably have gone far, for his theoretical knowledge of strategy was unrivalled, and his letters of the last few months showed his deep interest in watching it in practice from the standpoint of a regimental officer."

Feb. —, 1917.—***Alwyn Percy Dale,** Capt. (Temp. Major), 5th Bn. P.W.O. West Yorks Regt. (T.), aged 36. In the School House, 1894-8, he graduated from Clare College, Cambridge, in 1902, During his College days he served with the Service Contingent of the C.U.R.V. (attached to the Suffolk Regt.), in the South African War, gaining the Queen's Medal with five clasps. He subsequently took a commission in the 1st V.B. West Yorks Regt., transferring to the Territorials in 1908, and being gazetted Captain in 1911, and Temp. Major, 23 Feb., 1916. By profession he was a solicitor at York, being admitted in 1906.

June 15, 1915. ***Walter Ambler Davies**, Lieut., 4th Bn. Loyal North Lancs. Regt (T.F.) (W.D.H.) 1907–12, aged 20. He enlisted at the beginning of the War, soon obtained his commission, went to France at the end of May, and was killed while leading his platoon. A shot went through his right arm, and immediately afterwards he was hit in the other, but though advised to take shelter in a trench he said " No, I'll lead my men up," and was still going on when he received a fatal wound in his body. He was employed at the Kiveton Park Colleries, Hull, and was the first Preston T.F. officer to be killed in action.

Oct. 9, 1915.—**Robert Arthur Demuth**, A.B., Hawke Bn. Royal Naval Division (F.E.B. 1890–3), was for five years in a London Merchant's office, but had abandoned it for a life of leisure in the Pyrenees. When War was declared, he at once returned home and joined the Public School Battalion. Though twice offered a commission he refused both times, and went out to the Dardanelles as an A.B. He was invalided home from Suvla Bay, and died in the Royal Naval Hospital, Haslar, aged 40 .

March 5, 1918.—**Walter Henry Densham**, *M.C.* (W.S.I. 1912-15), gazetted 2nd Lieut. 3rd East Lancs. Brigade (16th Batty.), R.F.A. (T.), Aug. 3, 1915 ; died from wounds received in action on March 5, 1918. He had been over two years at the front in France.

Oct. 2, 1917.—**Geoffrey Garbutt Dickinson,** 2nd Lieut. R.F.A., killed in Flanders, aged 19. He came to Shrewsbury (Mr. Haydon's House) in Sept., 1912, and left in Dec., 1916.

.—***Arthur Hubert Dickson** was a member of the School House from 1899–1902. He died from illness contracted while engaged in recruiting duties, with the rank of 2nd Lieutenant.

March 6, 1917.—**John Vibart Dixon,** 2nd Lieut. 3rd North Midland Brigade, R.F.A. (T.), Ammunition Column (attached 2nd North Midland Brigade R.F.A.), to which he was gazetted Sept. 4, 1916. He was in the School House (leaving in 1915), and in the 2nd Cricket XI., and won the Bentley Elocution Prize three years in succession. He was sent to the front in August, 1916, and was killed while in charge of a Trench Mortar Battery.

June 17, 1917.—The well-known Rugby International **G. E. B. Dobbs,** Lieut.-Col. R.E., was struck by a shell on June 17, 1917, while returning from prospecting a new cable trench in the front line, and died the same day. George Eric Burroughs Dobbs was the Devon Albion and England forward of 1906 against Wales and Ireland. He used also to play for Llanelly about that time. He passed direct from school (G.T.H. and W.D.H.) 1898–1901 into Woolwich and was gazetted to the R.E. in March, 1904. He had served at home and at Singapore, and at the outbteak of war went to France as 1st Lieut. For valuable work during there treat from Mons he was awarded the Cross of Chevalier of the Legion of Honour, became Captain soon after, and obtained his brevet majority in 1915. He was three times mentioned in despatches, was made Assistant Director of Signals and received the temporary rank of Lieut.-Colonel in Nov., 1916.

Nov. 17, 1918.—Of pneumonia at Queen Alexandra's Military Hospital, Millbank, S.W., Major **Malcolm Douglas,** " D " Company, 46th Machine Gun Batty., who was at Shrewsbury (D.B.) 1907–9, then entered the service of the National Provincial Bank of England, and in the very early days of the war joined up as a private in the University and Public School Corps. He was given his commission in the 11th (Service) Battn. (St. Helen's) of the Prince of Wales' Volunteers (South Lancashire Regt.), and soon afterwards (June 29, 1915) promoted full Lieutenant, being transferred as Temp. Capt. to the M.G.C. on Nov. 29, 1915. He took a course at Camberley and later a certificate in machine gunnery at the works of Messrs. Vickers, and in 1916 went out to France where he had a year's service, and was invalided home with trench fever. He was mentioned in Sir D. Haig's despatches, May 26, 1917. He rejoined his unit at Grantham, where he went in for an examination for an instructorship in machine gunnery, and came out one mark behind the top man. Later he applied to go out to France again, and returned to active service. In June, 1918, he was promoted Major, and went out with the 46th Machine Gun Battery.

July 7, 1916.—**Charles Dutton,** Temp. 2nd Lieut. 10th (Service) Bn. Lancashire Fusiliers, was at Shrewsbury (F.E.B. and C.J.B.), 1905–7, and was gazetted to his commission 26 Sept., 1914, from the P.S. Bn., Royal Fusiliers. After being for a year in the Ypres salient, he was killed in action on the Somme.

Nov. 17, 1916.—*Charles Henry Dwyer,** 2nd Lieut. Worcestershire Regt., and Temp. Capt. 10th (Service) Bn. At Shrewsbury (F.M.I.), 1909–14, he was Captain of the Gymnasium (representing the School for two years at Aldershot), in the Football XI., and a Gentleman of the Runs ; he left intending to qualify for the Army as a profession, but was unable to pass, owing to weak sight. He therefore accepted a temporary commission in the 5th (Service) Bn. K.S.L.I., but was shortly afterwards transferred to the 10th Worcesters. Again nominated for a commission in the Regulars, he returned from the Front, whither he had proceeded in July, 1915, to go through courses of instruction, but eventually went back to his old Bn. as Captain and Adjutant, and was killed by a sniper while on very difficult reconnaissance work, aged 21.

July 15, 1918.—**Arthur Noel Ealand,** 2nd Lieut. R.A.F., accidentally killed on July 15 while flying at the front, was at Shrewsbury (E.B.M.) 1899–1902, and became a solicitor. At the time of his death he was in partnership at Thetford, Norfolk. After serving for two years with the Red Cross in France as driver of the O.S. Motor Ambulance, in 1917 he obtained a commission in a Dragoon regiment, but subsequently transferred to the R.A.F. Wireless Section. He was exceptionally sturdy and thick set, an " oar " of Nature's own making and a " full-back " whom no one tackled lightly or without thinking twice. He belonged to a golden age in the annals of " Moser's," and rowed bow in the House Four, which won " the Oars " in the Spring of 1902. From the outset of his aquatic career Ealand was a boy who seemed incapable of rowing wrong, who had practically nothing to learn from his coach, and the form and power, that he showed in the above race, made his place at bow in the School Eight a certainty. Five members of " Moser's Crew," Max Jourdier, C. F. Leake, J. Summers, W. Cooke, and H. Shimwell, did actually row in the Eight that year, an *annus mirabilis* indeed for the house! but Ealand, perhaps the best oar of all, was prevented at the eleventh hour by the doctor's orders; and so the astonishing record of six out of the eight was just missed.

Sept. 8, 1918.—**George Keith Elliott,** Lieut. Royal Welch Fusiliers was killed on September 8, aged 20. While at Shrewsbury (D.B.) he gained Dr. Bright's Science and History Prizes, the Dukes' French Prize, the Darwin Prize, the Turnbull Scholarship (Science), and in 1916 an open Science Scholarship at University College, Oxford. He did not go into residence, but joined the Oxford University O.T.C. in August, passed on to the cadet unit at Lichfield in November, and was gazetted to the R.W.F. in March, 1917. He served in Egypt and Palestine until May, 1918, when he went to another front, and only rejoined his battalion after his first home leave when he was killed during an attack. His Colonel wrote :—"Only a few days before he had carried out a very valuable patrol in the face of heavy machine-gun fire. His corporal got badly hit, but Elliott and one man got the corporal back between them under most deadly fire, as well as bringing back most important information as regards enemy dispositions. When he was in my company in Egypt and Palestine I always regarded him as my best platoon commander." His former C.O. wrote :—" He had lately very much distinguished himself at an instructional school for physical training and bayonet fighting, at which he had gained the highest praise, and returned as battalion instructor of bayonet fighting."

June 16, 1915.—*Basil Herbert Ellis, Temp. Lieut., 5th (Service) Bn. King's Shropshire Light Infantry, entered the School House with a Scholarship in 1909 ; was in the Cricket XI two years, in the 2nd XI at Football, and Captain of his House Boat. He gained a Scholarship at Wadham Coll., Oxford, and left in 1914. He enlisted with the other O.SS. in the 5th K.S.L.I., and, having been a keen member of the School O.T.C., was almost immediately made a 2nd Lieut., being promoted Lieut. on Oct. 1. He was killed by a shell while lying wounded, aged 20.

March 14, 1915.—Killed in action, *Frank Harold Elwin, in his 20th year, who entered the School in 1909, rowed for two years in the Eight, and was Captain of the Headroom Boat. He left at the end of the Summer term, 1914, intending to go to King's College, Cambridge, in October and read Science, but enlisted instead in the Shropshire Light Infantry, and at once became as popular in the ranks as he had been at school. He accepted a Commission some months later in the 3rd (Reserve) Batt. of the Wiltshire Regiment, and had just been transferred to the 2nd Battalion when he moved up to the firing line some ten days before his death. To quote *The Salopian*—

Easy going and kindhearted, a genial critic of rules and regulations though first-rate at carrying out any piece of work that he was given, he influenced others by the charm of his character, not by force. No one was better loved in his house, or carried more weight in its counsels.

Oct. — , 1919.—Arthur Frederic Evans, was at Shrewsbury (F.E.B.) 1900-4 : was gazetted 2nd Lieut. in the R.W.F. (T.) in 1915, and Lieut. in 1916. He joined the R.A.F. in March, 1918, and was killed in an aeroplane accident, while acting as Flying Officer.

.—Charles Wilmot Evans came to Shrewsbury (Mr. Haydon's House) in 1903, and left in 1909. At the time of his death he was a Captain in the South Staffordshire Regt., had gained the M.C., and had been mentioned in despatches for valuable service.

July 16, 191 .—Rees Tudor Evans, Temp. Capt. and Adjt. Welsh Regt. (S.H. 1901-6), and Richard Stanley Evans, Lieut. Welsh Regt. (S.H. 1905–11), reported missing, now reported killed in action in Gallipoli.

Sept. 16, 1916.—Killed by a shell at Martinpuich, aged 30, *Thomas Rubie Fawsitt (A.F.C.), 1900–3, 2nd Lieut. 3rd (S.R.) Bn. York and Lancs. Regt. (attached 9th Service Bn.). Leaving school he went up to Christ's Coll., Cambridge, where he coxed his College Boat and one of the Trial Eights, and obtained his commission in the 3rd York and Lancs. on June 29, 1915, having previously served in the ranks of the P.S. Bn. Royal Fusiliers.

July 24, 1915.—*George Rudolf Fielding, Capt., 1st Bn. Sherwood Foresters and Temp. Major, 9th (Service) Bn. ; at Shrewsbury (E.B.M.), May 1896-Dec., 1898.   He was gazetted from the Militia as 2nd Lieut. in the Sherwood Foresters in May, 1902, and served with the West African Regiment, 1911–14.   He was killed in action at the Dardanelles, aged 34.

March 28, 1918.—Philip Gerard Finch, M.C., Lieut. Northumberland Fusiliers, was reported missing on March 28, but is now known to have been killed in action on that date.   He was at Shrewsbury (F.M.I.) 1911–15 and Sandhurst, and obtained his commission in August, 1916, joining in the following month a battalion of the Northumberland Fusiliers at the front, where he had seen a good deal of fighting.   His Colonel writing at the time he was reported missing, said :—" He always did consistently well in every action. I twice put him in for a Military Cross and the last time I am glad to say he got it."

Nov. —, 1917.—Godfrey FitzHugh, D.L., Capt., came to Shrewsbury (C.J.S.C.) in the Michaelmas Term of 1888 and left in 1890. He served with the Montgomeryshire Yeomanry in the South African War, was mentioned in despatches and awarded the Queen's Medal with four clasps.   On the death of his uncle he succeeded to the Plas Power Estate near Wrexham, where he became a Justice of the Peace for Montgomery and an authority on agriculture.   He fell in action, aged 44, in the middle of Nov., 1917, while serving with the Welsh Regt., to which he was seconded from the Yeomanry.

March 25, 1918.—Reported wounded and missing on March 25, now officially presumed killed in action, John Herbert Fitzmaurice, 2nd Lieut. 6th (Service) Battalion K.S.L.I., aged 19, only son of JOHN RUPERT FITZMAURICE (O.S.),   He was at Shrewsbury (J.B.O.) 1912–16.

March 20, 1915.—Killed in Action near Bois Grenier, France, *Walter George Fletcher, B.A.., Oxon., second son of C. R. L. Fletcher, of Norham End, Oxford, aged 26.   Mr. FLETCHER, who was educated at Eton and Balliol, was a Classical Master at Shrewsbury 1911–13, when he was appointed to a Mastership at his old School. While at Oxford he served in the O.T.C. Cavalry, and subsequently held Commissions in the O.T.C. both at Shrewsbury and Eton.   On the outbreak of the War he was selected as an interpreter in the Intelligence Corps, went to the Front with the first Contingent

and saw almost every action in the retreat, and in the sub-
sequent advance to the Aisne. In September he was attached as
2nd Lieut. to the 2nd Batt. Royal Welch Fusiliers, and constantly
employed on patrol work, in which his accurate knowledge of
German proved of great service (he taught English at the Real-
Gymnasium, Schleswig, for six months, 1910–11) : he was mentioned
in Sir John French's Despatch of February, 1915.

May 13, 1918, killed in action in France, **William Robert Foldys,**
who was at Shrewsbury (W.S.I. and W.D.H.) 1901–4. He was
serving in the ranks of the Royal Fusiliers.

June 10, 1915, at the Dardanelles, aged 28, ***Stanley Foster-
Jackson,** Capt., 6th Bn. Manchester Regt. (T.F.), (C.J.S.C. 1901–4),
and in the School Cricket and Football Elevens. On leaving he
became a member of the Manchester Stock Exchange, and joined the
Territorials almost immediately. He was a fine athlete, distinguish-
ing himself at cricket, football, and golf, and also an excellent horseman.

April 16, 1918.—2nd Lieut. **Heaton Foster** entered the School
(Oldham's) in January, 1913, and left to coach for the Army
Examination in July, 1916. He went to Sandhurst that autumn
and was gazetted to the 1st Batt. East Yorkshire Regiment in
September, 1917, going out to France in the following month. He
was reported missing on April 16, 1918, but it proved that he had
been killed, while holding with his platoon a position which became
isolated owing to the withdrawal of its flank.

.—**Arthur Fox,** *M.C.*, Capt. K.S.L.I., killed in action
(S.H.) 1911–5, received his commission in March, 1915, and was
promoted Captain in November of the following year. His award
of the Military Cross for conspicuous gallantry and determination
was gazetted in May, 1916, the official account stating : " When he
found his half company too weak to carry out an assault, he went
back under heavy fire and brought up his supporting half-company,
equipped with bombs and shovels. After the assault, in which he
captured a trench, he beat off two counter attacks, and consolidated
his position in very difficult circumstances."

.—**Arthur Leslie Fraser,** Lieut. R.G.A., was at
Shrewsbury (F S. and C.J.S.C.), 1903–6, and Pembroke College,
Cambridge. He chose the Army as a career, and passed into
Sandhurst, but was there rejected owing to defective eyesight.
Possessing a spirit of adventure, he travelled a good deal and spent
a considerable time in Canada. Soon after the outbreak of war he
was gazetted, going out to France in 1916. He took part in many
heavy actions before meeting with the wounds to which he succumbed.

April 23–May 1.—*Charles Stockley French, Lieut., 2nd Bn. Royal Dublin Fusiliers (C.J.S.C., 1905–10). He took his *B.A.* at Trinity College, Dublin, in 1914 ; was gazetted on August 26 from the Dublin University O.T.C., 2nd Lieut. in the 2nd Bn. of the Dublins ; he was wounded in December, 1914 ; left again for the front on March 23, to meet his death in action near Ypres on some date between April 23rd and May 1st. He was a younger brother of Capt. C. A. French, and was 22.

June 1, 1915.—*Claude Alexander French, Capt., 2nd Bn. Royal Irish Regt., aged 35 (C.J.S.C. 1894–9), Stroke of a School Trial VIII, and in the Crew. In 1899 he went up to Trinity College, Dublin, and in 1900 joined the Derry R.G.A. Militia. In March, 1901, he was seconded as Lieutenant, 35th Co. 11th Bn. I.Y., for service in South Africa, where he was severely wounded at Twefontein in December, 1901 (King's Medal, 3 Clasps). He was gazetted 2nd Lieut. in the R.I. in 1903 ; Lieut., 1904 ; Capt., 1909 ; went out to Flanders, September, 1914 ; was wounded at Le Pilley, October 20 ; rejoined in January, 1915 ; was wounded by a shell on May 8 ; and died at the Australian Hospital near Wimereux.

November 3, 1914.—Edward Hugh Mainwaring Furley, Corporal, Bowker's Horse, East African Mounted Rifles (F.S. 1900–1901), aged 29. Soon after leaving school he joined the Montgomeryshire Yeomanry, and, after farming in Cheshire and the Argentine, went out to British East Africa in 1912. He at once enlisted in the forces raised for the defence of the Colony and took part in the fight on Lake Victoria Nyanza, in September. After the action at Longido, on November 3rd, he was officially reported " missing " and in February " killed." In the retirement of his troop from a kopje, he remained to see everyone mounted and away, and was probably shot while so doing. He was a keen sportsman and an excellent horseman.

Harold Penry Garnons-Williams was at Shrewsbury (W.S.I. and S.H.) from 1911–1915. At the time of his death in action he was a 2nd Lieut. in the R. Welch Fusiliers.

.—Holbrook Lance Gaskell, Flight Sub.-Lieut. R.N., killed in action, was at Shrewsbury (A.F.C. 1912–15), and was entered at Pembroke College, Cambridge, but joined the R.N.A.S., getting his pilot's certificate in June, 1916, and left for active service at the end of December.

Oct. —, 1918.—2nd Lieut. James Bainton Stowell Gell was killed on the Western Front after only a few weeks' service in France. He entered the School (Prior's) in September, 1913, and worked his way steadily to the top of the Modern Side, leaving in 1916.

Oct. 30, 1917.—**Stanley Gething,** Private, Artists', Rifles was killed during an attack in Flanders on Oct. 30, aged 27. While at Shrewsbury (1905–8) he developed his marked musical ability and became one of the best pianists the School has had in recent years. After leaving he studied in England and abroad intending to devote himself to a musical career.

.—**James Houghton Getty,** Capt., the West Yorkshire Regt., and a Staff Captain, came to Shrewsbury (C.J.S.C.) in the Michaelmas Term, 1901, and left in 1907 to go to Caius College, Cambridge. On the outbreak of the war he obtained a commission in the Lincolnshire Regt. in which he became Adjutant of his battalion.

July 7, 1915.—*****Bernard Gibbs,** 2nd Lieut., 6th Bn. Rifle Brigade (S.R.) (attached 1st), who was at Shrewsbury, 1907–12 (D.B. and F.T.P.) and a great gymnast in the days when the School did so well at Aldershot in the Public Schools Gymnastic Contests. On leaving he went up to Pembroke College, Cambridge, and represented the University against Oxford. He obtained his commission on the outbreak of the War, and three days before his death was awarded the Military Cross for coolness and gallantry in the face of an attack in force by the Germans. He was 23.

—, 1916.—**Richard Francis Gillett,** Private R.A.S.C. At Shrewsbury (E.B.M., 1903-7), he rowed in the School VIII., and on leaving was studying law, when the War broke out. Prevented from gaining a commission by weak eyesight, he enlisted as a private. A shell hit his lorry, and he was instantaneously killed.

April 30, 1915.—*****William Miller Major Gilliland,** Lieut., 1st Bn. Royal Inniskilling Fusiliers (S.H., 1909–12), who left Shrewsbury to go to Sandhurst. He went out to France at the very beginning of the War, was wounded and back in England within a week. As soon as his recovery was complete he was specially selected to go to Egypt with another battalion and was killed in the Dardanelles, aged 20.

July 13, 1916.—Killed in action, **Hugh Gerald Godber,** Temp. Capt. 15th (Service) Bn. (attached 12th (Service) Bn.) Northumberland Fusiliers ; aged 25. He was in the School House 1906-7, and was gazetted Temp. Capt. in the 15th Bn. 18 Jan., 1915.

Aug. 14, 1916.—Killed in action, aged 21. *****Donald Charles Goolden,** 2nd Lieut. 6th (S.R.) Bn. (attached 4th Bn.) Royal Fusiliers. A member of Haydon's 1909–14, he was a Præpostor, and enlisted at a Private in the Public Schools Bn. of the Royal Fusiliers, being gazetted to a commission in the 6th Bn., 14 April, 1915. He was killed by a shell while going up to the trenches near Guillemont.

July, 19-20, 1916.—**Norman Gough,* 2nd Lieut. (Temp. Lieut.), 7th (T.F.) Bn. Worcestershire Regt. At the School (T.E.P.), 1910-11, he joined the Worcestershire Territorials, his commission being dated 22 March, 1915, and fell in action.

August 14, 1915.—**Albyn Evan Powell Grant,* 2nd Lieut., 7th Royal Welch Fusiliers (A.F.C., 1908–12), who was in both the Cricket and Football Elevens. He left to take up Land Agency, was gazetted to a commission in the 7th R.W.F. (T.F.) and fell in action in the Dardanelles.

—.*Cyril Seaton Gray,* Lieut. Wilts Regt., died in hospital abroad from wounds received in action. He was at Shrewsbury (S.H.) 1909–12, and shot twice for his School at Bisley in 1911 and 1912. On the outbreak of war he enlisted in the Shropshire L.I., received his commission in the Wilts Regt. in Nov., 1914, and went to the front in March, 1915.

September 20, 1915.—*William Stewart Mial Green,* Lieut.-Commander, Royal Naval Division (E.B.M., 1897–8). Invalided home from the Dardanelles, he died on board the Hospital Ship, *Aquitania.*

June 28, 1916, aged 26.—**Edward Maurice Gregson,* Lieut. (Temp. Capt.) 4th (T.F.) Bn. Loyal North Lancs. Regt. At Shrewsbury (E.B.M.), 1903-6, he left to become a Surveyor and Mining Engineer, and, when the War broke out, was an Associate of the Surveyor's Institution, and was reading for the Fellowship. Gazetted 2nd Lieut. April, 1914, Lieut., April, 1915, he was promoted Temp. Capt. in the following June, had been at the front since May, 1915, taking part in the fighting at Festubert in the next month, and met his death while leading a reconnaissance party near Rivière, below Arras, on the night of June 28.

August 16, 1915.—*Charles Grundy,* Private, Canadian Expeditionary Force (W.D.H., 1894-7), who after being Head of his House for a year, went up to New College, Oxon. He then studied Law and was admitted a Solicitor. About three years ago he emigrated to Kootenay, British Columbia, and in October, 1914, enlisted in Princess Patricia's Regt. He was killed near St. Julien, while on duty in the trenches, aged 37.

Oct. 9, 1916.—**Philip Norman Gordon,* Lieut. and Double Company Officer, 14th, King George's Own, Ferozepore Sikhs. He was in the School House, 1907-10, then went up to Sandhurst, and was gazetted Lieut. 11 Jan., 1914. He was killed at Kissengere, 70 miles south of Dar-es-Salaam. His O.C. wrote that " he behaved with the greatest gallantry, the magnificent manner in which he led his men over two lines of trenches, and then on to the final assault could not have been exceeded." In recognition of his skill and dash he was recommended for the Military Cross.

—, 1916.—***Donald Campbell Hair,** 2nd Lieut. 3rd (S.R.) Bn. K.S.L.I. ; in the School House 1910-15 ; gazetted 2nd Lieut. on probation, 7 July, 1916 ; killed by a shell on his first day in the trenches.

June 28, 1915.—***Arthur Frederic Halstead,** Temp. Lt., 15th (Service) Bn. Rifle Brigade, attached Royal Dublin Fusiliers (F.B.M. and F.T.P., 1908–12), aged 22. He left School to become a Chartered Accountant, enlisted in the Rifle Brigade in August, 1914, being promoted 2nd Lieut. and later Temp. Lieut. He was killed in action at the Dardanelles.

June 6, 1917.—**Harold Hamer,** Lieut. R.F.C., reported missing on June 6, is now reported killed on that date, in his 26th year. Was at Shrewsbury 1906-10, and enlisted in the Loyal North Lancashire Regt. in Aug., 1914, being shortly afterwards gazetted. In 1915 he transferred to the R.F.C., and saw active service in the Sudan, being engaged in the battle which resulted in the break up of the forces of the Sultan of Darfur. In the summer of 1916 he was at Salonika, but returned to England in Sept. He obtained his wings in 1917, and left for the front in May. He was killed while flying.

—, 1916.—**Archibald Hamilton Hamilton,** Temp. Capt. 13th (Service) Bn. (1st County Down) Royal Irish Rifles. At Shrewsbury (G.T.H.), 1891-3, he left to join the engineering works of Harland and Wolff at Belfast, and, after serving his apprenticeship, started in business himself. At the outbreak of the War he received his commission, was promoted Lieut. in 1914 and Capt. in 1915. Invalided home from the front, he died of an illness aggravated by his work in the trenches.

May 18, 1915.—***Norman Hammill,** Private, 30th Bn. Canadian Expeditionary Force (C.J.S.C., 1895–9), was in the Football XI. in 1897 and 1898. Some years ago he went out to farm in British Columbia, and in 1914 enlisted in the 88th Victoria (British Columbia) Fusiliers. being sent to the front on April 29, 1915. On arrival in France he was posted to the 16th Bn. Canadian Scottish, ordered straight up to the trenches, and was killed by shrapnel on May 18.

—, 1918, killed in action, **Gerald Learoyd Hammond-Fisher** (E.B.M. and F.T.P., 1910-1912), Temp. 2nd Lieut. The King's Liverpool Regt. (T.), attached to the Machine Gun Corps.

Nov. 10, 1917.—**Cecil Rochfort Harman** entered the School House in Sept., 1912, and left in July, 1914, for Sandhurst. He obtained a commission in the 1st Bn. Gloucestershire Regt. in April, 1917, and was serving with it when he was killed on Nov. 10, 1917. He was a Præpostor, and in the 1st Cricket and 2nd Football Elevens.

Dec. 1, 1917.—**Ralph Walter Hargreaves** entered Mr. Chance's House in Sept., 1905, leaving in July, 1910. He went to work in a tea merchant's office in London, and after about nine months there, sailed in Nov., 1911, to Colombo, where he became sub-manager of a tea estate. On the breaking out of the war he joined the Planters' Rifle Corps, and proceeded with the foreign service section to Gallipoli, where he gained a stripe. After the evacuation he was given a commission in Egypt. but joined the Welsh Guards in June, 1916. He was in command of a company when he was killed in action, Dec. 1, 1917.

July 10, 1916.—In action in France, aged 23, ***Brian Harrison,** Temp. 2nd Lieut. 14th (Service) Bn. Royal Welch Fusiliers, who was in Haydon's 1906-10, and then for some time in the L. & N.W. Rly. District Superintendent's Office at Liverpool, which he subsequently left to become a partner in the firm of Pollock & Co., Birmingham. He was gazetted to the 14th R.W.F. 28 Jan. 1915.

April 17, 1918.—**John German Harrison,** Capt. R.F.A., was dangerously wounded while in action on the Western Front, and died from gunshot wounds in the head, from which he did not regain consciousness. He was at Shrewsbury (w.d.h.) 1905--9, and subsequently studied music with the intention of following it as a career. When war broke out he was in America, but returned at the call of duty and joined the Inns of Court O.T.C. from which he obtained a commission in the R.F.A. He left for the Western front in February 1917, and was all through the fighting of that year, and up to the time of his death was in command of a heavy trench mortar battery. He was a good all-round sportsman and a fine oar, rowing in the crew, and being Captain of Boats. His only brother, Lieut. Brian Harrison fell while leading his men in the taking of Mametz Wood in the battle of the Somme in July, 1916.

.—**James Harold Hartley,** Lieut. Royal Munster Fusiliers, attached R.F.C., killed in action. At Shrewsbury (F.T.P.) 1912–15, he passed through Sandhurst into the Munster Fusiliers, and served with them some time on the Western Front. Then he joined the R.F.C. He was out with a squadron of seven British planes and encountered 28 Germans, and a chance shot struck him soon after the fight started, and killed him instantly.

Feb. —, 1917, killed in action, aged 34.—**Bernard Nowlan Harvey,** Private, Canadian Grenadier Guards, who was at the School (c.j.s.c.), 1899-1902.

Nov. 20, 1917.—**William Hereward Haseler,** Capt., who was killed in action near Cambrai, Nov. 20, 1917, came to Shrewsbury (C.J.B.) in Jan., 1906 and left in Dec., 1910. He was in the School Football XI. and a Præpostor. On leaving he matriculated at the Birmingham University and entered the firm of Buncher and Haseler, Birmingham. At the outbreak of war he enlisted without waiting for a commission in the Oxford and Bucks Light Infantry, but transferred to the Shropshire Light Infantry to be with his schoolfellows. Volunteering for motor cycle work, he was transferred to the Motor Machine Gun Corps. Going to France in Feb., 1915, his first engagement was at Hill 60, where the work of his battery was commended. He subsequently saw much fighting, including the second battle of Ypres. He was granted a commission in Dec., 1915, and afterwards was transferred to the Tank Corps and took his tank into action at Messines Ridge. He was promoted to a Lieutenancy and afterwards to a Captaincy. He was in the leading tank of his section, doing splendid work, when a shell struck the tank, killing him.

Nov. 10, 1917.—**Charles Stanley Haslam,** Lieut., Yeomanry, attached West Yorkshire Regt., killed when leading his men in a raid on Nov. 10, 1917, aged 36, was at Shrewsbury (F.E.B.) 1895-9, and rowed in the School crew. He received his commission in the Yorkshire Hussars in Aug., 1914, and went to France in the following April. For a few years before the war he had been farming in Yorkshire. He was a keen sportsman, for many years a member of the Cheshire Hunt, and latterly of the York and Ainsty.

January 25, 1915.—Killed in Action, *****William Leonard Ringrose Hatch,** Lieut. 2nd Batt. Royal Irish Fusiliers, elder son of *Lieut.-Colonel WILLIAM KEITH HATCH (O.S.), Indian Medical Service (retired), of Earlham Road, Norwich, aged 24.

Lieut. HATCH who was born in 1890, was at Shrewsbury 1904-7, obtained his Commission in 1911, and two years later was promoted Lieutenant. When the War broke out the Royal Irish Fusiliers were stationed in India, and he returned to Europe with his regiment to take part in it. From an interesting letter written by one of his brother officers, who was nearest to him when he fell, it appears that, while taking observations of the enemy from the trenches, Lieut. HATCH was first hit in the shoulder and disabled and then, a few hours later—

The next burst put a shell right in the trench. Some of the men had got along near him to try and move him at great risk just before, but he ordered them back, and was alone with one other man, a Private, who must have tried to get to him, when the next rounds commenced. Both must have been killed instantaneously. Five other men were buried with the falling parapet, but afterwards safely rescued. The men ordered back realize he saved their lives, for the shell burst before they could have moved him.

The foregoing extract is taken from *The Salopian* which, in a previous Number, said of him—

Those of us who recollect him as a member of the Army Class. . . . will feel sure that he died, as he lived, a sportsman, a gentleman, and a loyal Old Salopian.

Aug. 8, 1916.—**John Plunkett Verney Hawksley,** D.S.O., Major (Temp. Lt.-Col.) R.F.A., killed in action, aged 38. In the School House 1891-4, he went up to Woolwich, received his first commission in 1897, and saw service in the South African War, 1899-1902, taking part in the defence of Ladysmith and various operations in Natal, the Transvaal, the Orange River Colony, and Cape Colony. He was mentioned in dispatches, and received the Queen's Medal with five clasps, and the King's Medal with two clasps. For seven years from 1905 he was attached to the Egyptian Army, and for his services during the operations in Southern Kordofan in 1910 he received the Soudan Medal with clasp and the Order of Osmanieh (4th Class). For his services in the present war he had been mentioned in dispatches, and made a Companion of the Distinguished Service Order.

Oct. 6, 1917.—**Douglas Heald,** died of wounds on Oct. 6, 1917. He came to Mr. Chance's house in Jan., 1906, and won his Trial Star, in 1909. He was above all a strong runner and for any course. He became Gentleman of the Runs in 1907, Senior Whip in 1908 and Huntsman in 1900, and won the Junior Mile and Weight-for-Age in 1907, the Junior Steeplechase in 1908, the Two Miles, the Mile and the Middle Quarter in 1909, in which year he was also 2nd in the Half-Mile. After leaving Shrewsbury at the end of that year he spent two years in the office of a firm of rubber-merchants in Liverpool, and in that period developed into a first-class golfer, carrying off the Captain's prize at the Ormskirk Club. In 1911 he accepted a position offered to him by Morrison & Co., rice-brokers in Rangoon ; here he returned to the recreation he loved best at School, was a prominent member of the Rangoon Boat Club, and won several prizes at the Boat Club's Regattas. Commenting on one of these events, the *Rangoon Times* expressed the opinion that " he was the best stroke that had ever been seen on the Lakes."..In the spring of 1916 he returned home, offered his services to the War Office, was accepted for a commission as he had had several years' experience as a Private in the Rangoon Volunteer Rifles, was gazetted in April, 1917, to the 6th Bn. Rifle Brigade and transferred to the 1st Bn. in France.

Jan. 4, 1917.—*Philip Ralph Heaton, D.C.M., 2nd Lieut. 1st Bn. 2nd African Rifles, British East Africa. He was in Churchill's 1906-11, and then settled at Naivasha, B.E.A. Before getting his commission, he saw much fighting as a trooper in Bowker's Horse, winning the *D.C.M.* in the first Longido fight. He died from an accidental wound at Kilwa, B.E.A.

April 10, 1917.—On the 10th April, 1917, at Homestead, Queen's Park, Bournemouth, **Frederick Thomas Henstock,** Col., late West India and West African Regts ; aged 56. He was at Shrewsbury (s.h.) 1877–9, a member of the 1st Cricket XI., and the 2nd Football and would have rowed Bow of the School Crew in 1878 and 1879 had there been a race. Col. Henstock entered Sandhurst in 1884, and passing out first, after gaining the Sword of Honour, was gazetted to a commission in the 2nd West Indian Regt. in 1886. He took part in the expedition against King Prempeh of Ashanti in 1895. Two years later he passed the Staff College and in 1900 he was appointed Staff Captain at Sierra Leone, and joined the expedition receiving the medal with clasp and the brevet of Lieut.-Colonel. In 1901 he was presented with a testimonial by the Cape Coast Chamber of Commerce in recognition of his services in suppressing a mutiny in the West African Regt. at Cape Coast Castle ; and from 1901 to 1905 he held the position of commandant of the West African Regt. In 1907 he was appointed a General Staff officer, first grade, and as such served in Cape Colony, but resigned the appointment in 1908, and shortly afterwards retired on a pension. In 1914, however, he rejoined for service on the outbreak of war, and was appointed as General Staff officer, first grade, to the Plymouth defences. Col. Henstock was invalided in May, 1915, but was reappointed in Sept. as A.A. and Q.M.G. In 1916 he was appointed A.A.G. at Aldershot, but was unable to take up the appointment on account of further illness which terminated with his death.

Nov. 9, 1918.—**William Hepton, Lieut.** 5th Dragoon Guards (e.b.m. 1899–1903), died on active service. Though a neat and taking oar he failed to reach the School Eight but had the honour of rowing in his House Four at the head of the river in 1902 and 1903, and in the latter year he obtained his Trial Eight Star. In the same two years he helped his House to win the Sports Cup, contributing as his quota the Senior High Jump and Senior 100 Yards. On leaving School he proceeded to Oriel College, Oxford, and thence, after taking his degree, into business. Yorkshire born and bred, he had all the true Yorkshireman's love of a horse, and so, on the outbreak of hostilities with Germany, he selected the Cavalry as his arm of the Service. Joining first of all the Yorkshire Hussars Yeomanry (Foreign Service Section), he was soon promoted Sergeant. Then he obtained a commission in the Reserve Cavalry attached to the Dragoon Guards and served with that regiment in France. He passed safely through all the perils of actual warfare only to fall a victim while on active service abroad to influenza on November 9, 1918, two days before the Armistice was signed and when fighting was practically over.

June 14, 1915.—*Cyril Gordon Reuss Hibbert, Capt., 4th Bn. Loyal North Lancs. Regt. (T.F.), (A.F.C., 1902-5), joined the Territorials immediately on leaving school, and was killed at Festubert in Flanders in a reconnaissance in force.

August 28, 1915, aged 34.—Thomas Halghton Trevor Hickman, Rifleman, Auckland (New Zealand) Mounted Rifles, who was at Shrewsbury as a Day-boy, 1893-8, and was admitted a Solicitor, 1905. For some time he practised in Shrewsbury, but about four years ago emigrated to New Zealand. He came over to Egypt with the first overseas contingent, and was killed in action in Gallipoli.

June 24th, 1915.—*Harold Lea Higgins, Private, 10th (Scottish) Bn. King's Liverpool Regt. (T.F.) (F.M.I., 1909-11). He was wounded in the famous charge of the Liverpool Scottish at Hooge, and died in hospital at Boulogne eight days later.

Oct. 3, 1918.—Killed in action on Oct. 3, Frederick Wystan Hipkins, Capt. The Sherwood Foresters, only son of the late Rev. F. C. HIPKINS (O.S.), Assistant-Master, House Master and Bursar of Repton School. He was at Shrewsbury (C.J.S.C.) 1899–1904, and a member of the School Shooting VIII. In practice as an architect at Sheffield when the war broke out, he at once enlisted as a private in the 12th (Service) Batt. (City of Sheffield) York and Lancaster Regt., and was gazetted 2nd Lieut. in the 6th (T.F.) Batt. Sherwood Foresters on July 2, 1915. He had been three years on active service at the front in France, and was awarded the *M.C.* after his death. He fell on Oct. 3 in the capture of Bellenglise. His battalion the 6th Sherwood Foresters, formed part of the famous 46th Division which had won undying laurels a few days before in the great series of attacks on the German positions north of St. Quentin ; and in the decisive action by which the Nord Canal was carried on Sept. 29, Captain Hipkins did some magnificent work which received official recognition after his career was so unhappily cut short a few days later. He met his death while attempting to secure a nest of 20 machine guns which by their fire were grievously hampering the advance of our troops at that point.

March 26, 1918.—Lieut.-Col. Philip Vaughan Holberton fell in action on March 26, aged 38. He was at Shrewsbury (D.B.) 1893-8, was Killing Hound, played in the Football XI., and would have rowed in the School crew had he not been prevented by examinations. He went up to Sandhurst, where he won the Sword of Honour presented by Queen Victoria. He joined his regiment, the 2nd Manchesters, in South Africa, where he was slightly wounded receiving the King's Medal with two clasps and Queen's with five. He held various appointments, including the Adjutancy of the West

African Regiment, and when war broke out was adjutant to the
6th Manchester Regt. (T.F.). He proceeded with his battalion to
Gallipoli and fought gallantly all through that campaign, afterwards
being appointed G.S.O. and Brigade Major. In October, 1916, he
was given command of a Lancs. Fusiliers Bn., with whom he was
serving at the time of his death. Col. HOLBERTON was four times
mentioned in despatches, receiving his brevet majority in 1915, his
brevet lieut.-colonelcy and a Serbian decoration in 1917, and
was on the waiting list for a brigade.

Oct. 4. 1916. Died of wounds received in action.—**Eustace
Addison Holt,** Lance-Corp., 10th (T.F.) Bn. King's Liverpool Regt.
He was a Day-Boy (1899-1902) and on leaving school served for
four years as pupil with a Liverpool shipping firm, by whom he was
afterwards appointed to a post, which took him to Spain for the next
five years of his life. He then received an appointment under the
Pacific Steam Navigation Co., in whose service he was employed
until, in May, 1915, he enlisted as a private in the Liverpool (Scottish)
Regt.

Jan. 15, 1918.—**Arthur Anthony Howell,** *T.D.*, *C.M.G.*, Brig.-
Gen., Commanding the London Reserve Brigade, died suddenly
at Aldershot, aged 56. He served with the C.I.V.'s in the South
African War, and also saw active service in the present war between
1914 and 1916, was three times mentioned in despatches, and made
C.M.G. in 1915. Col. Howell was then gazetted Brigadier-General
in command of the 1st London (Reserve) Infantry Brigade, and had
the Order of St. Anne presented to him by the Czar of Russia. He
was at Shrewsbury (C.J.S.C.) 1876-8, and at the London Hospital
(*M.R.C.S.*, 1886 ; *L.R.C.P.*, 1891).

December 30, 1915.—**Cecil Barton Hudson-Kinahan,** Lieut.,
4th King's African Rifles, aged 32 (F.E.B., 1897-1900). In 1902 he
joined the 4th Royal Munster Fusiliers (Militia) as 2nd Lieut,. but
after two years' service went out to British East Africa, where he
engaged in rubber and cocoanut planting. When war broke out he
obtained a commission in the African Rifles, took part in several
engagements with the enemy, and died in hospital in B.E.A., of
fever contracted while on active service.

June 28, 1915.—*Christopher Tatham Devy Hughes,** Private,
5th (Service) Bn. King's Shropshire L.I. (C.J.B., 1909-13), stroke of
the School VIII in 1912 and 1913. He enlisted in the K.S.L.I. with
so many of his schoolfellows in September, 1914, and died in hospital
in France from shell wounds received a few days previously.

Oct. 17, 1918.—Suddenly at a nursing home, Shrewsbury, **Joshua Bower Hughes-Games,** *M.C.*, late Capt. Durham Light Infantry, aged 30, who had been temporarily on the teaching staff at Shrewsbury. Capt. HUGHES-GAMES had been twice wounded in France and gassed, and was in hospital for 20 months, from which he had only just returned to school work, and died as much from his wounds as from influenza. He was at Shrewsbury (S.H.) 1902–7, and was head boy in 1907, leaving as a scholar of Queens' College, Cambridge. He was gazetted Temp. Captain in the 18th (Service) Batt. (1st County) Durham, L.I. on Oct. 4, 1914, and did some brilliant work in the Eastern Campaign, where he gained his M.C. Before the war he was an Assist. Master at the Forest School.

Oct. —, 1918.—**James Malcolm Inglis,** 2nd Lieut. (A.F.C. 1913–17), killed in action.

.—**Arthur Keedwell Harvey James** (A.F.C. 1888), Lieut. 9th (Service) Bn. the Buffs (East Kent Regt.), killed in action.

September 28, 1915.—**Charles Edward James,** Private 13th (Service) Bn. Middlesex Regt. (S.H., 1900), eldest son of the Rev. *C. H. JAMES (O.S.), Haigh Vicarage, Lancs. On leaving he entered upon a business career, and was for some time in Paris and later in the branch of the Credit Lyonnais at Valencia, in Spain, subsequently representing a Manchester firm in Brazil. This post he resigned and enlisted early in Oct., 1914, refusing to apply for a commission because, as he said, " he knew nothing about the job, so would go and learn it." As he spoke French, Spanish, and Portuguese fluently, and also knew German, he was attached to the Brigade Intelligence Department in France (whither he had gone on Sept. 1), and was killed in a front trench near Loos during some hard fighting less than a month afterwards, aged 31. Two of his brothers had previously fallen in Gallipoli, but they were not at Shrewsbury.

July 1, 1916.—Reported missing July 1, 1916, now reported killed on that date, **Robert Salisbury Jeffcock,** Lieut. South Staffordshire Regt., aged 38 (C.J.S.C., 1890-4). He was an artist by profession.

June 4, 1915.—**John William Jessop,** Lieut.-Col., 4th Bn. Lincolnshire Regt. (T.F.), aged 55. He was at Shrewsbury (Doctor's) 1877-9, stroked what would have been the School crew, had there been a race, in 1878 and 1879 ; won the School Pairs ; was in the Football XI ; and won the Up-river Swimming Cup three years in succession ; being also in the 2nd Cricket XI. He left to study medicine at St. Bartholomew's Hospital, London, where he was in the Rugby XV, and also played for the South of England XV against the North. He had for many years a medical practice at

Horncastle, and went out to France in command of the 1/4 Lincolns. He was killed by a stray shell " from a distant and random gun that the foe was sullenly firing," while in a Rest Camp far behind the lines.

July 4, 1918.—**Gilbert Ernest Johnson,** Capt. Army Cyclist Corps, was drowned in Lake Garda, Italy, in attempting to rescue a comrade. He was at Shrewsbury (D.B.) 1902-7, and a Præpostor. On leaving he entered Birmingham University, where he graduated B.Sc. and M.Sc., and was placed on the staff as Protozoologist. He obtained a Board of Agriculture biological research Scholarship, under the terms of which he worked for a time at the Kaiserliche Biologische Anstalt at Dahlem, near Berlin. He joined the Army in September, 1914, as a private in the Birmingham (University) Batt. Royal Warwickshire Regt., being promoted Temp. 2nd Lieut. May, 1915, and transferring to the Cyclist Corps in the following October. He served on the Somme and in Flanders, for which he was mentioned in despatches, and was awarded the Croix de Guerre. He went to Italy with the first contingent of British troops in November, 1917.

Sept. 7, 1916.—*****John Johnstone,** Temp. Capt. 7th (Service) Bn. Leinster Regt. Killed at Guillemont, aged 27. At Shrewsbury (C.J.S.C.), 1902-6, he enlisted in the Norfolk Regt. in Aug. 1914, was given a commission in the Leinsters in Oct., 1915, and was promoted Capt. in April, 1916. His devotion to duty and great gallantry on June 26, 1916, were ordered to be entered in the records of the Irish Division.

May, 1916.—*****Edward Pitcairn Jones,** 2nd Lieut. Rifle Brigade, died of wounds received in action. He was in the School House, 1910-15, and won an Exhibition at Oriel College, Oxford.

April —, 1918.—**Eustace Gabriel Lawrence Keatinge,** Lieut., Northumberland Fusiliers, attached Durham L.I., fell in action in the attack on Zeebrugge and Ostend, aged 26. He got a commission in the 5th Batt. (S.R.) Northumberland Fusiliers soon after the outbreak of war, and was wounded in 1915, near Ypres. He was at Shrewsbury (A.F.C. and D.B.) 1906-11, and Keble College, Oxford, where he took his B.A. degree with honours in 1914. He rowed in his School and College Eights, and won the Oxford High Jump, representing his University in that event against Cambridge.

.—**Edward Hext Kendall,** Flight Sub-Lieut., R.N. while at Shrewsbury won the School quarter-mile swimming race. He went to Salonika with the Duke of Cornwall's L.I. Regt., from which he was invalided home, and on recovery joined the R.N.A.S., and had only been eight days at the front. When flying at a height of 13,000 feet he was attacked by an enemy machine, had his petrol tank fired, and was killed.

September 25, 1915.—*Anthony Walter Brook Kitchin, 2nd Lieut., 7th (Service) Bn. Royal West Surrey Regt. (s.h., 1910-14) son of *Brook Taylor Kitchin (O.S.). He enlisted in the Public School Bn. of the Royal Fusiliers, and served in the ranks till January, 1915. He was then gazetted to the Royal West Surreys, went to the front with them in July, being in charge of a machine gun, and was killed in action in France, aged 18.

Aug. 18, 1916.—*John Lyndon Knowles, 2nd Lieut. 5th (S.R.) Bn. Rifle Brigade, killed in action, aged 19. He was in the School House 1911-15, and obtained a commission in the Rifle Brigade, 15 Sept., 1915. He was Junior Whip, and rowed in his House Boat.

Sept. 14, 1918.—Gerald William Lancaster, *M.C.*, Capt. Monmouthshire Regt., attached Welsh Regt., who died on Sept. 14 of wounds received in action on Aug. 27, aged 29, was at Shrewsbury (c.j.s.c.) 1902-6. In September, 1914, he obtained a commission in the Monmouthshire Regt., and was dangerously wounded in March, 1915, during the mining of Hill 60. He went out again to the front in Oct., 1917, was attached to the Welsh Regt., and wounded for the second time in April, 1918.

May –, 1915.—James Lancaster, Capt., 3rd Bn. Monmouthshire Regt. (T.F.) (c.j.s.c., 1893–6), after travelling in America, became a mining engineer. He was gazetted 2nd Lieut. Oct. 16, 1914, and gained rapid promotion. He was killed in action near Ypres.

August 10, 1915.—*Denis Digges La Touche, Capt., 8th (Service) Bn. Welsh Regt., son of T. H. D. La Touche (O.S.), at the Schools (f.m.i.) 1909-14, a Præpostor, Capt. of the Shooting VIII three years, Huntsman and good cross-country runner. He had won a Scholarship at C.C.C. Cambridge, but enlisted as a private in the 5th K.S.L.I., in which he was promoted 2nd Lieut. He was soon transferred to the 8th Welsh, became Capt. in February, 1915, and sailed for the Dardanelles in the summer, where he was killed after the landing at Anavarta : he was reported missing (later presumed killed) after the attack on Chanok Bair.

March 6, 1917, killed in action, aged 25.—*Francis John Graham Leadbitter, 2nd Lieut. King's Royal Rifles, who was at Shrewsbury (e.b.m.), 1895–9, and rowed Bow of the crew. He had been a most regular and valued member of the Executive Committee of the O.S. Club for some years, and was greatly respected by all his colleagues.

He rowed in the Thames R.C. VIII. at Henley, and in the O.S.R.C. crew ; and was admitted a Solicitor in 1904. Enlisting in the Inns of Court O.T.C. in December, 1915, he obtained his commission in December, 1916, and went out to the front a month later.

Sept. 30, 1918.—**Robert Edward Holt Leech,** (C.J.B., 1911-16), after a period of training with the Inns of Court, was given a commission in the 4th King's Shropshire Light Infantry, and from the spring to the autumn of 1918 was engaged in the battles on the Southern front of the Line in France. During the critical engagements in the Champagne he was with his battalion (1/4th K.S.L.I.) when, for its splendid fighting qualities and successes, it was awarded the Croix de Guerre with Palm leaf.

Oct. —, 1918.—**Richard Walter Leedam,** Private Canadian Expeditionary Force, killed in action, was at the School (C.J.B. and S.H.) 1900-4.

Sept. 24, 1918.—**John Dunning Gaunt Lewis,** Capt. 3rd (S.R.) Batt. K.S.L.I., killed on Sept. 24, aged 26, was at Shrewsbury (S.H. and D.B.) 1908-11, being in the Cricket XI., and a good fast left-handed bowler ; he then went out to a sugar plantation at Water Valley, Albany, Jamaica. Returning home, he obtained his commission in March, 1915, went to Gallipoli the same year with the North Staffordshire Regt., and was there at the time of evacuation of Suvla Bay and Cape Helles. With the same regiment he went to Mesopotamia, where he was severely wounded in the lung, during one of the attempts to relieve Kut. After his convalescence he served with his own regiment at Pembroke Dock and in Ireland, going out to France in Nov., 1915, to the 2nd Batt., and falling whilst leading his company into action.

Sept. 17th, 1917.—**Nevill Graham Newcome Hart Lewis,** Capt., entered the School as a member of Mr. Sergeant's House in 1907, and left at Christmas, 1910. He served with a commission during the war, first in the Monmouthshire Regiment, but was subsequently attached to the Royal Sussex at the front, and was killed in France, on the Menin Road.

March 22nd, 1918—**Frank Darley Livingstone,** *M.C.,* Temp. Capt., R.A.S.C. (E.B.M., 1900-4). He was a Scholar of Peterhouse, Cambridge, President of the Cambridge Union., and one of the most brilliant of recent Salopians. On leaving the University he studied for the Bar: his ambition was ultimately to enter Parliament and all who knew him predicted for him a distinguished career. Then came the War : never athletic in his tastes, a man of letters rather than of action, he overcame all difficulties, and showed qualities which are thus recorded by the Adjutant of his Corps: " a man of sterling value, and of such cheerful, virile, energetic disposition that we feel lost without him. He had the great gift of obtaining the love and devotion of those serving under him: both N.C.O.'s and men are broken-hearted at his loss."

February 22, 1915.—**Gilbert Kingsley Lloyd** (s.h., 1894-9), served through the South African War with the Shropshire I.Y. as Lance-Corp. in charge of a machine-gun (Medal with 3 clasps). He was gazetted 2nd Lieut. 2nd Bn. K.S.L.I., and saw much fighting in France. He died of disease while serving at Salonika, aged 36.

Oct. 17, 1916, in action, aged 21.—*****Kelyth Pierce Lloyd-Williams,** Temp. 2nd Lieut. 11th (Service) Bn. Welsh Regt., at Shrewsbury (s.h.) 1909-14. He went up to Clare College, Cambridge, where he served in the O.T.C. until commissioned, 26 Feb., 1915.

June 28, 1915.—**George Eimer Locket,** 2nd Lieut., 1st Bn. Suffolk Regt. (s.h., 1905-7), He studied engineering at the Central Technical College, South Kensington, joined the Public School Bn., was gazetted 2nd Lieut. in the 3rd Suffolks in October, 1914, was drafted out to France in May, 1915, and attached to the 1st Bn. as Signalling Officer.

Aug. —, 1916.—*****Eustace Counsellor Longworth,** Temp. Capt. 9th (Service) Bn. Lancashire Fusiliers, instantaneously killed in the capture of a German trench at Thiepval. At Shrewsbury (e.b.m.) 1904-8. He was a Præpostor and rowed Bow of the School crew. He took his degree from King's College, Cambridge, and then entered his father's business as a Cotton Manufacturer. Enlisting in the P.S. Bn. Royal Fusiliers, he received his 2nd Lieutenancy in the 13th Lancs. Fusiliers in Oct., 1914, being promoted full Lieut. in Feb., 1915. In Sept., 1915, he went out to Gallipoli attached to the 9th Bn., and was present at all the actions at Suvla Bay till the evacuation. He was promoted Captain 6th Sept., 1915, and went to France in July, 1916.

April 20, 1916, shot by a sniper in France.—*****Richard Arthur Maurice Lutener,** Temp. 2nd Lieut. 6th (Service) Bn. K.S.L.I., who was in the School House 1904-14, and then went up to Keble College, Oxford. He obtained his commission in December, 1914, and went out to the front in July, 1915.

April 25, 1918.—**Horace Macaulay,** Lieut. Seaforth Highlanders, killed at Wytschaete on April 25, aged 23, was at Shrewsbury (f.m.i.) 1910-12. He joined the H.A.C. on the outbreak of war, and was gazetted into the Seaforth Highlanders in September, 1915.

July 2, 1916.—**Reginald Squarey MacIver,** 2nd Lieut. Lancs. Fusiliers, aged 24. At Shrewsbury (E.B.M.) 1906-11. He left as a Præpostor with a Science Scholarship at Christ Church, Oxon. He rowed in his college boat at Henley in 1913 and 1914, and was a member of the Leander Club. He left Oxford to take a commission in August, 1914, in the 4th (S.R.) Bn. Lancs. Fusiliers ; was promoted Lieut. on March, 1915, transferred to the Regular Bn. as 2nd Lieut. from 15 Feb., 1915, and had been at the front since May last year.

May 12, 1915.—*****John Aquila MacMahon,** Lieut., R.A.M.C. (A.F.C., 1903-7). He went up to Trinity College, Dublin, taking his *B.A.* in 1912 and *M.B.* in 1913. While in residence he acted as Local Secretary of the O.S.C., played (centre forward) for the University Hockey Team (being Vice-Capt. of the Club), for the University Lawn Tennis Team, and also frequently for the Association Football XI. (as goalkeeper). MacMahon possessed exceptional gifts as an actor, and amateur humorous singer and reciter, and was a valued member of the University Dramatic Society. Joining the R.A.M.C. he was sent to a Field Ambulance, at Armentières in October, 1914, on March 17, 1915, was attached to the Somerset L.I., and while serving with the Regt. was wounded at Ypres on April 29, and died from his injuries on May 12.

—Died on active service, **Cecil Richard Maddox,** Capt. and Quartermaster 63rd Palamcottah Light Infantry, Indian Army, (S.H. 1901).

August 26, 1914.—Killed in action at Le Cateau, France, *****Wilmsdorff George Mansergh,** Lieut. the Manchester Regiment, aged 34, who was at Shrewsbury 1895-6. He obtained a Commission in the Militia Battalion of the Manchester Regiment, and was employed in the South African War, taking part in the operations in the Transvaal and Orange River Colony, including the action at Wittebergen. He received the Queen's Medal with three Clasps and the King's Medal with two Clasps, and, in 1901, his Commission as 2nd Lieut. in the Manchester Regiment. He was promoted Lieutenant in 1903, and seconded for service, under the Colonial Office, with the West African Field Force, in which he held local rank as Captain. When the War broke out he re-joined the Manchesters and proceeded to the Front.

In the battle at Le Cateau, after being himself wounded, Lieut. Mansergh gallantly met his end when giving shelter at the risk of his own life, to another wounded man. The manner of his death was thus graphically described by another Old Salopian—R. T. Miller, 2nd Lieut. in his regiment—who was also present and severely wounded in the right leg in the same engagement but happily survived (mentioned in Despatches), and whose account was published in *The Salopian*—

I am sorry to have to record the death of one Salopian. It is W. G. MANSERGH, at the time of the battle a Lieutenant in the Manchesters. He was advancing quite near me when he got hit in the leg and could not get further. He had chanced to fall near an enemy trench and managed to crawl into this, where he was comparatively safe. But shortly after a soldier, also in the regiment, crawled up to the same trench, whereupon MANSERGH pulled him in, and got the fellow underneath him—it was a short " two-man " trench for kneeling. MANSERGH was now exposed to shrapnel, though still protected by the trench-parapet from rifle fire. You will guess what happened : a shell burst just in front of the trench, quite low down. MANSERGH was killed on the spot.

Jan. 9. 1918.—Lieut. **Roger Charles Marshall,** who died of wounds on 9th January, 1918, was the only son of the late Rev. F. C. Marshall (O.S.), of Doddington Rectory, Cambs. He came to Shrewsbury in 1903 (School House). On leaving in July, 1907, he went to Pembroke College, Cambridge. At the time of his death he was a Lieutenant in the R.F.A.

April 14, 1916, of wounds received in action.—*Arnold Mathews, Temp. Lieut. 14th (Service) Bn. Cheshire Regt. At Shrewsbury (C.J.B.) 1908-13, he was Huntsman, and in the Football XI. and was one of the best runners the School has had in recent years, excelling in long distances and in cross-country races. He went up to Corpus Christi College, Cambridge, with a Science Scholarship, and in Sept., 1914, with many other O.SS. enlisted in the ranks of the 5th (Service) Bn. K.S.L.I. After a few weeks he obtained a commission in the 14th Cheshires, and was made full Lieut. 18th Dec., 1914. In Nov., 1915, he left for the Dardanelles, but before he arrived the evacuation was ordered, and he was sent to Mesopotamia. He took part in the fighting on the Tigris front on April 5th and 9th, in the latter receiving wounds, from the effects of which he died five days later.

Nov. 15, 1918.—**Geoffrey Lamb Maule,** Capt., R.A.M.C., who died from pneumonia at Baghdad on Nov. 15, aged 26, was at Shrewsbury (W.D.H.) 1906-9, and Christ's College, Cambridge, where he took his M.B. degree. He was a M.R.C.S. (Eng.) and L.R.C.P. (Lond.), and for two years before joining the Army in 1916 was house surgeon at Manchester Infirmary.

Oct. —, 1918.—**Lawson Tait McClintock,** Capt., died from pneumonia following influenza. Dr. McClintock was at Shrewsbury, (G.T.H.) 1893–5, and Edinburgh, where he took the M.B. and Ch.B. degrees at the University. He came to London in 1902, and was appointed Medical Officer of Health for the Loddon and Clavering Rural District Council and Medical Officer to the Loddon and Clavering Union Workhouse in the year 1910, and he held other local appointments with an extensive private practice. On the outbreak of war he organised the Loddon Red Cross Hospital, of which he was medical officer, and was in 1917 appointed R.R.C. Medical Officer, with the rank of Captain. He coxed the School Crew for two years.

Aug. —, 1916.—*George McConnan, 2nd Lieut. and Temp. Capt. 10th (Scottish) Bn. (T.F.) King's Liverpool Regt. At Shrewsbury (G.T.H. and W.D.H.) 1900–1, he left for business in 1914 ; enlisted as a private in the Liverpool Scottish Territorials and was promoted 2nd Lieut., 18 March, 1915, after having served in the ranks in France for some months. Invalided home in 1916, he was made Temp. Capt. 18 Feb., 1916. He went out again to the front as Lieut. at the end of July, 1916, and was killed early in August.

March 21, 1918,—Maurice Anderdon McFerran, M.C., 2nd Lieut. Royal Irish Rifles, who was killed on March 21, near St. Quentin on the first day of the big attack, was at Shrewsbury (S.H.) 1911-15, and was gazetted to the Royal Irish Rifles in Sept. 1916. He went to the front in Jan., 1917, and took part in much of the fighting during that year, being present at Messines Ridge, the Third Battle of Ypres, and at Cambrai, being awarded the Military Cross after the last. He was killed instantly by a shell while acting as scout-officer.

July 1, 1915, aged 26.—*Edward Guy Melland, Lieut., 8th Bn. Cheshire Regt. (A.F.C., 1904–8), went up to New College, Oxon., where he took a 2nd Class in Lit. Hum. in 1911. He was gazetted as an Ex-Cadet of the Oxford O.T.C. as Temp. 2nd Lieut. in the Cheshires on August 22, and was posted to the 1st West Yorkshire Regt. in October, in order to go to the front. He was shot by a sniper in Flanders.

July 18, 1916.—*Henry Robert Miles, Temp. 2nd Lieut. 6th (Service) Bn. Connaught Rangers, killed in action, aged 50. He was in the School House, 1883-5, in the Football XI, and Captain of the Cricket XI. Going up to Pembroke College, Cambridge, he was in both teams at his College. On taking his degree MILES was for a short time an assistant Master at Dulwich, then he went out to the Argentine, subsequently going into business at Saskatchewan, Canada, but returned to settle in England. Though 49 when the War broke out he joined the Bristol O.T.C., and applied for a commission. Refused on account of his age, he enlisted in the Sportsman's Bn. in Dec., 1914, and was eventually gazetted 2nd Lieut. in the Connaughts, on 18 Aug., 1915. His Colonel wrote " I know no one who was so universally popular—always the same, always cheerful and devoted to duty. Had he lived he would very shortly have been gazetted captain. He was a most excellent officer, and losing him is a great loss to the Regiment and to the country. It is small comfort, but it is true, that he had done more than one man's share in bringing us to victory."

1918.—**Tom Illingworth Mitchell,** Major Middlesex Regt. killed in action (s.h., 1898–1902), joined the 16th (Service) Battn. Duke of Cambridge's Own, Middlesex Regt., but, on being wounded, was, on Nov. 13, 1915, transferred to a Temporary Captaincy in the 24th Reserve Service Battn. When again passed for general service he was attached to the Line Battn. of the regiment with which he was serving when he fell.

July, 1918.—*James Adolph Moir, Lieut. R.A.F.

May 4, 1916.—**David Henry Carmichael Monro,** Lieut. Canadian Infantry, died of wounds. He was at Shrewsbury (s.h.), 1899–1903, and then at Oriel College, Oxford ; was called to the Bar in Lincoln's Inn, and obtained an appointment in the Nigerian Civil Service, in which he remained three years, and left owing to ill-health. He went out to Canada, and joined the Canadian Army early in Sept., 1914, when he was given a commission. He came to England in May, 1915, with his regiment, and went with it to the front on Sept. 17 the same year.

July 1, 1916.—*Richard Moore, 2nd Lieut. 6th West Yorks. (T.F.), aged 19, killed in action, after serving in France since April, 1916, his commission being dated 31 Aug., 1915. He was in the School House, 1911–15, Secretary of the Boat Club, and a Gentleman of the Runs.

Jan. 28, 1918.—Killed by a bomb in an air raid on London, on Jan. 28, 1918, the Rev. **Edward Henry Mosse,** *M.A.*, who was at Shrewsbury (D.B.) 1870–5, and Christ's College, Cambridge (*B.A.*, 1879). He was Vicar of Woburn Sands 1884–99, and of St. Paul's, Covent Garden, since that date.

March 3rd, 1918.—Died in hospital in London from pneumonia after influenza, **Cecil Mountford,** Lieut. Royal Army Service Corps. Mechanical Transport, who had served in the Balkans and in France. He was at the School (F.S.) 1906–8, and in the Cricket XI.

Oct. 12, 1916..—At a casualty clearing station, *John Kingsford Mylius, 2nd Lieut. King's Shropshire Light Infantry, aged 21. He was at Shrewsbury (s.h.) 1910–14, and after passing through the Royal Military College, Sandhurst, was gazetted to the K.S.L.I. in May, 1915, and was sent to the front at once. He had been twice wounded, and was mentioned in despatches.

June —, 1918.—**Trafford Nadin,** Capt. 5th Sherwood Foresters (T.F.), died from pneumonia after wounds received in action on the Western Front. Coming to the School (E.B.M.) in the Michaelmas Term of 1891, he achieved between that date and the Summer of 1896, when he left, a great reputation both as an oarsman and as an athlete. The son of an old Rowing Blue, he took to the water naturally, was three years in the crew, won the Sculls and the Challenge Oars and finally stroked his House Head of the River for the first time in 1896. Going on to Pembroke College, Cambridge, he stroked them from the bow side very successfully, rowed in the 'Varsity Trials and subsequently in an excellent crew, hailing from Burton-on-Trent, with which he won the Wyfolds in record time. As a runner he won many athletic prizes, and finally became Huntsman. By profession he was a Solicitor at Derby.

Sept. 18, 1918.—**Frank Shirley Nalder** (S.H. and J.B.O., 1910-14), reported wounded and missing in the last week of the Salonika operations, is now believed to have been killed on Sept. 18, while leading his company in an attack. He was Choregus and first Head of Oldham's. About to go up to Christ Church, Oxford, when hostilities broke out, he joined the K.S.L.I., being gazetted to the 8th (Service) Batt., with which he went to out France, and thence to Salonika. Invalided home with malaria, he was 18 months in England, and went out again in June, 1918.

—Missing, believed drowned : **Richard Owen Nelson,** Capt. R.A.S.C. (Mechanical Transport), was at the School (A.F.C.), 1901-4, and was a Carpet Manufacturer at Kendal, Westmorland.

September 11, 1915, aged 20.—*****Thomas Arthur Nevett,** Corporal, 5th (Service) Bn. K.S.L.I. (W.S.I.) 1911-13, left at Christmas, 1913, to take up farming, and joined the Army in September, 1914. He was offered a commission, but declined it in order to stay with his fellow O.SS. For three months he was at the front with the machine gun section ; was very seriously wounded at Hooge on August 8 ; was brought to the Edmonton Military Hospital, and died there after terrible suffering heroically borne.

—**Walter Adams Nicholson,** Lieut.-Col.,R. F.A., killedin action ; was at Shrewsbury (G.T.H.) 1883-4, and the R,M.A., Woolwich. He served in the South African War, receiving the Queen's Medal with four clasps. In 1904 he was promoted Major, and commanded a battery in Egypt, afterwards going to India, where he served until he retired in 1909 with rank of Major. He rejoined immediately on outbreak of the present war, and in Feb., 1915, took a battery out to France. He was wounded at the second battle of

Ypres, and after recovering he was made temporary Lieut.-Col., and given conmmad of a Brigade R.F.A., which he took to the front in August, 1915, and was still commanding when killed.

August 25, 1915.—*William Forbes Norris, (A.F.C.), 1907-12, Lieut. 5th Bn. Norfolk Regt. (T.F.), Cyclist Co. He was in his House Boat and an Editor of *The Salopian.* Going up to Trinity College, Cambridge, he took Honours in Part I. of the History Tripos, and having enlisted in the ranks on the outbreak of the war, obtained a commission as 2nd Lieut., and was promoted Lieut. December 1, 1914. In April he was seconded to the 54th Divisional Cyclist Co., and went out with them to the Dardanelles, where he fell in action.

August 9th, 1915.—Francis Brendon Ely O'Carroll, Temp. 2nd Lt., 6th Bn. Royal Dublin Fusiliers (F.M.I., 1911–13), who left at Christmas, 1913, for Dublin University. Having been in the O.T.C. at Shrewsbury and Dublin he had not to wait long for his commission in a Service Bn. He took part in the landing at Suvla Bay, and was killed there three days afterwards.

Oct. —, 1916.—*Richard Edward Deane Oliver, Temp. Lieut. Royal Engineers. In Churchill's 1904-7, he left for Trinity Coll., Dublin. Was gazetted Temp. 2nd Lieut. R.E., 4 Aug., 1915, and Temp. Lieut. 23 June, 1916, and was killed in action in France after he had been some months at the front.

June —, 1915.—*Samuel O'Neill, Lieut., 6th Bn. Lancashire Fusiliers T.F. (E.B.M., 1908–11). Killed in action in the Dardanelles, aged 21. He was a tube merchant at Castleton, Rochdale.

Jan. 6, 1917.—In action, aged 19, *Thomas Onslow, 2nd Lieut. K.S.L.I., who was in the School House 1911–15, and had gained a Scholarship at Magdalene Coll., Cambridge. He was in the Cricket XI, and a præpostor.

The death has also been reported (date uncertain) of **Francis Reginald Orme,** 2nd Lieut. 2nd Batt. Royal Welsh Fusiliers, who was at Shrewsbury 1907–12 in Mr. Haydon's House, and obtained his Commission early in 1914.

.—Edward Leslie Orme, his younger brother, reported missing, believed killed in action, was at Shrewsbury (W.D.H.), 1911-14; at the time of his death he was 2nd Lieut. in the 3rd Bn. of the R. Welch Fusiliers.

Oct. 26, 1918.—Arthur Banks Owen, came to Shrewsbury to the School House in September, 1912, and left as a House Monitor in April, 1917. After passing through Sandhurst he was commissioned to the K.S.L.I., and joined the 3rd Battalion at Fermoy. From there he went to France in July, 1918, and was wounded in action in the chest on October, 23rd. Though the wound was serious, it was hoped that all would be well, but unhappily he got rapidly worse, and died on October 26.

March —, 1918.—**Humphrey Francis Owen,** reported killed in action (A.F.C. 1901–5).

October —, 1915.—**William Henry Kenrick Owen,** Temp. Lieut., 9th (Service) Bn. Welsh Regt. (S.H., 1908–13), who went up to Clare College, Cambs., and died in hospital at Rouen of wounds received in action in France. His C.O. said he displayed the greatest gallantry all the time he was at the front. He was 21.

.—**Alan Reynolds Padmore** was in Mr. Baker's House from 1912-1917. On leaving school he joined the R.A.F. with a commission, for which, before his death he had shown himself well qualified.

March 8, 1916.—*****Alfred Henry Parsons,** Capt., 9th Gurkhas (S.H., 1896–1900), *B.A.*, Keble Coll., Oxon., was present with his Regt. at Festubert and Givenchy Wood ; was severely wounded in Mesopotamia in Jan., and fell in action just after he left hospital.

May 16, 1915.—*****Leslie Arnott Paterson,** 2nd Lieut., 3rd Bn. Essex Regt. (S.H., 1903-08), died of wounds received near Fromelles, . aged 24. He was a Member of the Surveyors' Institute.

Sept. 27, 1916.—*****Henry William Bourne Palin,** Private, New Zealand Contingent, aged 32, was at Shrewsbury (S.H.), 1899–1901, then went out to India as Assistant Traffic Superintendent of the Great Indian Peninsular Railway Co., afterwards joining the firm of Finlay, Muir & Co., of Calcutta. He was killed in action in France.

June 24, 1915, aged 20.—*****Eric John Keefe Pembertom Pigott,** 2nd Lieut., 1st Bn. Royal Irish Regt. (D.B., 1908–12), went up to Sandhurst, where he was an Under-Officer, and was out at the front very early in the war. He was invalided home suffering from frost-bitten feet, and had only recently returned to France.

—Killed in action, **James Adams Penell de Wood-ston Partridge** (W.D.H., 1909–13), only son of the late James Adams Partridge (O.S.). He was serving in the ranks of the Canadian Overseas Forces.

—, 1918.—**John Humphreys Plummer,** Lieut. Gordon Highlanders, who has died of wounds, was at Shrewsbury (F.E.B.) 1902, and after serving for two or three years in the Cheshire Regiment, went to Canada. Shortly after war commenced he returned to England, travelling 7,000 miles to join the army, being gazetted to the 3rd (S.R.) Batt. Gordon Highlanders on Jan. 2, 1915, and attached to the 8th (Service) Batt.

October 25, 1916.—*****James William Prior Ponsford,** Sergeant, 20th (P.S.) Bn. Royal Fusiliers, was at the School (W.D.H.) 1911–14 : being too young to join the Army when the War broke out, he joined an O.T.C. until he was of military age. Then he enlisted in the 20th Bn. Royal Fusiliers, became Lance-Corporal two days after joining, and Sergeant eight weeks later. He never wished for a commission, but preferred to serve in the ranks. He was shot by a sniper when in charge of his platoon.

Feb. 6, 1916.—At Witney, Oxon., aged 32, **Harold Garnock Potts,** Lance-Corporal, R.A.S.C., Mechanical Transport. He left Shrewsbury (where he had been a Day-boy and afterwards a member of Churchill's) in 1901 ; was admitted a solicitor, and practised at Broseley, Salop.

April 28, 1915.—*****John Russell Pound,** Capt., 3rd Bn. K.S.L.I. (Special Reserve), who came to Shrewsbury as Master in 1908, aged 27. He was educated at Merchant Taylors' School, was a Scholar of St. John's College, Oxford, and graduated with First Class Honours in Mathematics. He rowed in his College Boat. and was a good " Rugger " player. From the School O.T.C. he was gazetted to the 3rd K.S.L.I. (S.R.) in August, 1914, and was attached to the 2nd Bn., with whom he was serving when killed in action.

July 14, 1917.—**Thomas Clark Powell,** 2nd Lieut. R.G.A., was at Shrewsbury, entering Major Ingram's house in Sept. of 1910. There he became a Præpostor and a Cadet Officer in the O.T.C. At the end of 1915 he was elected to an Open Mathematical Scholarship at New College, Oxford. On leaving school at Easter, 1916, he was selected for an Artillery Cadet Unit, and, passing out with distinction, was sent at once to the front with a Commission in a heavy battery of the R.G.A. in Sept. of the same year. He was wounded early in 1917, and again on the night of July 14, dying shortly after reaching the Casualty Clearing Station.

September 26, 1914.—In camp at Epsom, suddenly, of heart failure, **John David Price,** second son of the late John Price of South Bank, Lansdowne Road, Wimbledon, who was at Shrewsbury 1898–1900 and then went to Trinity College, Cambridge.

Sept. 28, 1918.—At Salonika, of influenza, **Percival Thomas Priestley,** Major R.A.M.C., who was at the School (E.B.M.) 1903–6, coxed his House Boat and one of the Trial Eights, and narrowly missed coxing the School Crew, for he went to Bedford with it but was rejected at the last hour.   Entering Birmingham University as a medical student he obtained his M.B., and Ch.B. there. Being a Lieutenant in the R.A.M.C. Special Reserve he was mobilized on Aug. 24, 1914, and shortly afterwards sent to the Western Front. He was promoted Capt. March 30, 1915, and was Acting-Major at the time of his death.

April 13, 1918.—**Thomas Tannatt Pryce,** *V.C., M.C.,* Lieut. and Acting Capt. Grenadier Guards, was at Shrewsbury (A.F.C.) 1900–04 : then he went on the London Stock Exchange.   He joined the army in August, 1914, and was in the Honourable Artillery Company. He was then gazetted to the 6th Gloucesters (T.F.), in October, 1915, and later transferred to the Grenadier Guards.   In November, 1915, he received the Military Cross for conspicuous gallantry at Gommecourt, and was awarded an added bar some time afterwards for further courageous acts, having been twice wounded.   He was reported missing on the Western front on April 13, 1918, but is now known to have been killed on that date.   He was awarded the *V.C.* in May (posthumously) " for most conspicuous bravery, devotion to duty, and self-sacrifice when in command of a flank on the left of the Grenadier Guards.   Having been ordered to attack a village, he personally led forward two platoons, working from house to house, killing some thirty of the enemy, seven of whom he killed himself.   The next day he was occupying a position with some thirty to forty men, the remainder of his company having become casualties.   As early as 8-15 a.m. his left flank was surrounded and the the enemy enfilading him.   He was attacked no less than four times during the day, and each time beat off the hostile attack, killing many of the enemy.   Meanwhile, the enemy brought up three field guns to within 300 yards of his line, and were firing over open sights and knocking his trench in.   At 6.15 p.m. the enemy had worked to within 60 yards of his trench.   He then called on his men, telling them to cheer and charge the enemy and fight to the last.   Led by Captain Pryce, they left their trench and drove back the enemy with the bayonet some 100 yards.   Half an hour later the enemy had again approached in stronger force.   By this time Captain Pryce had only 17 men left, and every round of his ammunition had been fired.   Determined that there should be no surrender he once again led his men forward in a bayonet charge, and was last seen engaged in a fierce hand-to-hand struggle with overwhelming numbers of the enemy.   With some 40 men he had held back at least one enemy battalion for over ten hours.   His company undoubtedly stopped the advance through the British line, and thus had great influence on the battle."

Nov. 13, 1918,—At Gosselines, near Charleroi, of wounds received Nov. 10, **John Edwin Pugh,** Lieut. R.A.F., of the 210th Squadron and of H.M.S. Princess Royal. JOHN EDWIN PUGH, who succumbed to wounds received whilst flying on the Western Front just before the Armistice, came to the School in Jan., 1913, and though a good allround athlete, was specially distinguished as an oar. In the summer of 1914 he rowed bow in his House First Boat at the Head of the River. In 1915 he won the Challenge Oars and rowed stroke in the Head of the River Crew. In the School Eight at Henley, rowing at 6, he was at once marked out as an oarsman full of promise ; but the war turned his thoughts, which had previously run on motor machines, to flying. Going to Hendon as a pupil, he soon became a most expert aviator, passed thence into the R.N.A.S., and joined the fleet, where he remained flying his fighting plane: a longing to get to closer quarters with the enemy took him to France, where he was brought down and taken to a military hospital four miles from Charleroi. From there he sent a message—" I am still alive, but one lung pierced, also right leg and shoulder."

Oct. 26, 1917.—Lieut. **Richard Standiford Pullen,** of the South Staffordshire Regiment, fell on Oct. 26, 1917, when leading his Company with the greatest gallantry in an attack which presented extreme difficulties, age 34. R. S. Pullen was at Shrewsbury (W.D.H.) from 1898-1900, and afterwards at Mason College, Birmingham. He joined the Army in Sept., 1914, being at that time Captain of the Sandwell Park Golf Club, as well as a member of the Wednesbury Golf Club. He had been twice mentioned in despatches.

—**Edward Francis Ratliff,** 2nd Lieut. Rifle Brigade was at Shrewsbury ((W.D.H.) 1911–14. Whilst at School he had won distinction as a promising Cricketer, and more especially in the Fives Team, in which he appeared for two seasons, and of which he ultimately became Captain. Enlisting early in the war in the 13th Northumberland Fusiliers, he soon became Lance-Corporal, was present at the battle of Loos, from which he emerged unscathed, was subsequently twice wounded, got a Commission, and was later made Captain and gained the Military Cross in the Rifle Brigade, in which so many gallant Salopians have met their deaths.

March 15, 1915.—Killed in action in France, **William Gray Rawlinson,** Lieut. 2nd Batt. Duke of Cornwall's Light Infantry, aged 24, who was at Shrewsbury 1904-6 in Mr. Moser's House.

—, 1917.—Killed in action near Arras, **Alexander Armstrong Rees,** M.B., M.R.C.S., Temp. Captain R.A.M.C., who was a member of Chance's 1900-3.

January 22, 1915.—Died of wounds received in action, **John Trevor Rees,** aged 21, who was at Shrewsbury 1908–11, and then went into business. At the outbreak of the War he enlisted in the Artists' Rifles (28th County of London Territorial Battalion) and having volunteered for the Front was sent with a detachment to France. Promoted on the Field, he received a Commission as 2nd Lieut. in the 1st Battalion, Royal Welch Fusiliers, and, during the sadly short time that he held it, succeeded in winning the esteem and affection of his men, one of whom wrote of him, after his death, in these terms, which might well serve for his epitaph—

In losing Mr. REES the Regiment has lost one of the most daring and bravest officers it has ever had. He knew no such thing as fear. . . . He made us all love him by his daring bravery, cheerfulness and consideration for the sick and weak; and I myself have lost the best friend I have ever had in my six years of soldiering.

May 4, 1916.—**Victor Eustace Reynolds,** Temp. Capt. 14th West Yorks Regt., in action, In the School House 1894-6, REYNOLDS entered the Slade Art School and worked for some years at painting in Florence and Paris. He then accepted the posts of Art Master at Aske's Haberdashers' School at Cricklewood, and Life Master at the Evening Classes at Lambeth Art School. On the outbreak of the War he enlisted in the P.S. Bn., obtained his 2nd Lieutenancy in May, 1915, in the 14th (Service) Bn. West Yorks, was promoted Lieut. in October, and Capt. four months later.

—**Watkin Leoline Tom Rhys,** died of wounds received while serving as 2nd Lieut. with the Rifle Brigade on the Western Front. In Doctor's 1905-8, he proved himself a valuable all-round athlete, being in the Football XI. and Killing Gentleman of the Runs. When the War came he enlisted in the R.A.S.C. (Mechanical Transport), and his intimate knowledge of mechanism proved very serviceable to him in the earlier part of his army career.

Oct. 7, 1917,—**William Quintus Newsum Richardson,** 2nd Lieut., entered Major Ingram's House in Sept., 1912, and left in April, 1917, to be trained for the Royal Flying Corps. He had only obtained his Commission a few weeks before he was killed in an accident on Oct. 7th, while he was out on a practice flight at his Wing Headquarters in Essex.

July 1, 1916, aged 35.—**Henry Davison Riley,** Temp. Capt. 11th (Service) Bn. (Accrington) East Lancashire Regt. He was at Shrewsbury (A.F.C.) 1895 8, and became a member of the firm of Messrs. W. & A. Riley, fancy cloth manufacturers, of Houlker Street Mill, Colne. He was also a director of the firm of Messrs. R. J. Elliott & Co. (Ltd.), cigar manufacturers, of Huddersfield and Leicester, and was a well-known and popular figure on Manchester Exchange. He took great interest in the Burnley Lads' Club, of which he was the founder, and also in the industrial school movement. In 1912 he was appointed a County Magistrate, and was gazetted a Capt. in March, 1915.

Oct. 9, 1918.—**Eustace Blackburne Ritson,** 2nd Lieut. M.G.C., was at Shrewsbury (w.d.h. and s.h.) 1896–1901, gained a prize at the Electrical Training Institution in 1901, and entered Faraday House in January, 1902. In May, 1905, he received an appointment with the Mexican Light and Power Company. After two years as engineer at Necaxa, he returned to England, and subsequently went to Messrs. Callendar's Cable and Construction Company (Limited), where he was employed when the war broke out. In September, 1914, he joined the Universities and Public Schools Brigade. When his battalion was disbanded, on leaving France, he went as a cadet to New College, Oxford, in 1916, and was gazetted to the Machine Gun Corps. He returned to France in 1917 as a 2nd Lieut. On October 9, 1918, he was in command of a section taking up ammunition to the guns at the front. He went forward to reconnoitre and never returned.

April 23, 1917.—**Noel Humphreys Roberts,** Lieut. Scottish Borderers, killed in action, April 23, 1917, aged 24. Was at Shrewsbury (d.b.) 1907-10), and at Exeter College, Oxford, where he played hockey for College and the University, and also represented his college at football, cricket and tennis. Soon after the outbreak of war he enlisted in the 13th Londons, was given a commission in the K.O.S.B. in Jan., 1916, and went to the front in August.

May —, 1915.—The Hon. **William Francis Rodney,** 2nd Lieut., 5th Bn. Rifle Brigade (s.h., 1909–14), stroke of the School VIII., who, after passing through Sandhurst, was gazetted to the Rifle Brigade, being subsequently appointed an Observer in the Flying Corps. His squadron leader was full of praise for his "superb contempt of danger."

July 3, 1916.—**Esmond Hallewell Rogers,** Temp. 2nd Lieut. 10th (Service) Bn. Royal Warwickshire Regt. killed in action, aged 25, was at Shrewsbury (f.e.b. and c.j.b.), 1905–10, in the Cricket XI. two years, and at Caius College, Cambridge. A keen golfer and cricketer, he captained his College Cricket XI. in 1913, and on several occasions played for the Warwickshire second team. He received his commission 11 Jan. 1915.

, 1914.—**Thomas Allen Rose,** D.S.O., Capt. Royal Scots, was at first reported wounded and a prisoner, but is now believed to have been killed in action in the first month of the war. At the School as a Dayboy 1890-1, he was gazetted from the Militia to a 2nd Lieutenancy in the Royal Scots Fusiliers in 1895, being pro-

moted Lieut. in 1898, and Capt. in 1901. Attached to the West
African Frontier Force in 1898 he served in the expedition of 1900
against the Chief of Taweri (being mentioned in despatches), against
the Emir of Yola (again mentioned and gaining the medal and clasp)
and in the Aro Expedition of 1901-2 (slightly wounded, again
mentioned and winning the D.S.O.). In 1907 he was attached to
the North Nigerian Regt. as Capt.

Oct. 10, 1918.—**Kenneth Sutherland Rudd,** Capt. West Yorkshire
Regt., who was killed in action on Oct. 10, aged 24, was at Shrewsbury (C.J.B.) 1908–13, whence he obtained a scholarship at Jesus
College, Cambridge, in 1913. He enlisted immediately war broke
out in the Shropshire Light Infantry, and was gazetted 2nd Lieut.
in Aug., 1914, and posted to the West Yorkshire Regt. He was
promoted Lieut. in June, 1915, and obtained his Captaincy in May,
1918. He went to France with his battalion in July, 1915, and was
severely wounded in April, 1916. He returned to the front in Oct.,
1917, and at the time of his death was Acting Adjutant to his
battalion. When home on leave owing to wounds he more than once
was one of the Staff at the Shrewsbury Club, Liverpool, Camp at
Frodsham.

June 7, 1917.—Killed in action at Messines, **Donald Campbell
Rutter,** *M.C.,* Flight Commander R.F.C. (F.T.P. 1911-17). On
leaving he was first gazetted as 2nd Lieut. 3rd Bn. (S.R.) Royal
Sussex Regt., and while with the Infantry won the *M.C.* ; later he
transferred to the R.F.C. and in it had a brilliant record.

April 12, 1918.—**William Stewart Mitchell Ruxton,** *M.C.,* Lieut.
Border Regiment, who was killed on April 12, aged 20, while at
Shrewsbury was captain of the school Gymnasium of his house
cricket and football teams, and Sergeant in the School O.T.C. He
passed into Sandhurst in Sept., 1915, and there became a sergeant.
Receiving his commission in Jan., 1916, he proceeded to the front
in July, 1916, was wounded in Sept., and returned to France in
Jan., 1917. He was awarded the Military Cross in Sept., 1917, and
had since Jan., 1918, been Acting Captain.

June 1, 1915.—*****Reginald Victor Rylands,** Capt. 7th Bn. Manchester Regt. (T.F.), was at Shrewsbury (W.D.H., 1906-8) ; was
promoted Capt. September 26, 1914, and fell in action in the
Dardanelles, aged 23. He was LL.D. of Manchester University, and
was admitted a solicitor in 1914.

Oct. 27, 1916.—**Walter Petit Salt,** Capt. 2nd Bn. Lancs. Fusiliers,
killed in action, aged 39, was at Shrewsbury (G.T.H.), 1892-7, and in
both Cricket and Football Elevens ; was gazetted from the Militia
2nd Lieut. Lancs. Fusiliers in 1899 ; Lieut., 1900 ; Capt. 1904.

Retiring with this rank, he entered into business at Gibraltar. On the outbreak of the War he came to England with a view to re-joining his old Regt., but at first was not accepted owing to an injury to his right arm. He thereupon joined the R.A.S.C. as Temp. Capt. in Dec., 1914, but was eventually transferred to the 2nd Bn., Lancs. Fusiliers, in April, 1915.

Oct. —, 1918.—**Richard Harry Sampson,** Temp. Lieut. Welsh Regt. (S.H., 1906-7), killed in action, was a son of R. H. SAMPSON, J.P. (O.S.), and was gazetted 2nd Lieut., 16th (Service) Batt. (Cardiff City) the Welsh Regt., June 23, 1915.

.—**Tom Burton Sampson,** came to Shrewsbury (Churchill's) in the Michaelmas Term, 1903, and left in 1907. He was engaged in business in Nottingham, where he made for himself a considerable reputation as a cross-country runner ; for some years he used to bring over a side to run against the School in preparation for the Rugby Run, and was always one of the first to come in. On the outbreak of the war, he was among the now sadly depleted band of patriotic Old Salopians who joined the ranks of the K.S.L.I. When he fell in action he was serving as a temporary 2nd Lieut. with the 9th Battalion.

Dec. 31, 1917.—**William Denys Samuelson,** Capt., entered the School in 1910, as a member of Major Ingram's house, and left at the end of the Summer Term, 1914. He represented the School in the Shooting VIII. in 1912. He was trained as an officer in the Liverpool University O.T.C. and gained a commission from there in the R.G.A., going out to France in a Heavy Howitzer Siege Battery in June, 1916. He was at the front through the Somme and Arras battles. Subsequently he was on more than one occasion in command of his Battery, and distinguished himself as a capable officer and efficient Commander, being mentioned in despatches a few days before he was wounded. He was wounded when in action on Dec. 30, 1917, and died in hospital the following day.

April 23, 1917.—**Francis Savage Nesbitt Savage-Armstrong,** *D.S.O.,* Lieut.-Col. South Staffordshire Regt., attached to and in command of a battalion of the Royal Warwickshire Regt., who was killed on April 23, 1917, aged 36, served with the 1st South Stafford-shire Regt. in South Africa from 1900 to 1903, and had the Queen's medal with three clasps and the King's medal with two clasps. In the present war he was mentioned four times in despatches, first by Lord French and afterwards by Sir Douglas Haig. He went to France on Nov. 1, 1914, and was with his own regiment at Fromelles, Neuve Chapelle, and Festubert, being severely wounded at the last-named battle on May 16, 1915. He was then acting as brigade machine-gun officer. After recovery he was ordered on light duty, but in the following Sept. he returned to the front, and was appointed to the command of a service battalion of the Rifle Brigade and afterwards of a battalion of the Royal Warwickshire Regt. He was at Shrewsbury (s.h.) 1895–9, and rowed in the Crew.

July 31, 1917.—**Reginald Scott-Deakin,** Lieut. R.F.A., killed in action, July 31, 1917, was at Shrewsbury (D.B.) 1907–12, where he served four years in the O.T.C. and won his Trial Star. He received his commission in the R.G.A. in Feb., 1913, but on the outbreak of war was transferred to R.F.A., and had commanded a battery for some months. He went to the front in March, 1915, and took part in the engagements at St. Eloi and Hill 60. He was also in the offensive of Sept., 1915; in the Spring of 1916 he was invalided home. After a period of convalescence he returned to the front, and had taken part in severe fighting.

June 5th, 1916.—*****John Furlow McConnell Sergeant,** Private, Winnipeg L.I., Canadian Expeditionary Force, was at Shrewsbury (F.S.) 1907–10, rowing in the 2nd VIII., and went out to Canada. Enlisting at the outbreak of war, he served in the ranks ; was reported missing in June, 1916; and some months later as killed.

May 11, 1917.—**Kenneth George Shackles** came to the School House in the Summer of 1910 : after three years at Shrewsbury, he began work in his father's office, in which he was at the outbreak of war. In Aug., 1914, he enlisted in the 10th Bn. of the East Yorks Regt., and after more than a year's training went out as a private. After six months' service both in Egypt and France he was invalided home and received a Commission in the same regiment in Feb., 1917. He died of wounds received in action on the 11th of May following.

Sept. 19, 1918.—**Ronald Guy Shackles,** . Sec.-Lieut., K.S.L.I. (S.R.), was killed by a shell in France on Sept. 19, while acting as Intelligence Officer. He came to the School House in January, 1913, and won the Military Cross after being in France for little more than a month. " He led a successful daylight raid against an enemy post which he had located by two days' careful reconnaissance in ' No Man's Land.' In the hand-to-hand fight which took place the whole enemy garrison was accounted for, and our own party suffered no casualties. Sec.-Lieut. Shackles handled his men with much skill, and displayed great gallantry and energy."

.—**Robert Shaw,** Capt., the King's Liverpool Regt., killed in action, was 25 years of age, was at Shrewsbury (E.B.M.) 1906–9, and at Corpus Christi, Cambridge, where he took his B.A. degree. Later he was articled to Messrs. Dawson, Chevalier, and Graves, Chartered Accountants, Liverpool. He obtained his commission in the December of 1913, and went out to France in the Spring of 1915, and again on 25 Dec. of the same year. Captain Shaw returned home on leave in May of 1916, and went out for the third time in June, 1917.

.—**Leslie Shorland-Ball** was at Shrewsbury (G.T.H.) in 1898–99. He was killed in action while serving with his regiment, the R. Irish Fusiliers.

Feb. 17, 1916.—***John Frith Sidebotham,** Temp. 2nd Lieut., 6th (Service) Bn. K.S.L.I. (S.H., 1905–10), left as a Præpostor and in the Cricket XI., and was afterwards on the staff of Messrs. James Greaves, East India Merchants, of Manchester and Bombay. He went up to Hertford College, Oxford, and captained the University Lacrosse Team twice against Cambridge. He enlisted in the 5th K.S.L.I. in September, 1914, and was gazetted 2nd Lieut. in the 6th in January, 1916.

June 4, 1918.—**John Basil Pulling Simms,** entered Mr. Chance's House at Shrewsbury in September, 1912. He left in December, 1916, and shortly afterwards began his service in the 20th Battn. Northumberland Fusiliers. When he returned to France from leave, May, 1918, he joined the R.A.F. as an observer in No. 4 Squadron. Though happy in the infantry, flying was the service he was most attached to, and he was looking forward to a return to England to get his Pilot's Wings, when he was shot down and killed with his pilot by five enemy scouts, on June 4, 1918.

Aug. —, 1915.—**Leslie Crozier Smale,** Private 5th Bn. K.S.L.I., missing, believed killed, was at Shrewsbury (C.J.B.), 1911–14.

.—**George Orme Smart** was at Shrewsbury (S.H.), 1901-03, and a member of the School Football XI. At the time of his death he was a 2nd Lieutenant in the R.A.F.

Oct. 16, 1917.—Killed in action, **Norman Smart,** Lieut. and Acting Capt. M.G.C. (W.D.H., 1908–9).

—, 1916.—**Charles Ledward Smith,** 2nd Lieut. East Lancs. R.F.A. (T.F.), who was at Shrewsbury (G.T.H.), 1894–98, in the Football XI., and then went into business in Liverpool.

April 28th, 1917.—Lieut. **John Adams Smith,** was at Shrewsbury (F.M.I.), 1910–12, and went into his father's business as a wool merchant. Following the outbreak of war, he joined the Army, but although he might have had a commission he declined the honour, saying that if he joined he should do so as a private, adding to a friend : " I shall get a commission in due course, but I shall work for it." He chose the Sherwood Foresters, joined as a private, was promoted corporal and then sergeant, and afterwards was posted as a lieutenant in the Northumberland Fusiliers. In due course, he went out to France, and quite early on in the fighting got a bullet wound in the shoulder. He soon recovered from that, and had been through most of the severe fighting, in which, when in command of a company of his battalion in the great fight which won Vimy Ridge, he received the wounds that proved fatal, dying at Camiers,

Aug. 18, 1916.—*Hugh Stewart Smith, 2nd Lieut. (Temp. Capt.), 4th Bn. (attached 2nd Bn.) Argyll and Sutherland Highlanders. Killed in action. He was at Shrewsbury 1902-8, where he was Head of Churchill's and Huntsman for two years. He went to Corpus Christi Coll., Oxford, whence he took his degree in Modern History in 1911. In 1912 he joined the Colonial Civil Service and went to Northern Nigeria. He was District Officer in one of the wildest districts when war broke out, and at once volunteered for military service in the Cameroons. He was not needed there, and coming home on furlough resigned his appointment under the Colonial Office early in 1915. In March 1915, he was given a commission in the Special Reserve of Officers, and was gazetted to the Argyll and Sutherland Highlanders. He went to France in September, 1915, and was promoted Capt. in March, 1916. He was killed at the head of his company, aged 27.

.—William Reginald Sturston Smith, 2nd Lieut. R.F.C., who was reported missing on Oct. 22, 1917, and has since been reported as having died a prisoner in German hands, entered the School (Mr. Oldham's House) in Sept., 1912, and left in Dec., 1916. Before he left he was a member of the Cricket Eleven and Senior Whip. His one season in the School Eleven was rather a remarkable one. He was first played as a bowler (and no one is likely to forget his extraordinary action which was calculated to put off any batsman), but in the course of the season he developed so much as a bat, that, though in his first match he went in last, in his last he went in first.

—Edward Hamilton Southcomb, 2nd Lieut. Manchester Regt. (T.E.P. 1910-12), killed in action. On leaving School he was for some time employed in a Bank in Cheltenham.

Sept. 15, 1916.—*Evelyn Herbert Lightfoot Southwell, Lieut. Rifle Brigade, was educated at Eton. From there he went to Oxford, and won an open demyship at Magdalen College and took a First Class in the classical schools. He stroked his college boat to the Head of the River, and rowed twice for his University at Putney, as his father had done before him. After leaving Oxford he held a classical mastership at Shrewsbury, where he took charge of the school rowing and helped to turn out some fine crews. He offered himself for active service at the beginning of the war, and had served abroad with his battalion for a year from Sept., 1915, being in the trenches for practically the whole of the time. He was twice appointed, as Captain, to the command of a company, but was superseded on both occasions by the return of a senior officer to active service. A brother officer writes : " The battalion advanced, and did splendidly. Southwell was in the front of them, with one sergeant, and another officer was close to him. They were, in fact, the furthest advanced of anybody, and they got into a shell hole for cover. He was shortly afterwards hit by a sniper's bullet, and died immediately." At Shrewsbury he was master of Form V.B., and under his tuition the boys of the Form broke out into poetry, and published a volume to which he wrote a preface. *Two Men*, a memoir with letters written by him and his colleague, Lieut. M. G. White, was published by the Oxford University Press.

—**Arthur Max Spencer,** 2nd Lieut. Rifle Brigade (F.T.P.), killed in action. He was a scholar of the School and a promising cricketer.

.—Lieut. **Thomas Charlton Spencer,** L.-Corporal. H.A.C., killed in action; was at Shrewsbury in Mr. Prior's House from 1910–1914.

Aug. 25, 1916.*—**Frederick William Sprott,** 2nd Lieut. Indian Reserve of Officers (attached 92nd Punjabis), died at Amara in Mesopotamia, aged 27 years. He was the son of Sir Frederick Lawrence Sprott (O.S.), of Bombay, and was admitted solicitor in October, 1912. His school years were 1903–6 (E.B.M.).

—**Charles Cecil Stanfield,** Capt. 1st Bn. The Buffs, East Kent Regt. (School House 1898–1901), died in hospital at Aldershot from illness contracted on military duty, aged 33. He went to the front with his regiment when war broke out, took part in the battle of the Aisne, and was badly wounded on Oct. 20, 1914. He afterwards served in the Dardanelles, was present at the evacuation, and later saw service in Egypt. In April, 1917, he was selected to train an Officers' Cadet Battalion.

December 26, 1915.—**Gordon Pemberton Steer,** Capt., 2nd Bn. Somerset L.I. (A.F.C., 1899–1903), played for the School at cricket in most of the matches (including the Rossall) in 1903, and went up to Magdalen College, Oxon. (*B.A.*, 1908). Gazetted as a University Candidate to the Somerset L.I., he served abroad from 1909 to 1915. Promoted Captain in June, 1915, he was ordered home from Quetta and joined the 3rd Bn. He went out to France in September, attached to the 2nd Bn. Wiltshires, was severely wounded at Givenchy on November 25, and died of wounds in hospital at Wimereux on December 26, aged 31.

July 7, 1916.—Reported killed in action, **Basil Stott,** who was at Shrewsbury (W.D.H.) 1902-4. He was serving in the ranks of the Royal Fusiliers and was reported wounded and missing on July 7, 1916.

June 4, 1916.—**Alexander George Stuart,** Major and Brevet Lieut.-Col. 40th Pathans, I.A., and G.S.O.I., killed in action, aged 43 years. At Shrewsbury (T.A.B. and C.J.S.C.), 1886-90, he was at Trinity College, Dublin, 1890-3 ; received his first appointment in the Royal Scots in December, 1893, and was gazetted Captain in November, 1900. In March, 1904, he transferred to the Indian Army and was promoted Major in December, 1912. He held Staff appointments in India, and in 1908 served in the operations in the Mohmand country, being awarded the medal with clasp. From 1911 to 1914 he was a G.S.O. at the War Office, and on the outbreak of war was attached to the General Staff as Chief Press Censor. He had been mentioned in despatches for gallant and distinguished service, and given the Brevet rank of Lieut.-Colonel.

September 25, 1915.—*****Andrew John, Viscount Stuart,** Temp. Lieut., 6th (Service) Bn. Royal Scots Fusiliers (S.H., 1894-9), the eldest son and heir of the Earl of Castlestewart, of Stuart Hall, co. Tyrone, was born in December, 1880 ; went up to C.C.C. Oxford, was gazetted Lieut. in Oct., 1914, and was killed in action in France. Lord Stuart possessed considerable literary skill, as may be seen from some verses in the *Times* of September 16, 1914, quoted in the *Salopian* of October 13, 1915.

August 11, 1915.—*****Cyril Adolphus Stuart,** Lance-Corporal, 5th (Service) Bn. K.S.L.I. (W.S.I.), 1907-14, a Præpostor and Senior Whip, representing the School against Rugby and Blackheath. He won 48 cups for running during his school career, and besides gaining many medals while in the Army, came in an easy first in the chief cross-country race at Aldershot, out of over 500 starters. The King started the race and the Queen gave away the prizes. C. A. Stuart intended qualifying for a Doctor, but enlisted in September, 1914 ; was promoted Lance-Corporal before the regiment left England ; was wounded on August 8, 1915, and died three days afterwards.

Nov. 13, 1916, in action, aged 34.—*****Gerald Henry Sulivan,** Temp. Capt. R.M.L.I. At Shrewsbury (S.H.), 1887-1891, he left for London University, where he took his B.Sc., and was subsequently Science Master at Sedbergh School. In July, 1915, he was gazetted Temp. 2nd Lieut. in the Royal Marines, and promoted Capt. May 30, 1916. His Colonel wrote " He and the men under him advanced further than anybody. Unhappily at the moment of his triumph he was struck down." He went out to Salonica in December, 1915, but was transferred to the Western Front in the following May.

Aug. 9, 1916, of wounds received in action.—*Joseph Leonard Swainson, *D.S.O.*, Lieut.-Col. Duke of Cornwall's L.I. (attached 4th Bn. Royal Lancs. Regt.). Col. SWAINSON, who was 39 years old, was the elder son of the late Joseph Swainson (O.S.), of Stonecross, Kendal. He was at Shrewsbury (E.B.M.) 1891–6, and King's College, Cambridge (B.A., 1899). He obtained a commission in the Lancashire Fusiliers in 1899, and served throughout the South African War (medal with four clasps). When his battalion was broken up under the reorganization scheme he was transferred in 1908 to the Duke of Cornwall's L.I., then stationed in South Africa. From there they were sent to Hong-kong. In May, 1914, he came home on leave, and on the outbreak of the war was sent to Aldershot to train men of the 6th Duke of Cornwall's L.I. In May, 1915, he went with the battalion to the front. He was in the attack on Hooge in August, 1915, and commanded the battalion from September, 1915, till the following March. He then had charge of a Military School of Instruction behind the lines till June, when he was given the command of a battalion of the Royal Lancaster Regt. Col. SWAINSON was twice mentioned in dispatches, and awarded to D.S.O. for his services in the present war. He died gallantly organising a second attack on Guillemont.

Aug. 27, 1917.—**William Gregory Terry,** Capt., the Lancashire Fusiliers, who died of wounds at a casualty clearing station in France on Aug. 27, 1917, was at Shrewsbury (E.B.M.), 1897–1900. On leaving he served his apprenticeship with Messrs. Browett, Lindley and Co., Ltd., Patricroft, going through the whole of the departments and completing his engineering course in the drawing office. He afterwards joined the staff of the Salford Corporation Electricity Works and after a few years' connection with them again rejoined Messrs. Browett, Lindley and Co., being appointed to their staff as outside representative of their Northern Section. He joined the Lancashire Fusiliers in June, 1915, and had been in France since the early part of 1917.

April 18, 1917.—**Foster Newton Thorne,** Lieut.-Col. Royal Sussex Regt., killed on April 18, was at Shrewsbury (A.F.C.) 1896–8, and joined the 1st Royal Sussex Regt. in 1900 from the Militia (South Wales Borderers). He served in the South African War (Queen's and King's medals), and was attached to the West African Frontier Force for two tours of duty in 1909 and 1910. He returned to the 2nd Royal Sussex Regt. in England, was transferred to the 1st Bn. in India in 1913, and fought on the frontier in 1914. In 1915 he was promoted Major, and subsequently proceeded to the front with the temporary rank of Lieut.-Colonel.

August 19, 1915, aged 22.—*Alexander Arnold Tippet, 2nd Lieut. 2nd Bn. K.S.L.I. (F.M.I., 1909–12), was killed in the trenches in

Flanders, was Choregus, and went abroad to study Languages and Music before going up to Cambridge. Enlisting in the Artists' O.T.C., he was gazetted 2nd Lieut. in May, 1915, and posted to the Rifles 2nd K.S.L.I. He was shot by a sniper, near Armentières, and was buried in the churchyard at Erquinghem.

Dec. —, 1918.—**James Herbert Treasure,** *T.D.,* Major R.G.A. (T.F.), died while on active service. He was at the School 1888-91 as a Dayboy ; was gazetted Captain in the Shropshire R.G.A. Volunteers in 1899, transferring with the same rank to the 3rd Kent R.G.A. Volunteers in 1905. Though he had retired to the Territorial Force Reserve, he at once rejoined on the outbreak of the War, and was appointed Major of the Home Counties (Kent) Brigade of Heavy Artillery (T.F.), Oct. 7, 1914.

Nov. 13, 1916.—***Cyril Claude Howard Tripp,** 2nd Lieut. Loyal North Lancashire Regiment, killed in action, aged 20. He was at Shrewsbury (A.F.C.), 1910-13, enlisted in the H.A.C. soon after the outbreak of war, and was wounded in June, 1915. In the following August he was gazetted to the Special Reserve of the Loyal North Lancashire Regiment, and left for the front in June, 1916.

June 5, 1917.—**Alan Roper Tudor,** 2nd Lieut. Seaforth Highlanders, killed on June 5, 1917, was at Shrewsbury (W.D.H.) 1907-8. Being in India at the outbreak of the war, he joined the Calcutta Light Horse, but returned home in the spring of 1916 to enlist in the Seaforth Highlanders. On receiving his Commission in Oct., 1916, he joined one of the battalions at the front.

—**Herbert Samuel Alston Turner,** Lieut. Yorkshire Regt., killed in action, aged 20.. Was at Shrewsbury (Mr. Prior's), and passed direct on his marks into Sandhurst, being gazetted to the Yorkshire Regt. in April, 1916.

November 17, 1914.—Killed in Action at Busra, on the Persian Gulf, while Commanding No. 2 Co. of the 3rd Sappers and Miners of the Indian Army. *Capt. **Arthur Montague Twiss,** *R.E.,* youngest son of the late E. C. Twiss, Stipendiary Magistrate of Hull, aged 33. He entered the School in 1895, steered the School Crew in the four-oared race against Bedford in 1896, and passed 19th into the R.M. Academy, Woolwich, in 1898 ; was gazetted 2nd Lieut. in the Royal Engineers in 1900 ; promoted Lieut. in 1903, and Captain in 1910.

Sept. 7, 1918.—**Roland Maddison Vaisey,** Captain R.F.A., who was killed in action on Sept. 7 was at Shrewsbury (S.H.) 1900-3, and was admitted a solicitor in 1909. Obtaining his commission in 1916, he immediately afterwards went to the front, where he served continuously until his death. His Colonel wrote :—" He has been my Adjutant for over a year, and had been a wonderfully good and efficient one. He will be a very great loss to me and all my brigade."

July 4, 1916.—*Albert Theodore Vardy, 2nd Lieut. 4th Bn. R. Warwickshire Regt. (S.R.), attached 2nd Bn., shot and killed instantaneously while binding up the wounds of a fellow officer. He was at Shrewsbury (s.h.) 1902–7, was in the Football XI. and the Fives Team, and a Præpostor, leaving as 3rd boy in the school for Pembroke College, Cambridge, where he had won a Scholarship. After gaining a First Class in the Classical Tripos, he became an Assistant Master at Highgate School, and acted as Hon. Sec. of the Football Branch of the Old Salopian Club. He enlisted in the 16th (P.S.) Bn. of the Middlesex Regt. at the beginning of the war, obtained a commission in the Special Reserve, R. Warwickshire Regt., 8 May, 1915, and went abroad in May, 1916.

Dec. 8, 1916.—*Wilfrid George Vint, Private, Duke of Wellington's West Riding Regt., killed in action, aged 31, was at Shrewsbury (s.h.) 1899–1904, and at Merton College, Oxford, graduating with honours in 1907. He was admitted as a solicitor in 1911, and after gaining experience in the office of the solicitor of the Great Northern Railway Company, joined his father's firm of Vint, Parkinson, Hull, and Killick, at Bradford in 1912. At School and Oxford he took a great interest in rowing and was a successful coxswain. He created a record at Shrewsbury by steering the School Eight to victory against Bedford in five consecutive years (1900-4) ; he also coxed the winning boat in the University Trial Eights in 1905, and his College in the Eights in 1907, when they made six bumps.

Feb. 19, 1916.—*John Arthur Walker, Temp. Capt., 10th (Service) Bn. Royal Welch Fusiliers (E.B.M., 1907-9) went up to Trinity Hall, Cambridge, and at the outbreak of war at once joined the O.T.C. ; was gazetted Temp. 2nd Lieut. in the R.W.F., Nov. 13, 1914 ; was promoted Lieut. some months later, and gazetted Capt. in July, 1915. He fell in action in France.

October 21, 1914.—Died of wounds received in action, *Reginald Fydell Walker, 2nd Lieut. the Manchester Regiment, who went to Shrewsbury in 1908 with a Mathematical Scholarship " and left at Easter 1913 (says *The Salopian*) after having played a considerable part in the life of the School : he was Head of his house (Major Ingram's) for more than two years, was in the Football Eleven in 1912 and was Choregus in that year." On leaving Sandhurst he was gazetted to the Manchesters, just as war was declared, and accompanied the regiment to the Front. He fell, mortally wounded, in the charge upon Les Trois Maisons on the 20th October, and died the following day. His gallant conduct on that occasion was specially commended by his Company Commander in these terms :—

He did most excellent work, so good, indeed, that I intended to bring his name before the Commanding Officer. . . . He led several bayonet charges, and inflicted heavy losses on the enemy.

April 9, 1917.—**Robert Hugh Walker,** Lieut. Seaforth Highlanders, who was killed on April 9 while leading his company in an attack in a village in face of very severe shell fire, came to Shrewsbury in the Michaelmas Term 1888 (Chance's and School House), and left in 1891. After serving five years' apprenticeship with Messrs. Marshall of Gainsborough, he was appointed by the Neuchâtel Asphalt Co. director of their mines at Travers, near Neuchâtel, where he remained until 1912. He subsequently served the Company in Australia and at Athens. Soon after the outbreak of the War he came home and obtained a Commission in the Seaforth Highlanders. He was mentioned in Despatches after the operations on the Somme, where he was slightly wounded.

July 14, 1918.—**Herbert Wynn Walton-Evans,** Private A.I.F., who was killed in France on July 16, 1918, was at Shrewsbury (F.E.B.) 1890-2. He had taken up land in West Australia, where he lived until shortly after the declaration of war, when he and his brother, also an O.S., volunteered for active service in France. He was fond of athletics, especially rowing.

March —, 1918.—Reported missing, now officially presumed killed in action, **Henry Stanley Webb,** 2nd Lieut. 9th Bn. East Surrey Regt. (F.M.I. 1910–12). For two years he served as a Private in the South Midland Field Ambulance, being present at the fighting at La Bassée in 1916. At the end of that year he came home to take a commission in the East Surreys. Going out again he was at first attached to the East Lancs. Regt., and was wounded at Monchy-le-Preux in April, 1917. Returning to active service, he was posted to the 9th East Surreys, and reaching the fighting line at the moment when the Germans were beginning to break through in March, 1918, was reported missing in the first casualty list.

August 10, 1915.—*****Norman Lancaster Wells,** Temp. Lieut., 6th Bn. Loyal North Lancaster Regt. (F.E.B., 1903-6), graduated from Caius Coll., Camb., in 1909, having been in the School Crew and Football XI, and also in his college " Soccer " team. Having spent some time in Germany to acquire the language, he was selected from among many candidates by the Asiatic Petroleum Company to represent their firm in Japan. He was at first reported " missing " after the action at Anavarta in the Dardanelles, but has since been posted as " believed to be killed."

—**Albert Neave Westlake,** 2nd Lieut. N. Staffordshire Regt. (S.H. 1907-12), killed in action. At Shrewsbury he was Head of the School, in the Cricket Eleven, the Football Eleven, Huntsman and stroke of the School Crew. He went up as a scholar to New College, Oxford, where he rowed in the VIII, and gained a First Class in Mods.

——, 1916.—*****Arthur Whale,** Private 30th Bn. Royal Fusiliers, was in Churchill's 1902-7, and in both Cricket and Football teams. On going up to Pembroke College, Cambridge, he obtained his Blue for Association Football.

July 5, 1916.—**Arthur Nevin Wheatley,** Major 5th Bn. West Riding Regiment (T.F.), died of wounds received in action. At Shrewsbury (F.E.B.) 1891–5, he left to become a member of the firm of Henry Wheatley & Sons, of Mirfield, and joined the Territorials. He was gazetted Captain in the 5th Bn. Duke of Wellington's West Riding Regt., 25th April, 1913, and Temp. Major, 12 Jan., 1916, went to France in April, 1915, was mentioned in dispatches, and at the time of his death was 2nd in command of the Bn.

July —, 1916.—*****Malcolm Graham White,** Lieut. 6th Bn. (S.R.) Rifle Brigade (attached 1st Bn.). A graduate of King's College, Cambridge, he came to Shrewsbury as a Master in 1909. For the first six months of the war he stayed at the School, having been gazetted Captain of the O.T.C., 13 Feb., 1915. Joining the Rifle Brigade in the summer of 1915, he left for the front in April, 1916, and went into action on the first day of the Battle of the Somme. A memoir, containing his letters with those of Lieut. Southwell, was published in 1919 under the title of *Two Men.*

Jan. 29, 1918.—**Alfred Gordon Whitehead,** came ιo Shrewsbury (Churchill's) in the Michaelmas Term, 1906, and left at the end of the Summer Term, 1911, as Head of the House, for Caius College, Cambridge. In 1915 he was given a commission in a territorial battalion of the West Yorkshire Regiment ; he was seconded to the R.F.C. in 1917, and early in January, 1918, gazetted temporary Captain while acting as Flight Commander. Later in the month he was reported missing, and a telegram from the Geneva Red Cross says that he was killed in action on January 29, and buried at Fresnoy le Grand. Gordon Whitehead was distinguished at school both in work and play, having considerable mathematical ability, and representing his House in Football, Fives and Cricket. In football he was a member of an exceptionally strong School Eleven.

Oct. 15, 1917.—**Geoffrey Nield Whitehead,** elder brother of A. G. Whitehead, 2nd Lieut. R.F.C., was at Shrewsbury (C.J.S.C.) 1901–7, and Christ Church, Oxford, and before joining the Army was associated with his father in the business of Messrs. W. and J. Whitehead, New-lane Mills, Laisterdyke, Yorks.

July 12, 1917.—**Hugh Holtom Whytehead,** 2nd Lieut. R.F.C., was at Shrewsbury (W.D.H.) 1910-12, where he shot for the School at Bisley. He entered Birmingham University as a student of oil mining in 1913, but joined the Army as soon as war broke out as a private in 5th North Staffordshire Regt. He obtained a commission in 9th North Staffordshire Regt., and served in France some months. Afterwards he served as a motor-dispatch rider, then joined the R.F.C., and went out to the front as pilot on June 23, 1917 He went over the lines with a patrol on July 12 ; he and another pilot failed to return. and since then news has been received from a prisoner in Germany that he was killed on that day.

April 7, 1918,—*Charles Leyburn Wilkinson,** Major R.F.A. (T.F.), killed in action. He was at Shrewsbury (S.H.) 1900-4, and in the Football XI. ; being subsequently admitted a solicitor.

——, 1916.—*Ernest Wightman Wilkinson,** Temp. 2nd Lieut. 11th (Service) Bn. Duke of Wellington's West Riding Regt. A Day Boy 1893-6, he left to enter the service of Lloyds Bank, being for some time in charge of their Whitchurch, Salop, Branch. When war broke out he enlisted as a Trooper in the 2nd Dragoon Guards, and gained a commission in the West Yorks, 29 Nov., 1915, being appointed as Instructor, 9 Feb. 1916.

— —, 1918.—**Arthur Edward Wilson,** was at Shrewsbury (F.E.B.) 1904-8, and left for Clare College, Cambridge, where he took his B.A. He was gazetted Temporary Lieut. in the 14th (Service) Battn. (1st Birmingham) Royal Warwickshires on Jan, 27, 1915, being subsequently attached to a Line Battalion of the same regiment. He had seen much service active, and had been wounded in 1916.

Aug. 25, 1916, killed in action.—*Arthur Stafford Wilson,** Temp. 2nd Lieut. 2nd Bn. Rifle Brigade. He was at the School (A.F.C.) 1907-10, for two years a Gentleman of the Runs, and stroke of the School VIII. in his last year. He went out to British Columbia with the intention of farming, and was on his way home for a holiday when war was declared. He enlisted Sept. 10, 1914, with the other O.SS. in the 5th K.S.L.I., becoming later one of the C.O.'s orderlies. The Bn. went to Flanders in May, 1915, and remained near Ypres for several months. In the Battle of Hooge (Sept. 23–25, 1915), WILSON was mentioned for his services as orderly. Returning to England, Nov. 11, 1915, with the two remaining O.SS., J. S. Corser and L. F. Forbes, he received a commission in the 4th Bn. Rifle

Brigade, Nov. 29, 1915. Going to the front again, June 21, 1916, he was posted to the 2nd Bn., and was killed on the night of Aug. 24–25, while looking after his platoon in the front trench near Vermelles.

April 21, 1918.—**Harold Barkley Winton,** 2nd Lieut. R.A.F. Gaining the Old Salopian Scholarship, he entered Mr. Chance's House in 1908. While there he was captain of Fives, and represented the school at football. In 1912, he went up to Cambridge as a Classical Exhibitioner of Magdalene College, and took his B.A. degree by proxy in 1915. In September, 1914, he enlisted as a private in the 16th Middlesex Regiment (Public Schools), and went to France in November, 1915, where he was wounded on June 28, of the following year. On August 13, 1917, he was transferred to the R.F.C.; obtaining his wings in February, he went to the front as a pilot on April 6, 1918, and was killed in an aeroplane accident on April 21, aged 24.

.—**Charles Ewart Wodehouse** was a member of Mr. Prior's House, 1913-16. On leaving school he joined the R.N.A.S., in which, at the time of his death, he held the rank of Flight-Lieut.

— — , 1916.—**Philip George Wolfe-Murray,** Lieut. R.N.V.R., aged 25, died of enteric fever, contracted on duty. At Shrewsbury as a Day Boy, 1890–9. He afterwards studied at Heidelberg University and the State School of Forestry at Eberswalde. Leaving Germany by the last train before the declaration of war by Great Britain, he obtained a commission in the R.N.V.R., and his proficiency in French and German qualified him for the post of Intelligence Officer on the Staffs of several Admirals, he being often employed in carrying special dispatches. His fatal illness was contracted while serving afloat.

Oct. 22, 1917.—**Matthew Rodney Wood** came to Shrewsbury in the Lent Term, 1910 (Pickering's), and left in April, 1914. At the beginning of the War he was given a Commission in the Lancashire Fusiliers : he was killed in action on the morning of Oct. 22, 1917, having been previously wounded and having gained the Military Cross.

June 4, 1916, of wounds received in action.—*Leslie Woodroffe, M.C., Temp. Capt. 14th Bn. (attached 8th Bn.) Rifle Brigade, and Capt. unattached list, Territorial Force. He was a Scholar of University Coll., Oxford, and gained a 1st in Mods., and 2nd in Lit.Hum. He came to Shrewsbury as a Master in 1909, and took a keen interest in the School O.T.C. in which he was a Captain. He had been some considerable time at the front, and won the Military

Cross at Hooge. He was the last of a brotherhood of three, one a
V.C., all Marlburians, to be killed in the war, each in turn having
been head of the School, and joining the Rifle Brigade.

——, 1916.—*William Thornley Stoker Woods, 2nd Lieut. R.F.A.
Special Reserve. At the School (T.E.P.), 1910–15, he was a Præ-
postor, Choregus, Captain of the Boats, and Cadet 2nd Lieut.
School O.T.C. Gazetted to the R.F.A., 23 Sept., 1915, he joined a
Battery in France, after a very short training in England, and was
killed by a shell which fell on his dug-out by the Somme.

September —, 1915.—*Thomas Worth, Temp. 2nd Lieut. 7th
(Service) Bn. Cheshire Regt. (E.B.M., 1910–11) fell in action at the
Dardanelles. On leaving school he entered the Agricultural College,
Aspatria, Cumberland.

September 22, 1915.—William Edward Bellyse Wright, Temp.
Lieut. 7th (Service) Bn. King's Own Yorkshire L.I. (D.B., 1910–13),
a Gentleman of the Runs, and Captain of Day-boys' Boat ; was at
Pembroke Coll., Camb., for a year before he obtained his commission.
He fell in action in Flanders.

www.ingramcontent.com/pod-product-compliance
Lightning Source LLC
Chambersburg PA
CBHW030402100426
42812CB00028B/2802/J

9 7 8 1 8 4 7 3 4 2 1 5 7